Make Your Writing Count

From Free Writing to Structured Composition

Second Edition

Make Your Writing Count

From Free Writing to Structured Composition

Second Edition

REGINA M. HOOVER
Central Michigan University

CLARKSTOWN SOUTH HIGH SCHOOL
MEDIA CENTER W NYACK, N. Y.

HOLT RINEHART AND WINSTON

New York   Chicago   San Francisco   Dallas
Montreal   Toronto   London   Sydney
Tokyo   Mexico City   Rio de Janeiro   Madrid

Library of Congress Cataloging in Publication Data

Hoover, Regina M.
  Make your writing count.

  Includes index.
  1. English language—Rhetoric. I. Title.
PE1408.H6834 1981   808'.042   81-7143
ISBN 0-03-058701-8

Copyright © 1982 by CBS College Publishing
Copyright © 1977 by Holt, Rinehart and Winston
          Address correspondence to:
          383 Madison Avenue
          New York, N.Y. 10017
All rights reserved
Printed in the United States of America
Published simultaneously in Canada
2 3 4 5   059   9 8 7 6 5 4 3 2

CBS COLLEGE PUBLISHING
Holt, Rinehart and Winston
The Dryden Press
Saunders College Publishing

810320

PREFACE

This text, like the first edition, is designed to meet one or more of the following goals:

1. To give teachers who wish to spend more time with individual students the freedom to dispense with the traditional classroom model involving lectures and discussions. Often, such lectures are addressed to all students regardless of whether they need the instructions or are ready for them. Because this text provides sequenced, self-instructional activities and assignments consistent with the most recent findings on how students mature in their thinking and writing, it allows individual students and their instructors to concentrate on particular problems while steadily improving general skills.

2. To allow the student to progress smoothly from personal writing—increasingly recognized as the logical starting point for developing improved skills—to more formal, structured essays without loss of personal involvement and intellectual control over the material. Although most teachers today understand the underlying values of such a sequence, the problem of transition remains a major one. Part II of the text helps students to move beyond merely personal viewpoints and to achieve the more sophisticated language flexibility needed in formal writing.

3. To cover a broad range of writing skills and strategies without "overloading the circuits." Students confronted with a multiplicity of demands can easily become confused and frustrated. This text proceeds in incremental steps from simple tasks in all areas (focus, organization, coherence, style, grammar, and mechanics) to increasingly complex activities, strengthening skills across the board without overtaxing the learner at any point. By linking skill development to the writing activities and assignments, the text avoids the trap of teaching through exercises unrelated to the student's own writing.

4. To introduce and reinforce an appreciation of the process of writing (prewriting, writing, rewriting) and its relevance to the completed product.

5. To help students overcome negative attitudes about writing. Graduated tasks allow an opportunity for success and personal satisfaction at each step, making writing more meaningful and pleasurable, making it "count."

The basic design of the course is the same in this edition as in the previous one: from free writing to description and narration, then "over the bridge" to more formal modes. Principles of grammar, mechanics, spelling, and style are introduced gradually as students gain confidence and fluency, and are integrated with the writing called for in the assignments. For best results, Parts I and II should be followed consecutively, although Chapters 4 and 6 can be omitted by the teacher who wishes to approach language flexibility differently. Part III, although also designed to bring the student step by step to greater verbal effectiveness, provides the instructor with further options: each chapter can be used or not as he or she deems best. Chapter 7, however, is particularly important, since it introduces the basic whole-essay skills of focus, unity, coherence, and development. Chapters 8 and 9 reinforce these elements and add new material; Chapter 10 is for review, permitting students to consolidate their achievements.

The sample papers, all student-written, have been updated, and an annotated research paper has been added as a new feature. My conviction that students react most favorably and productively to writing by their more accomplished peers has not wavered. Throughout, an attempt has been made to give students more assistance in specific writing problems, particularly in Part III, which has been almost totally rewritten. As in the first edition, all the material has been class-tested. Although the text remains basically self-instructional, reinforcement by the instructor at key points helps.

During the past few years, student response to this text has been overwhelmingly positive. Not only do students find it easy to understand and follow, but they surprise themselves by beginning to like to write. Once that happens, the outlook for both student and instructor brightens considerably.

My thanks to all, students and colleagues, who in the past years have expressed their appreciation for this text and to the many who have offered helpful suggestions to improve its usefulness.

RMH

CONTENTS

PART I Developing Your Ideas

PART II The Bridge

PART III Focusing Your Ideas

MINIGRAMMARS

Minigrammar A
Agreement between Subjects and Predicates   17ᴸ

Minigrammar B
Verb Forms and Tense Shifting   183

Minigrammar C
Sentence Fragments and Run-on Sentences   193

PART I:

Developing Your Ideas

The best way to begin writing is to do simply that: begin writing ideas, words, and so forth, rather than sit and wait for an inspiration When you write, remember you can "brainstorm" more easily by groping in the dark until the ideas develop. It's like standing outside a room totally dark. You'll never find the light in the room by standing outside. You must go into the room in search of the light switch.

A STUDENT

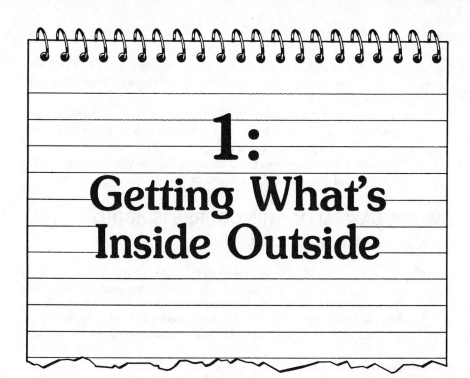

1:
Getting What's Inside Outside

S o. You are in a composition course, and if you are like many of the people around you, you will more or less cheerfully admit that (1) you hate English or (2) you can't write or (3) both of the above. A few—probably not more than 25 percent of you—like English and would be in the course, required or not. But if you are not among these few, you are not alone. You needn't be afraid that you are the only one in the class who comes in feeling uneasy, doubtful of your ability to make it through the course, perhaps even somewhat hostile if you are here solely because your curriculum requires it.

If you are mathematically inclined, you probably have figured out that if only 25 percent of the class likes English, or at least sees the necessity of a composition course in college, only two or three out of ten come into the class feeling fairly comfortable. Unfortunately, even some of you in this small minority also have a few attitudes toward English that will rise up to plague you, at least at first. You have perhaps had English composition psyched out since the fifth grade. You know that if you put the commas in the right places and spell words correctly and understand how to use the approved footnote form, you have it made. That is all well and good, but prepare yourself for a bit of a shock. College writing is more than researching and rewording encyclopedias, more than achieving perfect mechanics, more than producing a neatly tied-up package. In college writing, you need to use your own mind, forming your own ideas and expressing them effectively in order both to interest and to enlighten your reader.

Probably many of you have not had much experience in expressing your *own* thoughts. It's not easy at first, and you may not like what you are asked to do at the beginning of the course. Students say, "But I never had to do anything like this in high school!" Maybe not, but give it a whirl. You'll find there's more to writing than putting that comma in the right place. You may even like what you find.

A few of you really "like to write." You enjoy sitting down, letting ideas and images take hold, and arranging your thoughts into a clear, organized, compelling whole. But maybe you can learn something, too; even Shakespeare grew more skilled as he grew more experienced. So can you, because writing is a cumulative skill, like playing the piano or skiing.

WHAT, BASICALLY, THIS COURSE IS ABOUT

A student once wrote:

> When I entered English 101 I thought I would have to write one large term paper, but to my surprise I was required to write many smaller papers. Now this seemed quite simple to me for college-level work, and it also frustrated me, because I had been taught to write large papers and use resources in my writing. But in this English class, the only resource needed was my mind.

He was actually complaining about a course similar to the one in this text, but the basic principle of this approach to writing could not be expressed better. *The only resource needed is your mind.* If that is working, all else follows.

Many students have not learned to trust their own minds. They have been told what to do and how to do it for too long. Most students are sharp enough thinkers when it comes to matters of their own interest—sports, the bad food in the dorms, problems of commuting—but to many, the idea of education as personally challenging and rewarding has not yet occurred. As for writing, they seldom think of it as something more than putting together a term paper.

To write well you must think well. You must formulate your scattered thoughts into well-organized and coherent wholes that reach across the barrier between you and your reader, so that your reader says, "Ah! I see exactly what you mean!" or "That's interesting!" Further, because writing well involves thinking well, a composition course affects everything else you will do in every activity of any kind the rest of your life. Taking a composition course isn't the only way to learn to think well, but it is one of the most efficient. Nothing is more mentally demanding than the challenge to say on paper exactly what you are thinking, so that anyone—even in your absence—can understand and respond to your ideas.

If your writing is not a product of your own mind, the picture you put on paper may be quite different from the image of yourself you intend to project. A neat paper, cribbed from two encyclopedias, on market conditions in Outer Mongolia may present the picture of a mind without a thought to call its own. Your flowery description of that perfect evening with the boy or girl of your dreams may reveal a mind convinced that romantic lady teachers like that sort of thing. A paper on justice (or peace or evil or death) heavy with big words and fine-sounding phrases may be the sign of a mind that doesn't think its own, real thoughts are worth writing down—certainly not worth handing in to a teacher!

You are what you are. You must start where you are and work from there. It's scary sometimes to say honestly what you are thinking. Let's face it; usually the first thoughts of your own that go down on paper aren't brilliant. But they are what you have to work with; they are the basic "resources." What you say has no meaning unless *your mind gives it meaning for you.*

When your mind is working, when it is taking hold of ideas and perceptions and turning them into meaningful information and thoughts, then it is possible to write convincingly and well about markets in Outer Mongolia or a tender evening or even justice. The key is to express the things that interest you in a way that is natural to you. If that sounds easy, don't be fooled. It's not.

Many of you can probably remember a time when writing was easy—even fun—way back when you first started school and were discovering the magic of being able to read and write. You put exactly what was in your mind on your piece of ruled paper, and the teacher said, "How nice!" Then something happened; it no longer seemed important that you put down what you were thinking. Good penmanship took over, along with where to put the periods and the capital letters. Later you had to learn to use the library. These skills are important, of course, but somewhere along the line you forgot *you* were doing the writing.

In a sense, this text tries first to take you back to where you began, when you wrote because you had something to say. As a reminder of those days, the next page shows how a third-grader described her school's Spring Festival in a letter to a faraway aunt. If your first efforts sound something like this letter, don't despair. This may have been the last time this third-grader would write naturally about things that mattered to her; already in the word "perform" there was evidence she was trying to conform to what her teacher had told her. Perhaps you have not said on a piece of paper exactly what is on your mind since the third grade either.

You may find the first activities in this text difficult, though they sound easy. But try to suspend your judgment for a while. If your initial response is "I took this course to learn how to write a good term paper for other college courses, and this isn't getting me anywhere," have a little faith. If you keep an open mind and follow along, things may turn out better than you think.

HOW, GENERALLY, THIS TEXT IS SET UP

If you have not already done so, it would be a good idea now to look at the table of contents, a practice that should become a habit; the table of contents gives you the first clue about what to expect of any text. Note that there is a center section consisting of two chapters, called "The Bridge"; the other chapters have titles like "Getting What's Inside Outside," "Drawing on the World around You," and Keeping It Your Own." Together with what you now know about the purpose of this text, you should realize that the overall on May 17 at 2:30 we had May day and first came the boys and then the girls and then the queens and court and at the end of the queens court was the person who crowned the queen and after her two grils and then a gril who held the mace and other girl held the crown and at the last was the queen. And then the lower school perforndances for the queen frist 10 little Indians that were the first grade boys and then the 2 grade grils did bow-bow-bow Belinda and then the frist grade grils did shoe fly and then the 5th grade did a sad dance and then the 3 grade boys and 4 grade grils did a cowboy dance and then the May pole dance and the 3 grade grils did it. That's the dance I was in.

Love Carol

plan is to move (across "The Bridge") from your unique personal experience to your equally unique relationship with information and ideas available around you.

Each chapter begins with an introductory discussion and then moves into a series of *Activities*. Some composition texts refer to such activities as "prewriting," a misleading term because it implies that only the finished product qualifies as "writing." Not so. Every time you write a single word that conveys a portion of your thoughts or feelings, you are "writing." The activities prepare you for the writing from each chapter that you will hand in as an *Assignment*. Every chapter is designed to help you build the kind of skills needed, not only to do your best on the particular assignment but also to use as a foundation for the *next* chapter and the next assignment. Neglecting the "prewriting" activities, *especially* if you find them hard, will almost certainly mean difficulty later in the course.

Each set of activities, then, leads to an assignment. Starting with Chapter 2, the explanation of the assignment will be followed by one or more *Revising Activities*. You will find a *Checklist* at the end of each chapter, to help you make sure you have completed all the activities and evaluate whether you have achieved the goals of the assignment. In Chapters 1-10, marginal checkmarks have been provided to help you locate the various assignments and activities.

✔ Keep everything you write for this course in a folder. Later you may be asked to look back at your early writing; perhaps it will provide ideas for future writing. Looking back occasionally will also help you gauge what you are learning in the course.

Activity 1-1   *To Get Started*

It requires practice to be natural and open: to say what you think and be willing to take the consequences. This activity should help—it's your first step.

✔ The idea is to write for fifteen minutes without stopping for any reason. (Well, you can stop to turn a page, and if you do, you can congratulate yourself, because writing more than a page the first time is very good.) Start in and keep writing. Never mind if you haven't anything to say. Almost no one does at this point; if others around you seem to be scribbling away in a manner that intimidates you, they may be writing, "I can't think of anything to say," over and over. You can do the same thing. Write it forty times if necessary, until something comes to you. Then keep that thought going as long as you can. Write whatever comes to your mind. Write "This is the stupidest thing anyone ever asked me to do," if that's what you're thinking. Write sentence fragments, write unconnected words, write nonsense. But don't stop. Above all, don't stop!

All but a few examples in this text were written by students. If some seem better than you can manage, don't let that worry you. The examples picked are, by and large, the better ones turned in. Beginning with Chapter 2, most examples of student writing are in typewriter type.

I can't think of anything to say.
I can't think of anything to say,
I can't think of anything to say.
Boy, this is hard to get used to!
I can't think of anything to say.
I can't think of anything to say.
Boy, rat, bird, smell, fart, big,
pig, tree house oh boy I. can't
think of anything to write but I'm
going to write and write and write
anyways the stars are pretty i
think, I got to write something
that makes sense or no sense.
The purple fog fell on top of the
refrigerator with such a large and
fat noise that I jumped into my
tomato and gasped for gasoline.
The bird didn't answer its pink
telephone call but a spoon fell
in a crack and said hi. I said
Hi back but I hardly knew the
cucumber. I just noticed that
there is a cute girl right across
from where I am sitting. She
doesn't have the slightest idea
that at this very moment I am

writing about her. She has a yellow top on and pretty blond hair. She just scowled while thinking and made the ugliest face. If I wanted to be completely honest and strip away all my masks and be a real person I would walk over to her and say, "I think your cute, and I have been writing about you and I noticed you made an awful scowl while thinking and it made you quite unattractive." Unfortunately I don't have the guts to say that to her face but wouldn't it be great if I could. That's the problem of society. It teaches us to suppress, withold, and play games. We must always wear our masks. If we feel awful we must always hide it and smile and say "I feel just fine." When we really feel awful and should say, "I feel shitty, partially because I want to and partially because I don't want to, I'm having all sorts of conflicts right now, and I feel lousy and I am playing games with you and myself."

You may recognize this voice here; it is probably something like yours: hav ing a hard time getting going, feeling foolish, writing nonsense because there doesn't seem to be anything else to write. Perhaps you have not yet achieved the next step: noticing something and starting to write about it, your thoughts suddenly taking hold of an idea and flowing, perhaps not elegantly but at least with direction, which is what happened to the student who wrote the next ex- ample. As this occurs, your thoughts are there, on the page to look at and build upon, not lost in the moment of their passing.

The chair across from me has a curved seat and it reminds me of a smiling face. Not those happy face things — they make me sick. They are trite & there are too many although I do believe it is a good gesture to smile. I wonder if "gesture" was the appropriate word for that. I have had a lot of Art and I believe I know what I do like. Instead of making millions of these them whatever cheepo happy faces I think some artist (not necessarily that good of one either) should have drawn a more realistic but still animated face. It would have shiney eyes with crinkles on the outside (sometimes known as crowfeet I think) When smiling the eye closes more than half so it would be a squinty smile. The nose would be crinkled the entire thing would make you feel great & feel like laughing. Now the mouth, being the most important factor, would be stretched from ear to ear. I havent decided whether or not to show teeth but there would be creases in the cheeks that run from chin to the eye. It reminds me of Mr. Hill (psychology) But it will be like an explosion. You will have to smile back. I wish I could do it but it'll take some more practice. Right Now if I drew the face, it would look like a man in agony. Maybe not really, but it wouldn't crack you up like I would like it to. Well, that's that isn't it?

Both the students quoted so far came upon an idea to explore *after they started writing*. If you are someone who "can't get started," this should be a clue to you: begin jotting down random thoughts until they begin to form into a coherent idea. The same student who wrote the first example wrote the excerpt with which Part I of the text begins. "The best way to begin writing is to do simply that," he says. Like most things, thoughts often get going when you least expect them to. If yours don't flow right away, don't despair. Most students are initially tongue-tied, like the student who wrote the following.

Here is Friday oh boy, can't wait until this class is over so I can head for home. My mother is a teacher and my father is an employee of Gibsons. My sister went to CMU and will graduate in December. Oh Boy, can Think of anything. Oh I have a dog named Toby who has been with me for sometime. It funny it really is nice having a pet that you can take care of, and just enjoy his company. Especially when he always is around to listen to my problems he is also a good listener. Because he knows not to interrupt. Well I'm blank again. What's new!

That's about five minutes' worth of the total free writing down by this student, but it never gets much beyond where it's gone already. Never mind; uninspired as it is and full enough of grammatical problems to send an English teacher up the wall, it is still a good beginning. This student ended up an excellent writer, as did the others—believe it or not.

See what you can do. Don't try to figure out what your teacher would like, however strong the temptation may be to try kinds of writing that have won you pats on the back (translation: A's or B's) before. In the long run, the most benefit will come from an honest attempt to get your thoughts—good, bad, or indifferent—onto paper. You will not be graded now on things you are used to being graded on: punctuation, spelling, good sentence structure, not even whether you have made sense. You will probably not be graded at all at this point. Of, if you are, it will be on whether what you have written sounds as if it comes out of your own mind or whether it has been filtered through preconceived notions of what writing "ought to be."

✓   Stop *now* and try some free writing for fifteen minutes.

Let what you have written sit a while after you have finished. Then go back and read it. Is there a sentence you like? A place where you had a train of thought going for a while? Even a short phrase that captures for a moment something meaningful to you? If so, congratulations. If not, maybe it will happen on the next try.

Activity 1-2   *To Keep Going*

✓   Do two more fifteen-minute writings. As before, write what comes to your mind whether or not it makes sense. If you write something you'd rather not have someone read, all you have to do is throw it away or put it in the back of your desk drawer. Do at least one more to keep.

Activity 1-3   *Something a Little More Focused*

✓   Do another fifteen-minute writing, but this time choose a subject that interests you. Be *sure* it interests you.

> **Principle 1** If what you're writing about doesn't interest you, it will bore your reader to death. It isn't good to bore a reader.

As before, don't worry if the details don't make much sense, just so long as they are all somehow related *in your mind* to the subject. As before, don't stop. If you have to, write "I can't think of anything else to say about this." Keep writing it until something else comes. Don't stop!

Again let your writing cool before you read it. Then look at it. Did something get going, even for a while? Did you write something a little unexpected? Did some new thoughts come as you wrote?

If not, did you let your true thoughts flow on paper? Or did you plan out ahead what you were going to say? Did you "write a paper" instead of "think on paper"? Were you perhaps reluctant to write what was really on your mind? Perhaps it seemed too trivial to put on paper, especially if the teacher was going to see it. Forget the teacher. For now, write about what interests or bothers you: your girl or boy friend, your wife or husband, your problems getting adjusted to a new term at college, your job, your roommates. Let other kinds of subjects wait for another time; for now, just write.

Many students are reluctant to write true thoughts not because they seem trivial but because they are too personal and intimate. Just as these students get going well, they stop themselves, often with a sentence like, "No, I don't want to write about that." But that is precisely the point at which you had better *keep going!* Otherwise you may prevent yourself from putting on paper that one thought or feeling that will free your mind and permit you to go on to other things. By writing out your thoughts now, you may come to a new and liberating understanding. If you don't let this one difficult or even frightening thought flow, you may inhibit all your thinking. You are all of one piece; you cannot shut off one part of yourself without limiting the whole of yourself. It takes a little risk to be honest—even with yourself. Now is as good a time as any to begin to take that risk.

Activity 1-4   *Now Try This*

✔   Think of a place or person that you feel strongly about and start to write. Don't plan ahead. Let it come. Have an experience on paper, revisiting that place or remembering that person. Let your mind explore, while you tag along and write down what it tells you. Keep going beyond the fifteen minutes if you get fired up.

Again, wait a while and then read what you've written, looking for spots where things seem to click. These are signposts toward good writing. Try to think how you felt, how your mind was working when they happened. Could you put yourself in that mood when you are writing about other kinds of things?

ASSIGNMENT 1   Two Free Writings

✔   Choose two pieces of writing you like best from the activities you have just completed. Hand them in. Don't recopy them. Don't, *under any circumstances*, revise or polish them. Just hand them in, sloppy handwriting and all. The important thing is that what you have said means something to you, not that you have written a "paper." None of the assignments in Part I of this book will be "papers"; they will be practice for papers to come, in which, ideally, certain skills will be developed. For this first assignment, the specific skill you want to have developed is the ability to write down what you are really thinking.

Note: Your instructor may ask you to proceed through these chapters more or less on your own. If so, you have a special responsibility that can provide big dividends. You must learn to read carefully and follow instructions exactly, both essential skills if you are to succeed in college. Be sure you *have* read and understood everything in each chapter; if you are confused at any point, ask your instructor. Under no circumstances should you skip any activity unless requested to do so by your instructor. Get the instructions straight and follow them.

After you have completed the work in each chapter, review the checklist at the end. Have you done all the activities? Have you achieved the goals of the chapter?

CHECKLIST   *Getting What's Inside Outside*

Preparations.   Check off each item when completed.

Activity 1-1   To Get Started . . . .
Activity 1-2   To Keep Going . . . .
Activity 1-3   Something a Little More Focused . . . .
Activity 1-4   Now Try This . . . .
Assignment 1   Two Free Writings . . . .

Goals to Be Achieved.   Write your answers on a separate sheet. Explain fully.

1. Do the writings you are handing in represent free-flowing thoughts and ideas just as they came to your mind?
2. When you sat down to do the pieces you are turning in, were you in a relaxed, easy state of mind, not "trying harder" because you knew a teacher would read them?
3. While you were writing the pieces you are turning in, did you develop new ideas that came to you while you were writing?

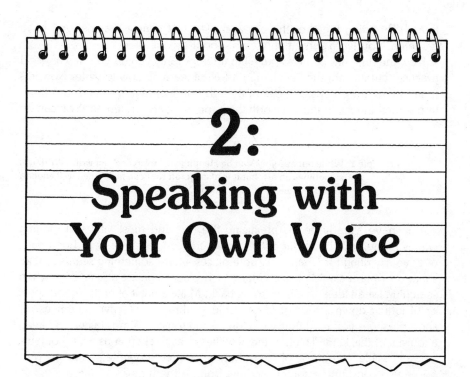

2:
Speaking with Your Own Voice

When we talk about "writing naturally," as we did in Chapter 1, there is a risk of confusion. More than likely, what you have written for this course so far, if you honestly tried to do what was asked of you, would earn you a failing mark in any class except a composition course run like this one. You may remember words about composition like "unity" and "coherence" and "transition"; unless you are unusual, what you've written doesn't have those things. Yet you have "written naturally."

In hundreds of ways in the past, you have perhaps been led to believe that what comes out of your own mind isn't worth the paper it is written on. That's one reason you may feel uncomfortable at first when you let your mind take its own course. Yet no writing is worth the paper it is written on *unless* it comes out of your own mind.

Does this mean that all you've learned until now is useless? No, it doesn't. There are good reasons for requiring you, for instance, to go to library sources for a term paper. All the world's information is stored in books somewhere; you need to learn to tap that information so that you can build on a firm foundation. Where would we be if every individual had to start over and discover everything again? Some of the information you obtain from an encyclopedia or an article sticks with you and is added to the store of knowledge you can build on. And if you copy it, using footnotes, you are introduced to words, sentence patterns, types of punctuation, and writing strategies that never come to your attention when you are "writing your own thing." By fitting together the bits and pieces of source material you have gathered, you learn some things, too, about organization.

Now the time has come to put all that temporarily behind you. It was good practice, but it is not the be-all and end-all of learning how to write. Now it is time to take the shreds and bits of thought that come to you and turn them into something that is indeed worth the paper they are written on. You can do it.

> *Principle 2* **While not everyone can be Hemingway, everyone can write. Writing is sometimes an art, but it is also a craft that can be learned well enough to suit the needs of most people.**

You have already begun practicing the first and most vital skill: getting what's inside your head out on paper where you can look at it. Look back over your writing for Chapter 1; note places where something seems to take shape, if only a single phrase. Mark such places against a later day, when searching for an idea, you may come back. Make a habit of noting good spots or of jotting down scraps of ideas, striking phrases, effective sentences, or short passages you read that seem interesting to you. Almost all writers keep a journal of this kind. Think of the activities in each chapter as a kind of journal, a possible storehouse of ideas that, while they serve the immediate purpose, also constitute a source to draw from in the future.

Be honest, though. Don't mark something because "the teacher will like it." Mark it because *you* like it. The teacher has more expertise and can give you the benefit of experience and knowledge, but he or she is just one person. So are the fellow students whose opinion you may ask from time to time. Listen, but make up your own mind. Possibly you will change your mind later, but if you don't start now to rely on your own judgment, you will never develop it fully.

THE PROBLEM OF "NATURAL VOICE"

All right. You say, "Well, I like what I have written, but you—the teacher—don't. You tell me to 'write naturally' and I do, and then you say there are ways to improve what I have written."

There is a difference among your various "voices." Although "voice" refers primarily to speaking, it applies also to writing. Speaking and writing are different things, though they share certain characteristics. Thinking is on a different level from writing and speaking, but it is the source of both. There is a reasonably direct line from the mind to what is written or spoken. The connection between speech and the written word is less direct; perhaps it could better be thought of as a broken line. Diagrammatically, we might visualize the three functions as a triangle with all parts interconnected (see the next page). But though speaking and writing are different, that doesn't mean one is "natural" and the other "unnatural." It means you have more than one "voice."

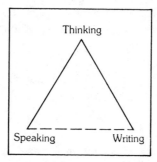

Even in speaking you have more than one "voice." The way you speak to your mother is different from the way you speak to a teacher. You do not speak the same way to your mother as to your best friend. You do not speak to a friend as you do to someone you dislike. You have innumerable voices, all "natural." Try an experiment. Listen to a group of your peers talking. Jot down a few expressions that strike you. Then listen during a class discussion and note how your classmates talk. Do you hear a difference?

Similarly, there are innumerable ways to write. Perhaps the most useful concept to understand is the difference between private and public writing. The most private kinds of writing are random jottings and diaries. If, when you are frustrated, angry, depressed, or just generally ready to burst, you have never experienced the release of letting it all spill out on paper, then you haven't experienced one of the joys of life. You need to get those private thoughts out of the vast echo chamber your mind becomes when something seems too big to handle.

In these private kinds of writing, it would be foolish to say, "Should I use a different word here? Should I put a comma there?" But when you begin to write something someone else will read, different principles take over. We talk about the truth, the whole truth, and nothing but the truth. Who knows what the whole truth is? You know what you think a part of it is at this moment, and that is the best you can do. In writing, you select from among the possible bits of truth and from among your various voices what best suits your purpose in writing and what best communicates that purpose to another person.

Look back again at what you have written so far. How much can you lift out, just as it is, for another person to read? The cornerstone of everything in this course is what comes naturally to you, what you say in one of your own voices, and what also can be read with profit and interest by someone else. You communicate to a reader some portion of your thought. For the time being, that is enough.

TYPES OF UNNATURAL VOICES

Although you have many different natural voices, you have a few that are unnatural, voices you assume to mask your own. The peculiar thing about these is that they call attention to you as writer rather than to what you are trying to say to a reader and so interfere with your line of communication.

> *Principle 3* **A primary criterion of good writing is its ability to communicate with a reader. Anything that interferes with that communication is poor writing strategy.**

With apologies to the bird world, here are handy metaphors for unnatural voices that produce unsuccessful writing:

Stuffed Owl

All puffed up, this one sits blinking on a branch, uttering pronouncements that sound more impressive than they are:[*]

> The two most familiar types of environmental pollution to the average citizen of today are air pollution and water pollution. Their familiarity is due to the fact that they are the types most commonly seen and noticed by the people and they are also the most publicized. But the majority of people's familiarity with these two types of pollution is more of an awareness of their presence than an understanding of what they are and what they mean to them as human beings. Here will be presented a comparison of air pollution and water pollution based on several major qualities which each possesses in one form or another.

Proud Peacock

This one struts, displaying beautiful plumage, but little else:

> I am a bud about to bloom. I am a child of the universe and I am on this lovely earth to do what God wants me to. I am sometimes meek and mild and other times can be outspoken and mean. I can be thoughtful and can be forgetful. I can love and hate. I experience many emotions every day of which I cannot fully understand. I am different things to different people. I have found that friendship is a great way to travel, and although sometimes friends get off during the journey, they stay a treasure within my memories and thoughts. I am reality. I can see pain and hatred. I can see my responsibilities and I know they must be done. I am fantasy. I am a child of the universe and I'm glad I am me.

Ungainly Ostrich

Clearly out of its element but unable to escape to any other, awkward though not necessarily incompetent, this one tries hard but rarely gets off the ground:

[*]The examples of student writing in typewriter type in this book are single-spaced to save space. The actual papers were, of course, double-spaced as all typed themes and papers should be.

Being is the full potential of all existence. It involves
itself into the flux of life. It is the opposite of non-being but yet
it still retains a close relationship with it. Being could never
have been created because by definition, it always was. Being has no
lack of completeness of itself and does not need non-being. Non-
being is the negation of being while it is in existence. Remove that
existence of it, and the activity of this life would come to a stand-
still. Being is the goal of itself which ultimately cannot and does
not follow any other objective or task. Non-being is nothing else
except the remainder of what is left over of Being. Where Being does
not invade, then Non-being has a niche of existence. Being is the
full development of its own self. The Ultimate Being is the plain
upon which all Being and Non-being rest. It is strange that Non-
being can rest on this plain, when, in fact, it is, by definition,
indefinable.

THE SIGNIFICANT DETAIL

One of the best ways to avoid being a Stuffed Owl, a Proud Peacock, or an
Ungainly Ostrich is to use concrete details, vivid and exact, that bring pictures
to the minds of your readers or that make them suddenly understand. Stuffed
Owl says nothing you might not have said yourself; Proud Peacock keeps
promising to, but, when you really take a good look, not much sparks
answering pictures in your mind. Ungainly Ostrich, for all those fancy words,
simply doesn't make much sense—or if he does, you have a hard time figur-
ing it out.

Suppose, on the other hand, Stuffed Owl had begun talking about the
stream on his grandmother's farm, pure and clear and bubbling, in which as a
child he had built dams and sailed paper boats. Suppose he had made you
see a weeping willow hanging over sparkling water. Suppose then he went on
to show you the stream now brown and cloudy, moving sluggishly between
blighted banks, the willow beginning to die, cans and bits of garbage swirling
in back eddies, a dead fish beached in the shallows? Wouldn't you have a
more vivid awareness of the present-day threat of pollution than from Stuffed
Owl's vague statements?

The first thing you must learn to do is to make what you are talking about
come "alive" for a reader through the use of *significant details*.

Activity 2-1   *Description of a Scene or Object*

✓   Wherever you are, look around you. Start to make a list—a sort of "fact
sheet"—of everything you see. *Be as specific as possible!* Don't say just "a
lake"; say "a small, jewel-like lake, shimmering in the afternoon sun." Try to
create a little picture or vivid image with every "fact."

An overwhelming silence, so different from the way I remember it
Long rows of gray, closed lockers (some partially open)
My footsteps echoing off the bare gray walls
Cold, gray tile floor with a crack running diagonally across it
My reflection in the window of the dark offices
Notices taped on the window: practice announcements, athletic
        scholarships being offered, a school dance, game schedule
Closed door of the office, looking both lonely and threatening
The hard glare of unshaded electric lights
Rows of benches in front of the lockers, nicked and scratched
The sound of silence: it keeps coming back
The clock on the wall clicking off minutes, suddenly loud
I open the door of my old locker. It creaks like a rusty crow
In the locker: blue shorts, white tee shirt, towel, tennis shoes,
        dirty white socks
On shelf: neat folded uniform
On door: Team schedule and coach's inspirational handout (same one
        she gave me!)
Smell of sweaty bodies even though no one is around
A kind of damp mustiness I never noticed before
Everything feels cold

After you have compiled a complete, detailed list of things you see, not forgetting textures and colors, think about your other senses. Try hearing first; many people find recording sounds the next logical step. When you can't hear anything more, can you smell something? Give it time; it may take you a while to get past an initial "blindness" before you become aware of what is going on around you. All right now, is there anything to taste? What about touch? People seem to miss the sense of touch more than anything else; perhaps we have an instinctive fear of emotions aroused by touch. But give it a try. Close your eyes and feel around lightly with your fingertips. Whole new vistas may open for you.

✓ By now, you should have a list that covers at least a page, even if you write small. Next write a description of the scene or object whose qualities you have been listing.

Locker 145

Walking into the empty locker room, I was engulfed in silence. My footsteps echoed hollowly as I crossed the tiled floor, while the familiar smell of sweaty bodies and musty dampness reached me. Glancing towards the dark office, I noticed my reflection in the window among the notices taped randomly on it. How many times had I walked by this same office and seen my reflection before? Only, then I had often been wearing a uniform when I went by. It seemed so long ago.

Glancing around, I noticed the tall, silent rows of lockers, some partially open, but most closed and locked. I scanned the numbers until I came to 145, my old locker. Slowly, I walked towards it and opened the door. The creak of the handle shattered the stillness, bouncing back and forth off the walls. Inside, a pair of blue shorts, a white tee shirt, and a towel hung on the hooks, while a pair of tennis shoes and dirty white socks lay at the bottom. Neatly folded on the top shelf was a red and gray uniform. Taped to the door was a copy of the team's schedule and an inspirational saying identical to the one I had received from my coach.

The locker brought back a flood of memories. So many times I had stood in front of this locker before a big game trying to quiet the butterflies in my stomach. Or laughed and joked with teammates while celebrating a victory. Or sat in weariness and misery on the bench in front of the locker after a defeat. This locker had even withstood a few kicks, particularly after we lost to Kalamazoo Christian in the state quarterfinals my senior year.

The memories were so strong I could see and hear the events just as they happened that night we lost. But gradually the voices in my mind faded, and I became aware once again of the silence. Taking one more look at the locker, I slowly closed the door, wondering whose locker it was now and what memories the girl would carry with her after graduation.

Perhaps you think you can't write a description like this. You may doubt it was written by a student, but it was. You can come a lot closer to writing like this than you may think.

Notice that the vividness of this description comes largely from a *judicious* choice of the *significant details* listed in the fact sheet: the emptiness and silence, the girl's reflection in the window, the notices, the shorts, shirt, and dirty socks in the locker. (Facts may mean something out of a book—statistics and the like—to you, but the silence and the writer's reflection in the window are facts, as are the items in your own fact sheet.)

Note too that in preparing her fact sheet, the student has rather systematically approached her task: first items of sight and impressions that came quickly, then sounds, later odors and a brief reference to the sense of touch.

If you have done your observing well, you will not use all the significant details or facts you have listed. In the description above, for instance, there is no mention of the crack in the floor or the glare of the lights. Even if you decide not to use some of the details you've recalled, your effort is not wasted. Your best writing always comes when you know far more about your subject than you write down. Hemingway once said that on paper you see only the tip of the iceberg; 90 percent of the author's total knowledge is below the surface, forming a solid base. If in your writing the top of the iceberg is all there is, your reader will sense the unsubstantial nature of what you are saying. It is important, therefore, to gather more facts and know more about your subject than appears on the page.

Two other elements deserve notice. (1) The fact sheet is *not* an outline; details have been rearranged to suit the writer's purpose, which is to follow a

CLARKSTOWN SOUTH HIGH SCHOOL
MEDIA CENTER W NYACK, N. Y.

time sequence: what she noticed first as she entered the locker room, what she next noticed, and so on. (2) In the writing, *new* facts have been added; the entire third paragraph demonstates this. One detail suggests others, and during the writing new ones may present themselves. Be alert.

When you have a good list, how do you choose what items to use? How do you make order out of the apparent chaos of your fact sheet? First, *decide what you want to say to a reader*. Do you want to create a *dominant impression*, like the feeling of nostalgia and loss that dominates the description of the locker room? Choose from your list those details that most effectively produce the impression you desire to convey. Discard others that do not contribute; add new ones that occur to you. Keep *everything* related to the *one* dominant impression you want to create.

There are other ways to organize your description. For instance, if you are describing a scene at the beach in the late afternoon, a *logical time order* might best suit your purpose: first details showing the activities of late afternoon—people romping in the waves, others sunbathing or playing volleyball, children building sand castles—and then details of people departing—folding up lawn chairs and blankets, gathering radios, suntan lotion, and coolers, calling the children away from their play. Finally, you could describe the beach deserted except for yourself: the sun sinking into the ocean, seagulls flying low, a feeling of peace and tranquility.

Another way is to choose a *particular point of view*. Sometimes you can try an unusual point of view, as does the student in the following example. He pretends he is a tiny organism, only returning at the end in his own person.

A crack in the sidewalk is quite mysterious when you think about it. If you were to reduce yourself to a microscopic organism you would surely see that the crack resembles an enormous canyon. Looking around the top of the canyon, you would see a rugged terrain of mountains and huge boulders. On down the jagged edge of the ravine you could catch a glimpse of the canyon floor, covered with large pieces of broken rock formations and divided through its middle with a raging river: a rapids, tormented by stones, that has probably carried many Protozoans and Amoebas to their death.

Thousands of caves line the walls of the canyon and go deep within the earth in a maze of tunnels. If only you could explore them and collect the bizarre pieces of stones and shining bits of quartz that glimmer like jewels! But remember, it is only a crack in the sidewalk. The shiny jewels are hardly visible to the naked eye and the terrain of mountains and rock formations is merely the nature of the cement. Still, although our size does not enable us to creep into cracks and small holes, our imaginations can explore even the tiniest cave.

Think about taking the point of view of something or someone other than yourself. It may make a big difference in your perception of something you have always taken for granted.

CLARKSTOWN SOUTH HIGH SCHOOL

The foregoing example also demonstrates another device that can be helpful in organizing your material: *the extended metaphor*. A comparison or analogy helps the reader see more clearly what the writer is trying to describe; everything is related to comparing the crack to an "enormous canyon" from a microscopic organism's point of view. Comparisons like these are helpful, if not overused, to make your description more vivid. From the standpoint of achieving order, however, it is the *extended metaphor*, which controls the whole piece of writing, that can pull your material together and establish which details to choose. We will get into the extended metaphor in more detail in Chapter 6.

Order that will focus your description can also result from using *some other sense than sight as the central device*. This may also open your eyes to things you don't usually observe, that you take for granted. In the following example, for instance, the focus is on sound.

The room is silent except for the ticking of a clock. I've begun to wonder if that is all the noise to be heard. Sitting with my head erect, I begin to listen closely. Straining my ears to hear sounds only brings me the frustration of hearing nothing. Relax, and let the muscles of your body flow as though you were just one blob of blackness. I hear the voice in my head telling me to relax. I begin to respond. My body begins to bend and become one. I can hear my own heartbeat seeming to thump at a slow pace.

My mind wanders around the room, listening for sounds otherwise never heard. My roommates are asleep and their breathing is one of the sounds I don't usually pay attention to. Thud, and there is the radiator heating up the room. There is another sound I can't quite place that sounds like the murmur of a car motor but yet is not a car. Screek, someone has begun to run water in the upstairs room. Tap-Tap-Tap-Tap-Tap. It's coming from the pipes lining the top of the windows. Tap-Tap-Tap. It sounds like a reply. Stretching myself, I listen for more. The drip, drip, drup, drip of our leaking faucet takes my attention from the pipes. I try to combine the sounds and call it "Silent Music." Drup, Drip, Drup. Tap, Tap, Tap, Tick, Tock. The muffled sound of a sleeping body. Drip, Drup . . .

Another device to help you achieve focus is to *think of your writing as the lens of a camera*. A camera lens can take in only so much, but what is shown is highlighted and made important. If you use a wide-angle lens, you get a broad view but often it lacks focus. In writing, at least for now, concentrate on a close-up. Choose a limited picture and show it as much in detail as possible. You may have to leave out some elements, but your reader will receive a sharper image. Remember too that a camera records *everything* that is within its range, every detail. If your description is focused to show exactly what you want it to, it also should show every relevant significant detail. Don't expect a reader to supply details you leave out. Don't expect a reader to "see the picture" if you leave out significant details.

✓   *Write your description*, remembering that you want your reader to experience the scene or object as you do. Keep three key terms in mind, all of
which will recur throughout this text:

1. Natural voice
2. Significant detail
3. Focus

Don't linger too long over this first description, trying to make it perfect.
Frederick S. Perls, the wise father of Gestalt psychology, calls perfection a
snare and a delusion. He is right. Probably no writer in the world, after the
first heat of creation has worn off, thinks he or she has written the perfect
passage. Some writing comes off better, that's all. Do the best you can in the
time you have and then go on to the next step; this is a cardinal principle not
only for learning to write well but in all learning.

If you have made an honest effort and this description still hasn't come off
well, *set it aside and go on!* Maybe you will come back later and see the problem. Maybe you will come back later and say, "Hey, that's pretty good. Did I
really write that?" Maybe you'll just not come back at all. Do your best. Move
on.

Activity 2-2   *Description of a Place You Remember*

✓   After you have read through the instructions for this activity, close your
eyes. Relax. Think of a place. Wait for it to pop into your mind. Some place
has real meaning for you. You may love it or hate it, but it counts in your life
somehow. Keep your eyes closed until the place becomes so real that details
are crowding through your mind. Begin making a fact sheet. List everything
that comes to you, without regard to order. Just get significant details down
as fast as possible. As in Activity 2-1, concentrate on senses other than
sight—sound, smell, taste, touch. Jot down metaphors that occur to you
naturally, but don't force them. Don't forget colors. Go beyond "bare" facts:
remember not just trees, but tall, pointed evergreens dark against a stainless
evening sky.

*Don't start your description of the place until you have at least twenty
separate items.* Too many people either get excited after listing a few or think
they can do just as well without bothering with the list, and start writing the
description too soon. Skilled writers invariably see the advantages of a fact
sheet; less skilled ones—who need them more—often don't. If you do not
make a generous collection, *more than you need*, you will run out of facts
and, by writing prematurely, will drain off the energy that was supplying them
as you made your list. Don't fall into this trap, or your description will end up
stunted.

When you have a full list of *significant details*, think how to *focus* your description. If a plan has already developed in your mind, good. Go ahead. If not, consider the ways of focusing suggested in Activity 2-1:

1. What is the dominant impression you wish to convey to a reader?
2. Will a *logical time order* help?
3. Can you take a *particular point of view*, perhaps high above your place or from the spot where you first came upon it? Or see it with the eyes of an outsider?
4. Is there an extended metaphor that will provide focus? Could you, for instance, compare a scene at dawn to a sleeper awakening?
5. Can you use *some other sense than sight* to give focus? Do the smells of a farm, perhaps, provide a way to select relevant details and give the impression you want to convey?
6. Will the "lens" of your "camera" limit your description to a single picture that will provide everything you need? The following description is a sample of how focusing on a single part of the whole tells you all you need to know.

The wallpaper was white, with clusters of faded green leaves, and flowers which had once been red but were now pink. Grayish-blue tiled floor was smooth underfoot, but surprisingly not worn through. The white, paint-chipped railing had often proven itself sturdy enough to prevent two rowdy boys from crashing down the stairway head first. At the end of the hallway above the stairs, a window let the sun pour light and warmth in. What sounds filtered up the stairs were so muted by the distance they traveled that they might have been the pulsations and sighs of the old house itself. Opposite the stairway were two doors leading to bedrooms, a doorless closet, and a vacant corner.

It was in this vacant corner that my father placed my child's table and chair set. While my brothers and sisters were at school, I entertained myself for tireless eternities in this corner. At my little work table, I invented the pattern of alternating objects and alternating colors. I contentedly filled page after page with designs, each design consisting of alternating squares and circles, hearts and diamonds, red and blue, green and yellow.

Often my works of art were not revealed to any human eye, but only to that of a reliably understanding and appreciative critic: my teddy bear. He had struggled bearfully through three other generations of loving and cuddling, and, much to his credit, he had emerged from the fray with only one eye missing. This disabled veteran endured even more from me. I thought our church had the most wonderful choir, and I often sang or hummed whatever snatches of the beautiful hymns I could remember to the old bear. As I was never asked to perform my solos elsewhere, his complaints were probably justified.

Next to my work table was the small, doorless closet. In the closet there was a seat-like shelf and an old brown chest of drawers. My imaginary wardrobe was housed in the old, scratched-up chest, and the shelf-seat was my canopy bed. One day my teddy bear was very tired and cross, but he would not take a nap. Being well versed in child psychology, I lay down with him and pretended to sleep. Soon the old bear was snoring.

When we woke up, I felt greatly refreshed (and so did my teddy bear, although he didn't want to admit it). We went downstairs, and found the whole neighborhood frantically searching for us--or, rather, for me. My mother had just come into the house to call the police. I explained that my teddy bear had needed a nap.

To this day my teddy bear is listed as lost in action. He was forgotten one night and left to fend for himself beneath the swing set.

The old table and chair set have rusted and been thrown away, and doubtless the faded wallpaper has peeled and been replaced, but those tranquil, secure days are safely printed on the pages of time.

As before, do the best you can with your description, but don't agonize over it. Remember these activities are basically practice sessions, designed to help you build gradually the skills you need.

Activity 2-3   *Description of a Person*

✓   This time, remember a person, someone who matters to you, someone you care for deeply or perhaps dislike intensely. Emotional involvement on your part is a key ingredient of any good writing, though of course you must not let your emotions overrule your good sense. If you are neutral about your subject — in this case, the person you are writing about — your reader isn't going to be much interested.

Prepare a fact sheet, only now as you list facts also be alert to *specific incidents* that reveal the person acting in a characteristic way. People are known more by what they say and do than by how they look. Develop the *incident* in a second fact sheet, listing all the significant details that come to you. A reader can understand more clearly if you *recreate a scene.*

Remember too that all people are many-sided; no one is perfect. (We would hate anybody who was!) Will showing another side of the person you are describing help a reader understand him or her better? Usually one event for each characteristic is enough; don't pile up instances showing the same thing over and over. But be sure you have told the incident you choose in enough detail for the reader to see it as you do, experience it as you did, really feel *there!* You may want to try some dialogue, as in the following example. Often it makes your writing livelier and more interesting.

✓   When you have the two or three specific incidents showing the most important characteristics of the person you have chosen and have developed significant details about those specific incidents, write your description.

Be Yourself

While browsing through the posters at the store one day, I came across one which caught my eye. Pictured on the poster were about sixteen rows and eight columns of oranges; however, directly in the center, instead of an orange, there was a big red apple. The wording at the bottom of the poster said, "Be Yourself!"

This poster intrigued me, reminding me how people usually try to be alike in the way they dress, think, and act. Occasionally along the way, however, one meets some self-actualized person: that is, someone who enjoys doing as he pleases and doesn't need to conform to the actions of the majority.

I have a friend, Kim, who is like the apple in the middle of the oranges. Sometimes she stands out in crowds by wearing styles of clothes different from the majority or by expressing her own views. Kim doesn't care what other people think about her; she enjoys being herself and doing as she pleases. For instance, one time three of us girls went to Kim's to pick her up for a high school dance. We nearly died laughing when Kim came out wearing a wild pair of pink flowered pants and a huge, yellow, floppy hat.

"What are you idiots laughing at?" she demanded.

Trying to answer with a straight face, I replied, "Kim, your clothes are a little bit wild, aren't they?"

"What's wrong with pink pants and a yellow hat?"

"Kids these days just don't wear those kinds of clothes, Kim," I answered a bit sarcastically.

"I don't care what kids these days are wearing," Kim replied angrily. "I like this outfit and this is what I'm wearing." Then she added, "If you don't want to be seen with me, I'll go by myself."

"Of course we want you to go with us. Come on and get in the car," the three of us cried simultaneously.

Kim is also an individualist in the way she expresses herself. She doesn't hold back any of her true feelings because of what others might think. One time Kim and I went to the movies. When we got up to the front of the line, the ticket seller said, "Three dollars each, please."

"But the sign says two dollars," Kim protested.

"Sorry," the ticket seller replied, "but we raised the price."

"I'm not paying three dollars for your dumb movie. The sign says two, and if you won't let me in for two, I'll call my lawyer. It's ridiculous to advertise a lower price than what you charge in order to get people to come here," Kim shouted.

Everyone in the lobby of the theater could hear her. I was turning red with embarrassment and told her, "Calm down. I'll pay the extra dollar."

"Heck no," she yelled at me. "They advertise two dollars, and I'm going to get in for two dollars."

The manager came over and, after arguing with Kim for a while, let us in for the advertised two dollars.

Kim and I had our differences, but I knew she was just being herself in acting the way she wanted to and not caring what others felt about her. Most people, including myself, wouldn't do anything out of the ordinary, because they are afraid of what others will think of them, but more of us would be happier with life in general if we didn't have to worry about what other people were thinking about us all of the time. A good philosophy to follow is "Be a red apple among all of the oranges. Be yourself!"

ASSIGNMENT 2   A Description

✓   When you have finished Activities 2-1, 2-2, and 2-3, choose the description you like best.

> *Principle 4* **If you like something you've written, the chances are better that others will like it too.**

There follow three revising activities. Exercises like these will be a regular part of most of the chapters from now on, and doing them is *a part of the assignment*. Perform each revising activity separately on the *one* description you have chosen, according to the instructions. Some of you are good at revising your rough copy, but some don't have much idea where to begin. Some of you spoil your original work by revising all the life out of it. At this early stage, *do only the specific things called for in the revising activities*.

For the time being, all revising will involve looking at individual sentences. The tediousness of this will decrease with practice and eventually revising will become second nature. *Look at every sentence!*

In general, you will be looking first for unnecessary words. Many of you have formed bad habits, some conscious and others accidental. Sometimes you fall into a pattern of repeated words that sets up monotonous echoes in a reader's mind. Sometimes you overuse words, usually rather small ones like *I, and, of,* or common words like *really* and *very*, or forms of the verb *to be* and *to get*. Often the words *that* or *which* (frequently in phrases such as *that is* or *which are*) can be eliminated easily, making your sentences tighter and more efficient. The best writing is writing that makes its point most economically with the least expenditure of empty words. Excessive wordiness is a disease that frequently plagues college writing.

> *Principle 5* **Treat words as if they were money; save them whenever you can. Make every word count.**

One word of caution: What you are looking for is *words* that can be eliminated without changing the meaning of your sentence, spoiling its structure, or ruining its rhythm. Do *not* leave out or remove good vivid *details* that give your writing its life!

> *Principle 6* In revising, eliminate insignificant words. Retain significant details.

✓   When you have completed the three revising activities, prepare a final draft of the description you have chosen to hand in.

Revising Activity 2-1   *Repeated Words*

✓   Go through the draft of the *one* description you have chosen for Assignment 2. Watch for and circle repeated words. Note in particular whether such small words as *I* or *the* seem to recur monotonously, especially at the beginnings of sentences. A rule of thumb to follow at this early stage is: *Never begin two consecutive sentences with the same word.* If you find two sentences in a row beginning with the same word, see if you can change the structure of one sentence or perhaps in some way combine the two sentences to avoid the repetitious sentence beginnings. Remember, however, that sometimes repeating is a good device, helping to give emphasis to some idea or point. Use your judgment. After you have examined your description for repetitiousness, revise as you see necessary.

Example

(We) also had to eat our (lunch) at (school) every day. (We) lived about a mile from (school) and they didn't bus kids attending Catholic (schools.) We would eat our (lunch) as fast as (we) could, then run out on the (playground) to play. At our (school,) we had two (playgrounds.) (One for the) girls and (one for the) boys. It was a federal offense if you played in the wrong (one.)

[72 words]

Revised

Because kids attending Catholic school weren't bused and we lived a mile away, we couldn't go home for lunch. We would eat as fast as possible and then run out to play. There were two playgrounds, one for girls and one for boys. It was a federal offense if you played in the wrong one.

[55 words]

Notice how the revised passage cuts down on the wordiness, from 72 words to 55 words. Can you do this with your description without sacrificing meaning, good sentence structure, or an easy rhythm of the words? (Try reading your revised passage out loud. Often you can tell better if you hear what you have written.)

Revising Activity 2-2   *Extra Occurrences of* Which *and* That

✓   Now go through your draft again and look at *every* occurrence of *which* and *that*. If any can be eliminated from your sentence without changing its meaning, structure, or sound, cross it out. If there is more than one *which* or *that* in a sentence and one cannot be eliminated, can you revise the sentence to make one unnecessary?

Example	Revised
Sister Margaret started screaming that we were over on the boys' playground, it when we knew ~~that~~ was against the rule. She went on to say ~~that~~ we had caused trouble all year. [32 words]	Sister Margaret started screaming we were over on the boys' playground, when we knew it was against the rule. She said we had caused trouble all year. [27 words]

Revising Activity 2-3   *Extra Words*

✓   Look once more at every sentence. Bracket any words you could leave out without changing the meaning or ruining the sentence structure. Watch out particularly for *really* and *very*. Often these words weaken rather than strengthen your writing. Eliminate those words in your final draft.

Examples	Revised
Jane and I were still [the] best [of] friends until [the] eighth grade. [13 words]	Jane and I were still best friends until eighth grade. [10 words]
It was [really] strange how [very] grown up I felt. [10 words]	It was strange how grown up I felt. [8 words]

CHECKLIST   *Speaking with Your Own Voice*

Preparations.   Check off each item when completed.

Activity 2-1   Description of a Scene or Object . . . .
Activity 2-2   Description of a Place You Remember . . . .
Activity 2-3   Description of a Person . . . .
Assignment 2   A Description . . . .
Revising Activity 2-1   Repeated Words . . . .
Revising Activity 2-2   Extra Occurrences of *Which* and *That* . . . . . .
Revising Activity 2-3   Extra Words . . . .

Goals to Be Achieved.   Write your answers on a separate sheet. Explain fully.

1. Does your final draft of the description you chose say something that matters to you in a voice natural to you?

2. Have you done your best to include significant details so that a reader can feel *there* with you, understanding what you are seeing, hearing, feeling?
3. Have you done the three revising activities carefully and revised your description accordingly? Are there words repeated so often as to become monotonous, unnecessary occurrences of *which* or *that*, extra words you can eliminate?

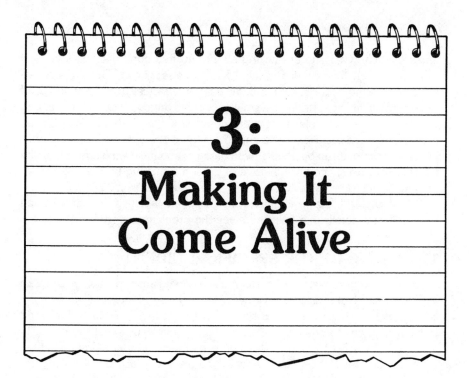

3:
Making It
Come Alive

You know that sometimes when you read you "can't put it down" and other times you yawn your way through, your attention wandering. You read a passage over and over without having the slightest idea afterwards what it was about. This may happen when you aren't concentrating or the material is too difficult; it also happens with perfectly clear passages. Nor does your degree of attention necessarily depend on whether the subject interests you: one article or essay on economics can be deadly dull while another commands rapt attention.

Where does the difference lie? Why does a subject come alive in a meaningful way one time and not another?

We have already discussed two ways to make *your* subject come alive. One is to *talk naturally* about it, in words that are simple and direct. The dull article on economics was probably written by a Stuffed Owl and is full of big words that send you running for the dictionary. Often the language employs jargon—terms and phrases that may make sense to another economist but to few others. The interesting article, on the other hand, may be no less informative, but the language, by and large, is clear and easily understood, with special terms defined for the ordinary reader.

The second way is to use *significant details* to put a reader *there*. Abstract, general statements tend to be boring and often confusing. Details help your writing come alive for a reader by providing sharp, easily remembered pictures. Suppose you are concerned about the population explosion. You could make a general statement: "Increasing pressures from the population explosion are ruining the quality of life in the United States." Your readers know vaguely what you are talking about but they don't become involved; more than likely they yawn and say, "So what else is new?" But suppose, instead, you begin by describing in detail a favorite picnic spot where·you used to go some years ago, perhaps a small, sheltered area of grass, sunshine, and shade, where a few tables and one outdoor stove were shared amicably by two or three families. Next, as a contrast, you tell how that picnic spot looks now: the area overrun by people, with garbage and trash lying around, all the tables taken, no space on the stove and people snarling at one another for moving a pan to one side. Now your readers nod and say, "Yes, I know exactly how that is." They understand; they become involved. You have given the significant details that help them see the problem as you do.

THE VALUE OF THE SPECIFIC INCIDENT

Often, however, even a description has a certain abstract quality. Or it can lack a sense of dramatic involvement. What really works may be to tell a *specific incident* to illustrate your point. People are interested in and respond to what happens to other people, real people involved in real situations. In addition, it is easier for you to describe something if you visualize an actual, typical occurrence. You have already had some practice in looking for specific incidents to make your point clearer in your description of a person for Activity 2-3 in Chapter 2.

In order to use this tool well, you need to develop skills of narrative, a step beyond description. Narrative is simply a telling of *what happens next*, of progressing logically from one point to the other so that a reader can see it all happening.

Although narrative has many uses in all writing, the easiest way to develop skill in narrative is to tell about something you have experienced. When using personal experience you have all the significant details available and can concentrate on how to select and order them for the greatest effectiveness. If you make events out of your past come alive for yourself, you are on the way to making them come alive for a reader, and beyond that, on the way to being able to instill life into all your writing.

The activities in this chapter are designed to help you develop narrative skills. As before, it is important that you do the activities carefully, even if your instructor never looks at them. The activities lead to the assignment; each assignment is practice for the next assignment; the whole course is practice for writing you will be doing the rest of your life. Like all skills—playing an instrument, painting a picture, participating in sport—writing takes steady practice. You cannot suddenly say, "Well, now I am going to write something really good." It would be like giving a piano recital or entering a tennis tournament without working and practicing beforehand.

> *Principle 7* **Very few things are achieved without hard work. Writing is hard work, not just for you—for everyone.**

Activity 3-1   *Narrating an Event*

✓   Relax. Close your eyes and wait for an event to pop into your mind, something that for some reason has special meaning for you. Open your eyes and begin a *fact sheet*. Write down the first thing that comes to you. What comes next? Write that down. Keep saying to yourself "What comes next?" until you have everything down that initally comes to mind.

By now the event should be taking shape. Keep writing down facts, even small ones that seem irrelevant. Irrelevant facts—like details in a dream—are often the clue to an inner significance not at first apparent. They don't seem to fit together; then suddenly something clicks, and you see totally unexpected meanings.

After you have done this first step, think specifically about significant details—sights, sounds, smells, tastes, touch—just as you did for the activities in Chapter 2. Fill a page, two pages. Maybe even three pages.

Put your fact sheet aside for a time. Let it cool. Leave it overnight or at least until after you've eaten or taken a walk. Let your subconscious mind work on the experience you have been thinking about. Then turn your full attention to it again.

The next step is crucial; it can make all the difference in your success in interesting your reader. Focus on the *peak moment*, the most vivid moment, the one that makes the experience live in your memory. It will be the moment of strongest emotion—excitement, fear, anger, happiness—whatever causes you to remember the incident. *Do a supplemental fact sheet featuring that moment.* Then review your original fact sheet for additional pertinent details. *Organize your narrative around the peak moment.*

What happened first? Is it important at this moment to record your own thoughts or feelings? If so, don't neglect to do so. But perhaps the events can be narrated so vividly that you will not have to explain your thoughts and feelings. Ideally your significant details should be so skillfully used that the reader *himself* will think and feel what you did. Avoid, if you can, *telling* a reader what to think. Show! Make him see! Make him feel!

Move on. What happened next? What happened after that? Don't leave gaps in your narrative that make it difficult for a reader to follow; on the other hand, don't include details that add neither to the vividness nor to the reader's understanding. Don't make a special effort to dredge up "colorful" details or you may sound like a Proud Peacock. A key word in all writing is *significant*. It takes practice to recognize what is significant, but you must learn to make that decision. Readers can say, "Well, this isn't important; the narrative drags here and I got bored," or they can say, "You've lost me somewhere; something's left out that I need to know." They can't supply the important details you've omitted, because only you know what they are.

When you've narrated the peak moment of your experience as well as you can, again let it cool. Then read what you have written, trying to see it as an ordinary reader would. Does it carry some of the emotional impact that characterized the actual experience? If not, have you failed to use significant details that created the impact for you? For instance, if you are writing about the moment your football team made the winning touchdown in the last two minutes, was there something that increased your own excitement and suspense—some momentary, intense silence in the crowd or, on the other hand, a rising roar of sound with a chant "We Want a Touchdown" coming through it? Did you describe that for your readers to help them experience what was happening to you?

When you feel you have done your best to make the particular moment come alive, ask yourself if there is any additional background information a reader needs. If you can't decide, ask a friend to read your narrative. Don't expect to be told what to do, but find out what kind of reaction you get. (Be cautious about a friend who says, "That's pretty good. I don't think you need to do anything to it." Such a statement often masks a feeling of boredom; you may not have brought the experience to life yet. No one is bored by a good story.)

It was the night of the football game between my high school and our cross-town rival. It was also my last game as drum major for the band. I already knew some simple twirls, but I wanted to be able to throw the baton in the air and catch it. Every morning before school for two weeks, I went out and practiced during band. The first week I didn't make any progress at all. The baton would come down to one side, or I would drop it. By the beginning of the second week I was ready to forget the whole idea, when, for the first time, I caught the baton. Slowly I started improving, but the game was only four days away. I worked, catching one out of every ten throws, then one out of eight, until the day of the game I was catching it once every three times I threw it up. The whole day I fought with myself. If I caught it, it would mean succeeding at a goal I had set and it would add considerably to my routine. If I dropped it, not only would my goal be shattered, but thousands of rival fans would use it to cut down our band. Just before the game, I tried again. Up it went, but it landed two feet in front of me.

I stood in my position waiting for the pre-game activities to start. They announced the band. Cheers from the home side met with jeers from our rivals and grew into one tremendous roar. The majorettes ran out. Then my turn came. "Our man-up-front . . . " I ran out into the noise. The band started playing. It was now or never. I started twirling the baton. In a few beats the point would come where I would have to throw it up or just hold on to it. I held my breath and threw it up. All noise was blocked out as I concentrated on the twirling piece of metal above me. Up it went, reflecting light with every turn. Then, slowly at first, it came back down. I stuck out my hand and waited and watched. I felt the cold baton hit my hand and my fingers clasp around it. It stung, but I had caught it. I turned around and gave the signal whistle to the band and we marched down the field. It didn't seem like my feet touched the ground the rest of the way.

Here the writer has chosen for his focus the peak moment when he threw the baton up during the game, not knowing whether he would be able to catch it. He begins at the "night of the football game" and then briefly sets the scene, describing the preceding two weeks during which he tried to perfect his skill and culminating in the day of the game when he still was not sure of himself. Immediately thereafter, he moves to the crucial moment: it is time to face the crowd and make his decision. Note how he sets the scene with the significant details that heighten his suspense as well as yours as reader, first concentrating on sounds (the cheers, the jeers, the roars, leading up to his running out "into the noise" as the music begins), and then, with the noise blocked out, shifting the emphasis to details of sight (the twirling of the metal, the reflection of light, the slowness with which the baton seems to fall). Finally, details of touch dominate (the coldness, the clasp of his hand around the baton, the sting).

Activity 3-2   *Using Dialogue*

Perhaps in Activity 3-1 you have naturally included some conversation. Although, as the example shows, effective narration can be achieved without dialogue, often the use of conversation helps bring an event to life in an almost magical way. A skill in using dialogue not only helps you with your narratives; it comes in handy in other ways. Notice how often an article or essay you read includes direct dialogue, a direct quotation of something someone has said that clarifies the idea and makes the passage more natural and interesting. A proficiency in using dialogue may prove useful later on.

Years passed and the friendship between Boag and me grew so strong it seemed we were always together, us against them. Everything we did we did together, like the time we sneaked into the woods after class to smoke our first cigarette. The excitement of something devilish and naughty filled our veins as we ran through the woods giggling. We sat puffing and coughing for about ten minutes, before some girls saw us and ran off in horror.

The next day when we entered the classroom—a few minutes late, as usual—our teacher told us the principal would like a word with us. Sure enough, it was about our smoking adventure. Cursing the girls who saw us, we sat and listened to that old man lecture for nearly an hour. Boag cut the sermon short, however, when he asked old man Wilson why he smoked. The principal choked on a few more words and spluttered for an explanation.

"Well . . . er . . . ah . . . it's bad, I mean it's different with adults."

"How different?"

"Adults smoked before they knew it was bad for them."

"If it's bad for you and you know it is, then why do you still smoke?"

"Never mind. Just don't let it happen again! You can go!"

> As we got up to leave, I noticed a slight smirk on Boag's face which seemed to say, "Another one for us, Dave." All I could say as we ran back down the long hall was, "You bust me up!"

This passage gains both its humor and its point primarily from the exchange of conversation at the end. Until then, it has a tendency to scoot along the surface, not involving a reader especially, although the visual picture of the two boys giggling and coughing in the woods, feeling devilish, is a good one. Probably this paragraph suits its purpose adequately. The next one, though, seems to drag. The teacher "told" the boys they were wanted by the principal. *Consider the possibility of using dialogue whenever you see a phrase like "the teacher told us" or "I said that" or "he explained that."* Perhaps this part of the story could be made more dramatic, more real, by using a bit of dialogue:

> The next day when we entered the classroom—a few minutes late, as usual—the teacher glanced at us over the top of her spectacles. "The principal wants you in his office right away," she announced grimly.

Another clue for some dialogue is the phrase "we sat and listened to that old man lecture for nearly an hour." Obviously the writer wouldn't include an "hour's" worth of lecture, but a few typical phrases might put the reader there with the two boys: "Against the rules . . . shocking at your age . . . what would your parents say? . . . ruin your lungs and stunt your growth . . ." Then, just when the reader is getting bored, Boag could break in with his question, deflating the pompous principal. It's something to consider.

Sometimes it takes a little practice to get your ear tuned to the real sound of conversation. The first thing to do is to listen and record.

✓ In two different situations during the course of a day, listen carefully to the conversation going on around you and try to jot down exactly what you hear. Make the situations different enough for you to get different patterns each time. Listen to people next to you in the cafeteria or commons, to people on a bus, to conversation in the classroom before the hour begins, to a teacher getting warmed up to lecture. Catch the hesitations, the repetitions, the slurred pronunciations. Don't worry if what you write down doesn't make much sense. The important thing is to capture the sound of real conversation.

> "Close the book, stupid. It's time ta party."
> "Whaddaya mean, it's time to party?"
> "The week's over. We gotta party down for the weekend."
> "But it's only Thursday night. I don't know about you but I got classes tomorrow."
> "Aw, nobody goes to classes on Friday."
> "I do."
> "Well, Christ, just because ya got classes don't mean you can't party."
> "I gotta read this book."
> "Hey, where's tha beer?"

"In the fridge."
"Let's have some music. Yah, yah, C'mon, party time."

✓ Next recall a situation involving a conversation between two people. Using a minimum of explanation, recreate the situation and people involved. This time don't reproduce the conversation word for word, as that is usually rambling and boring. Suggest the speech patterns so that a reader can recognize them, without necessarily using the exact words.

Around noon, floating down the river in our canoe, we opened up some pop and ate our bologna sandwiches.
"Jackson!" I announced. "You stink! You profuse with odor! Jackson! You smell!"
"Oh, ya?"
"Ya!"
"Oh, ya?"
"Yah!"
"Walters! You reek with perspiration! You smell so bad that if the wind changed and blew your odor my way, it'd burn my eyeballs purple! Walters! You're nothin' but a sorry-sack-a-shit!"
"What're we gonna have for supper, Jackson?"
"How 'bout beans and hamburgers?"
"O.K."
In the late afternoon, we chose a campsite. Jackson built the fire and I did the cooking. After he ate his first forkful, Jackson looked at me. "Walters, you may smell bad but you're a darn good cook."
"Gee, Jackson. T'anks. Seein' as how I cooked the food, you can do the dishes."
"I'll tell you what, Walters. I'll wash my dishes and you can wash yours. How's that grab ya?"
"It doesn't grab me at all."

Activity 3-3 *Bringing Life through Dialogue*

Go back to the experience you wrote about in Activity 3-1. Look for at least one place where you could have used dialogue but did not. In the drum major's story, for example, the narrative might have been livelier if, during his practice, someone had come by and ridiculed his efforts with some remark such as "Wow, you really gonna try that Friday night?" Or instead of writing "They announced the band," the student might have included actual words coming over the loudspeaker.

Watch particularly for signals such as "my sister said it was time to go," or "the policeman told us to pull over." Such signals don't necessarily mean you want to use dialogue, but consider the possibility.

✓   Revise your narrative to bring in dialogue. If you can't remember exactly what was said, fabricate some dialogue, as long as it seems natural and right. The point is to give you a feel for the way dialogue can help bring an event to life.

ASSIGNMENT 3   A Narrative

✓   For this assignment, you will revise and submit a narrative of a personal experience. You may choose anything you have written so far, as long as it includes at least one *specific incident*, *one* event that actually happened. A good source for this assignment may be the sketch of a person you wrote in Activity 1-4, which you might improve now by using specific incidents told in significant detail and with dialogue. But almost any of the writing activities you have done so far, which have not already been used for assignments, may yield a good beginning for Assignment 3. If nothing you have written seems appropriate and interesting, recall another event out of your past, do your fact sheet, and write a first draft trying to keep in mind the things discussed so far. If your narrative includes more than one incident, be sure *each* incident clearly serves the overall purpose you have in mind (what you want to communicate to a reader) and *each incident* is told with sufficient detail to make a reader feel *there*.

Review your choice of a narrative carefully for the following points:

1. Is this an incident that had some emotional impact on you, an emotional impact you wish to communicate to a reader?
2. Have you chosen the *peak moment* of each specific incident to write about and have you developed that thoroughly?
3. Have you included all the significant details needed to bring your narrative alive for a reader, without piling up irrelevant details?
4. Have you used dialogue effectively where appropriate? Have you missed opportunities to use dialogue effectively?

Rewrite the narrative to make full use of the techniques of focusing on the peak moment, using significant details, and employing dialogue. When you have done the best you can, revise it as suggested in the revising activities that follow, make a clean, neat copy as a final draft, and hand in your narrative. As before, don't agonize too long over this. Do your best and, even if it doesn't satisfy you entirely, *move on!*

Introduction:
sets background so
that reader can
understand the story

In elementary school I was the school's athlete. Because of my athletic abilities, I felt that fat people were inferior to me. There was this kid named Herbie Jorgenson, who started school a week after it opened. He was pretty big for his age and walked clumsily. I guess the reason for his clumsiness were those two canoes he called feet.

When it rained and the streets were flooded, we
would ask, "Herbie, take us across the street in
your canoes."

Despite our harassment he seemed never to be
upset or angry; he acted as though we weren't even
there. I guess that's the reason I pestered him so
much. He would sometimes wear his father's clothes
and shoes, which we would naturally tease him
about. Herbie constantly ignored me, which ir-
ritated me, so one day I ran up and pushed him
down. Believe it or not, this guy actually rolled
about five yards before he came to an abrupt stop.
We stood there and just laughed at him.

Incident 1

Herbie finally got fed up with my little
tricks and started chasing me. I was only toying
with him, running backwards, stopping until he
caught up with me. Then I took off running again.
Herbie ran like a penguin and with every step he
made, the fat on his body went up and down. I could
see that he was tiring so I picked up more speed
and left him blocks behind. All I could see then
was a fat out-of-shape object with his hands wav-
ing in the air as though he were saying, "I'm going to get you yet, Red Baron."

Incident 2

The following morning during class I sat
directly behind him intentionally, so I could ag-
gravate him. Teasingly I said, "Good morning,
Herbie." He turned his fat round head around and
said, "We'll finish where we left off yesterday
when class is over." His serious tone put a little
fear in my heart, but I knew my speed would help me
escape. One thing I was always afraid of, and that
was the day he ever caught me while I was playing
games on him.

Incident 3
Peak moment 1

Class was over. Everybody crowded out on the
playground. I was there showboating, showing the
spectators what I was going to do to Herbie. In a
way I was worried about him because it was unusual
for him to invite me to a rumble in a public place.
Finally he came stumbling through the doorway and
out onto the playground. When he approached me I
confronted him by telling him his mother wore army
boots, and that started the rumble. I was circling
him, hitting him all over his body, but his fat
just absorbed the impact of my blows. I was tiring
and Herbie knew it. He rushed me like a charging
elephant, sending me running backwards to escape.

Unaware of a low fence behind me, I backed
into it and went flying over on my back. Coming
directly at me was two hundred and about forty

pounds. I had a split second to react. All I could
think of was "Roll! Roll!" and without a moment
to lose, I rolled over just in the nick of time,
sending Herbie crashing to the ground on his face.
When he got up, he looked like a clown, with dirt
smeared on his nose and fat cheeks. Tears came
rolling down his face.

"Someday I'll get even with you," he swore.
We all laughed.

Transition

Soon after that day his family moved to the
other side of town. But I continued picking on fat
people. I suppose you could call me a bully,
because I only picked on fat, helpless people.

Incident 4

A year passed. Word was around that Herbie
was back in the neighborhood and was going to
enroll in school the next day. So I plotted against

Peak moment 2

him. The following morning I went to school about a
half hour earlier than usual, along with my spectators to witness the coming massacre. Herbie was
spotted about a block away by one of my fellows. We
waited like impatient vultures. Suddenly somebody
shouted, "He's here!" Everybody scattered to
hiding places. As Herbie entered through the doorway, I jumped him from behind. All I can remember
then was being tossed through the air like a dummy.
When I landed I was scooped up and shaken by two
gigantic hands.

"Remember me?" Herbie said.
"Herbie! Is that you?" I answered.
"Who were you expecting? Santa Claus?"
"But, but, but . . . Herbie, I didn't know."
"You didn't know what?"
"Herbie! Please put me down."
"On one condition."
"Anything, Herbie."
"You agree to stop picking on fat people."
"It's a deal. Just put me down!"

He eased me gently to the floor. Later he told
me he had joined a weight reducing club that turned
his fat into muscles.

**Conclusion:
writer's purpose
emerges**

After that day he and I were like brothers. We
went all the way through high school together.
Every now and then we joked about that little incident when we were young. After high school graduation I decided to go to college, while he joined
the Army, which came as a shock to me, because Herbie didn't like violence.

A year passed after Herbie joined the Army.
It was on a hot summer day when his parents told me
he had been killed in the line of duty. They also

> told me he died with honor. That made the burden a
> little lighter but it couldn't bring Herbie back.
> Oh, fat humble Herbie, I miss you.

This is an example of a narrative that uses several incidents and covers a long time period without becoming superficial. The passage of time is handled easily, with quick, efficient transitions. The writer lingers, however, over the specific incidents, giving the reader a vivid picture of each: in the first, for instance, we can see Herbie running "like a penguin" with his fat going "up and down." Dialogue adds to the lively effect at every point. When the story is over, the underlying purpose is clear; there is a clear and effective picture of the developing and changing relationship between the writer and Herbie. The narrative is funny, but in addition it satisfies another criterion of a good story: there is conflict in it—between the writer and Herbie, between the writer and himself, and between a story humorous on the surface but underneath not funny at all. This student, by not being afraid to tell the truth in detail, has approached a point where writing becomes art, and has produced a story that will not die in the reader's mind, that has truly come alive.

Revising Activity 3-1   *Conventions for Dialogue*

✔   Read the following discussion of how to put your dialogue in proper form; then revise your draft of Assignment 3 accordingly. (If you have included no dialogue in Assignment 3, use the third conversation you wrote in Activity 3-2, the one where you tried to create a situation through the use of dialogue. Put that in proper form and turn it in with your Assignment 3.)

It should perhaps be noted that, as with almost every "rule" in English, there are exceptions to those that follow. "Rules" should not be taken as arbitrary never-to-be-broken precepts. Conventions of dialogue form have been adopted for good reason: they establish quick communication between writer and reader. This is the basic reason for all rules of punctuation and grammar. You can deviate from them, but you must first know the conventions and rules, so that your deviation is intentional, not an accident. How does a reader know whether your deviation is intentional or accidental? In the same way that a listener knows whether a pianist is slowing down over a complicated passage of music because it is too difficult for him or because he wants to create a mood. In the same way that someone in the gallery knows a professional golfer's unconventional stance is his style and not a result of ignorance. If you know what is expected and then choose to ignore it—and experienced writers break nearly every "rule" in the book—people will recognize your skill. But there is no way you can fake it.

1. Conventional Paragraphing in Dialogue

As a general rule, *paragraph when attention shifts from one person to another.*

"I'm going up on the tricksters," I announced. "Keep me in the smooth and take it easy on the speed." Pulling on the skis and jumping in the water, I grabbed the line. "Take out the slack," I yelled to the boat. "O.K., hit it!" The line snapped tight and I glided up. I skied backwards for a while and then decided to do some fancy stuff. "Hey, watch this!" I did my helicopter, spinning around on the skis several times in a row. It's a classy move and the crowd was impressed. I was dizzy. I dropped off. "How'd I look?" I asked when I got into the boat.

"Pretty decent, but you should see that other guy. He's on one ski."

"Oh, yeah? Well, I'm going up again then. I'm going to do my toe trick."

"O.K., but don't blow it."

"Hey, don't worry, man. Take out the slack . . . . O.K., hit it!"

This passage demonstrates the shifting of attention from speaker to speaker by the use of new paragraphs. Notice that because the reader is accustomed to this device, the writer can go on for quite some time without indicating who is doing the speaking, thus avoiding awkward dialogue attributions like "I said" or "he cautioned."

Note carefully: *Dialogue paragraphs are exactly the same as other paragraphs.* Do *not* indent anything except the first line, which is what you do with any paragraph. *Do not single space if you are double spacing the rest of your narrative.* (If you are indenting and single spacing, you are confusing dialogue with material quoted from a book or article. They are two entirely different things.)

2. Use of Dialogue Attributions

As a general rule, *place dialogue tags or attributions in the middle of a conversation or at the end, not at the beginning.*

One day after collecting money from our Karate Club members, Gwendolyn and I went downtown to buy our instructor a birthday gift. After browsing around a while, we decided on cuff links.

"Miss," Gwendolyn said, walking up to the lady behind the counter, "do you have any handcuffs?"

The clerk looked at her in surprise. "What did you say?" she asked. "I didn't quite understand what you said."

"Do you have any handcuffs?" Gwendolyn repeated.

"That's what I thought you said."

"You know what I'm talking about? The things you wear on your arms."

"Yes, I know what you're talking about, but I'm sorry," the clerk replied, looking strangely at Gwendolyn, "we just don't sell them. As a matter of fact, we never have."

Starting to laugh, I broke into the conversation. "Miss, she means cuff links."

"Oh! Cuff links! Right this way, please."

In this passage, all the dialogue tags such as "Gwendolyn said" and "the clerk replied" are either inserted during the speech or are at the end. The main reason for this is that the first part of a sentence always gets more attention from a reader, and since what is more important is what is said in this case—*not* who is saying it—the dialogue tag is relegated to a secondary position later in the sentence. Sometimes of course it works just as well to put the dialogue attribution first; for instance, Gwendolyn's first speech might have been introduced in the following manner:

Walking up to the lady behind the counter, Gwendolyn said, "Miss, do you have any handcuffs?"

But even here the dialogue tag is put in an inconspicuous spot; the action of walking up to the clerk is emphasized in this version. What would not have worked would be to have put the dialogue tag first, like this:

Gwendolyn said, walking up to the lady behind the counter, "Miss, do you have any handcuffs?"

---

3. Verb and Adverb Usage

Make the verbs you choose do the work for you; be careful about overusing adverbs.

"I'm King of the Mountain!" Jim boasted pridefully.

"Not for long!" I shouted loudly. Jumping off the white snowbank, I ran like a bullet up the side of the hill. Jim sidestepped me and I flew over the hill, missing his body completely. When I got up, Jim sneered from the peak, "I'm King of the Mountain! You can't get me!"

"I'll get you yet!" I ranted furiously.

"Kill 'im, Jim!" George screamed at the top of his lungs.

If you take away the adverbs (*pridefully, loudly, furiously*) and the adverb phrase (*at the top of his lungs*), this passage emerges cleaner and more effective. But even when you do that, there is the impression of a mad scramble for verbs, producing Proud Peacock language. Keep in mind that the verb *said* can be used quite often before a reader notices it and becomes bored, but when you reach too far for a "different" term, whatever it may be, the reader is more apt to be noticing your virtuosity at finding "colorful words" than to be reacting to what is said.

Principle 8 **Language that draws attention to itself and away from what is being said should be avoided.**

4. Punctuation of Dialogue

The following are the conventional ways to punctuate dialogue. As always, keep in mind first that every rule has its exceptions, and that there is no attempt in this book to tell you *all* the possibilities and problems, just the common ones. If you run into something not covered, check your handbook. If that doesn't answer your question, ask your instructor.

a. If the speech within quotation marks is a complete sentence ending in a punctuation mark other than a period, put the end punctuation for the speech inside the quotation marks.

"What did you say?" she asked.
"I'm King of the Mountain!" Jim boasted.

---

b. If the speech within quotation marks is not a complete sentence or is a complete sentence that would normally end in a period, it is separated from the dialogue tag by commas.

"I'm going up on the tricksters," I announced.
"Miss," Gwendolyn said, walking up to the lady behind the counter, "do you have any handcuffs?"

---

c. Quotation marks go around only the part that is actual dialogue, even when the speech is split by a dialogue tag.

"Take out the slack," I yelled to the boat. "O.K., hit it."
"Miss," Gwendolyn said, walking up to the lady behind the counter, "do you have any handcuffs?"

---

d. Enclose in commas (or other punctuation) names and substitutes for names used in direct address.

"Watch out, Jim, when you climb that hill."
I jumped up and cried, "Let's go, man!"

✔ To recapitulate, revise your narrative to conform to the "rules" explained under the headings (1) Conventional Paragraphing in Dialogue; (2) Use of Dialogue Attributions; (3) Verb and Adverb Usage; and (4) Punctuation of Dialogue.

Revising Activity 3-2   *Basic Punctuation*

Most people who have trouble with punctuation do so because they try to memorize many rules in a vacuum, then forget them, retaining only a confusing and vague collection of trailing vestiges. There are logical reasons for the conventions of punctuation, and all are aimed at trying to establish better communication between a writer and a reader. Like all other rules, punctuation conventions can be be bent almost out of recognizable shape, but first you must get a few in mind. The most confusing problems involve commas, so let us leave those for later.

We will talk first about the semicolon (;), the colon (:), the dash (—), and parentheses (). In experienced hands, all these have multiple uses, but you should stick to *one use for each*.

1. Semicolon (;)

Use a semicolon to separate two units of words—each of which is a complete sentence that can stand by itself—when the two are so closely united in thought that you would rather not divide them into two sentences.

Two sentences	Combined with a semicolon
My row was the last to get in line. There were about fifteen kids already up at the chalkboard when I got behind Mary.	My row was the last to get in line; there were about fifteen kids already up at the chalkboard when I got behind Mary.

Each of the original two statements could stand by itself and therefore can be ended with a period. But if this writer wants to associate closely the fact that his row was last and the fact that there were already fifteen kids in line, this is an excellent place to use a semicolon.

2. Colon (:)

Use a colon to introduce a list or series that explains what goes ahead of the colon.

The natives brought us four kinds of fruit: mangoes, bananas, pineapples, and pomegranates.

3. Dash (—)

Use a dash only to enclose or set something off that is unusual, extraordinary, or surprising. Make it a rule never to use a dash if some other form of punctuation is available; students typically use dashes indiscriminately.

I put my lips to the horn only to hear a sickly hiss of air—not a note came out!

Note: When typing dashes, be sure to use *two* hyphens (--). Do not put extra spaces between the dash and the words on either side.

4. Parentheses ()

The general rule here is: *Avoid parentheses!* Experienced writers know how to use them, but few students do. Work *all* your information smoothly into your sentence structure.

Poor use of parentheses	Better
At school (Illinois College of Optometry) this fall, he met a student who was bragging about being accepted with a 2.0 average.	When he entered the Illinois College of Optometry this fall, he met a student who was bragging about being accepted with a 2.0 average.

5. Comma (,)

We now come to the comma. Some comma usage, as in addresses and dates, is strictly conventional; consulting a handbook on style will give you the answers. The handbook will also help you make other decisions about commas. There is no one simple "rule" that will give you all the answers, but if you keep in mind that, in general, *commas signal logical pauses*, it may help. A distinction must be made, however, between a *logical* pause—where the thought or idea takes a turn—and what is called a *rhetorical* or *speech* pause. Speakers pause for various reasons, some logical and some not. If a phrase is long, they may pause simply to catch their breath. Or for emphasis. Or they may make pauses dictated by the dialect of the area where they live; many northerners, for instance, were initially surprised by unexpected pauses in the speech of Jimmy Carter, when he was running for the office of President.

The chief purpose for commas in writing is to help make the meaning as clear as possible. Most so-called rules simply facilitate this purpose. For instance, the purpose of a "rule" about placing a comma after a long introductory phrase or clause is to tell a reader that the introductory material is completed and the writer is beginning his or her main thought.

After John understood that Sally's bad temper resulted from her argument with his mother, he forgave her.

Here you have two ideas, one minor and one major.

Major idea: he forgave her
Minor idea: After John understood Sally's bad temper resulted from her argument with his mother

The comma following "mother" helps a reader see that the minor idea, contained in a dependent clause, is finished. The writer is about to express the major idea—that John forgave Sally.

Sometimes incorrect placement of a comma can create confusion by seeming to indicate a pause at an illogical place.

Incorrect use of comma	Correct
John came but, he didn't stay long.	John came, but he didn't stay long.

Try saying these two sentences out loud. It is awkward to pause after "John came but." On the other hand, it is natural to pause after "John came." The comma is correct after "John came."

Very often the lack of a comma, not the incorrect insertion of one, causes the trouble. The following sentences would be easier to understand if commas were used.

Confusing	Better
To win his father required a keen appreciation of horseflesh.	To win, his father required a keen appreciation of horseflesh.
We looked at snowshoes and snowmobiles and skis and what we wanted we bought.	We looked at snowshoes and snowmobiles and skis, and what we wanted we bought.

✔   As a bit of practice, punctuate the following sentences, using the foregoing principles of punctuation. Then turn to the key on **p. 250** to check yourself.

1. The student should be required to type every paper he hands in particularly for the English class.

2. This would not only conserve the eyesight and sweeten the disposition of the professor but it would help the student learn.

3. He will no longer be able to hide his spelling errors behind blots and erasures and unrecognizable squiggles and he will learn to spell better.

4. If he can't fatten his essays simply by enlarging his handwriting he may be forced to come up with some real ideas.

5. And he will be less likely to dash off just any kind of nonsense in order to fill up space silly statements have a way of looking very silly indeed even to their author when they are neatly lined up in precise and impersonal black type.

6. Thus he will be able to see his own errors in a new and painful clarity deprived of his usual subterfuges unrecognizable handwriting great scrawls and lots of empty words to make up the required five hundred.

—A student

6. End Punctuation

Although most of you are familiar with the marks at the end of sentences, there are some problems to keep in mind. A *period* (.) as end punctuation usually marks the end of a complete statement; if you are not sure what constitutes a complete statement, be sure you master Minigrammer C when it comes up later in the text. *Exclamation points* (!) indicate emphasis or surprise; use them sparingly and never more than one at a time. Overuse gives your writing a frantic air, weakening the impact rather than strengthening it. The most troublesome piece of end punctuation, rather surprisingly, is the *question mark* (?). Everyone knows it comes after a question, but students constantly forget to use it. Check yourself carefully until use of question marks becomes automatic.

7. The Apostrophe

Apostrophes trip up almost everyone at some time or another. They are used in two principal situations. The first is in *contractions*, to show the absence of a missing letter. If you place the apostrophe *where the missing letter was*, you should have few problems with contractions.

Examples		
are + not	aren t	aren't
There + is	There s	There's
they + are	they re	they're
Class of 1972	Class of 72	Class of '72
Rock and roll	Rock n roll	Rock 'n' Roll

The other principal use of apostrophes is to show *possession*. The "news of today" becomes "today's news"; the "house of Mrs. Jones" becomes "Mrs. Jones's house"; the "ball of the children" becomes the "children's ball." Notice that *in every case* the apostrophe comes *after* the complete word: *today, Jones, children*. When the word ends in *-s*, you add another *s only if, in pronouncing the possessive, you hear an added "s" sound*: for instance, *"boss's desk," "Sphinx's smile," "mistress's keys."* But there is no added *s* when you hear no added sound: *Euripides' plays," "a five years' accumulation," "in several judges' opinion."* Once the principle is grasped, use of apostrophes to show possession presents little difficulty—except that of oversight; we simply forget the apostrophe. As with the question mark, watch yourself until you've formed a habit.

A special problem: The apostrophe that gives people most trouble involves the "its/it's" conundrum. Which do you use when? Two little rules of thumb may help. *No pronoun ever shows possession by use of an apostrophe!* Associate *its* with *theirs, his, hers,* and *ours,* other pronouns which never use an apostrophe. The second little rule: *the contraction rule always takes precedence over the possession rule.* Therefore: *it's* means *it + is.*

Examples
It's a fine day for a picnic. (Contraction: it + is)
This law has outlasted *its* usefulness. (Possessive: no apostrophe)

✔ Now examine your own narrative, sentence by sentence. Try to reword any sentence with a parenthetical statement in it. Examine any use you have made of a dash; would a comma or a semicolon do just as well there? Read your sentences aloud or *listen* to them in your mind. Have you put commas in places where, when reading, you would not pause? Have you left out commas in places where they are needed to help your reader grasp your meaning more easily?

Revising Activity 3-3   *Grammar (Minigrammars A, B)*

✔ Check through your narrative carefully, sentence by sentence, for the following:

1. Agreement in number between subjects and their predicates.

2. Agreement in verb tense.

If you are not sure what you are looking for or need some refreshing, work through Minigrammars A and B, beginning on pp. 171 and 183.

The *Minigrammars* are provided to help you review certain principles of grammar and style about which you may be uncertain. Most of the minigrammars begin with a *Diagnostic Section*, which you should go through whether or not you feel confident of your grasp of the principles involved. Don't worry if you have trouble; the purpose is to *find out* what you know. When you have finished, consult the *Key* section. If you have done the diagnostic exercises correctly, you probably can skip the minigrammar. But even one or two mistakes should convince you to work through the exercises in the minigrammar and take the *Check Yourself* test at the end. If, after doing the exercises and consulting the keys, you still feel uncertain, consult your instructor for further assistance.

Follow this plan throughout this text wherever your attention is directed to the minigrammars. Be very sure you understand *as you go along*, because each minigrammar builds on the one that precedes it. If you work conscientiously, consulting your instructor when you perceive problems, you should find yourself increasingly sure about your control of the basics of language.

Revising Activity 3-4   *Wordiness*

✔   As a final revising activity on your narrative, check it for wordiness, as you did your Assignment 2. Are there words that are monotonously repeated? Are there consecutive sentences beginning with the same word? Are there unnecessary occurrences of *that* or *which?* Tighten your sentences where you can.

✔   **Note:** When you have finished Revising Activity 3-4, you should make a final draft of your narrative. This assignment will show whether you have absorbed the techniques presented to this point in the course. Since it is a more formal "paper" than anything you have done so far, think seriously about the appearance of your final draft. This is a much less trivial matter than you might think.

The moment anyone — including an instructor — looks at your paper, a first impression is formed, a preliminary judgment both of you as a writer and of what can be expected from the paper. A sloppy paper gives off sloppy vibrations; you may have trouble overcoming the first negative evaluation of your work. Don't put an unnecessary hurdle between yourself and your instructor/reader by not taking the time and effort to produce neat, easily readable copy.

Furthermore, your attitude toward your writing and your perception of your writing problems are vitally affected when you take the extra time and effort to "clean up" your work. It is easy to say, "Well, a few crossouts won't hurt. Why copy it all over for that?" This kind of self-indulgence, however, can lead to further self-indulgence; instead of moving steadily forward, you may begin to slide into other kinds of carelessness. Discerning read-ers—including your college instructors—notice careless mistakes. If you start now to be careful, to produce clean copy to hand in, to look up words you can't spell, if you watch punctuation carefully and think about the logic of your paragraphing—then you will build habits that will become part of your writing.

> *Principle 9* Good mechanics and spelling and a neat appearance don't make a good paper, but the lack of them can make a good paper something less than it is.

Ideally, you should type your papers, on one side of the page only, double spacing them and leaving adequate margins so that the page does not appear cramped or crowded. If you can't type, you should learn to do so. Having someone else do it for you may help present a good first impression, but it does not help in the second and more important aspect—forcing you to look carefully at your own work and to start building better habits.

CHECKLIST   *Making It Come Alive*

Preparations.   Check off each item when completed.

Activity 3-1   Narrating an Event . . . .
Activity 3-2   Using Dialogue . . . .
Activity 3-3   Bringing Life through Dialogue . . . .
Assignment 3   A Narrative . . . .
Revising Activity 3-1   Conventions for Dialogue . . . .
Revising Activity 3-2   Basic Punctuation . . . .
Revising Activity 3-3   Grammar (Minigrammars A, B) . . . .
Revising Activity 3-4   Wordiness . . . .

Goals to Be Achieved.   Write your answers on a separate sheet. Explain fully.

1. Does your narrative contain specific incidents told in enough significant detail to come alive for a reader?
2. Have you incorporated dialogue judiciously to help make the narrative more alive and interesting?
3. Have you carefully checked your narrative for dialogue form, punctuation, and wordiness?
4. Have you typed or at least made a neat, legible copy of your final draft?

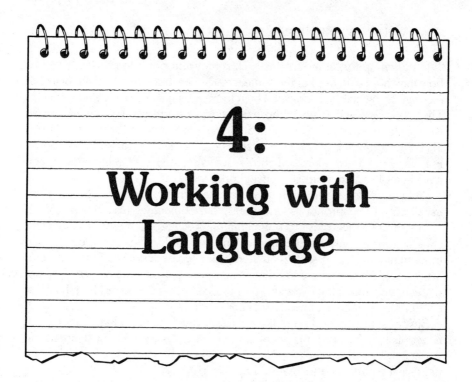

4:
Working with Language

I n Chapter 3, you began to work seriously with grammar and mechanics, and perhaps you groaned a bit, thinking, "Here we go again on the same old stuff." Perhaps you've already learned the so-called basics so a rehash is boring. Or if you didn't learn how to locate subjects and predicates, how to punctuate, or how to spell, what makes your instructor think you can learn it now?

If you're already in control of language, you have nothing to worry about. You can read the explanations in the main text or the minigrammars to refresh your memory (and possibly correct some misconceptions you've picked up) and move on.

If you still have problems, perhaps you should first think about why you should learn how to control language. Contrary to what you may think, what is called "correct" grammar, together with "correct" mechanics, is not merely a collection of hard-to-remember rules; it is a codification of certain agreed-upon conventions by which we attempt to make ourselves understood. This mutual understanding is achieved differently in different languages. In English, our grammar is controlled chiefly by word order. For instance, we say something like this: "I took him up to the mountains on our holiday." We would not say, "Him took the mountains I to holiday on our up."

Other languages *can* scramble the words in sentences, because they have different forms for the same word and you can tell from the form how the word is being used. In English, we have something of the same in our pronouns; we use *I, he,* or *they* to show the doer of the action, as in "*I* took him up to the mountains." We use *me, him,* or *them* for the receiver of the action:

"I took *him* up to the mountains." Thus the form of some pronouns tells us how they are being used in the sentence. (Notice that frequently the object or receiver of the action is indicated by a form ending in *-m: him, them, whom.* This is one way to help you choose the "correct" form.) But for the most part, word order provides the clue to meaning in English, and one reason for learning correct grammar is simply to be sure you are making yourself understood. For many of you, the kinds of choices just discussed are largely natural; you have been learning them since babyhood.

Problems come where there are alternate forms of words to choose from, usually involving pronouns and verbs, but sometimes also the plurals of nouns. If you have mastered Minigrammars A and B, many of your word choice problems, grammatically speaking, are under control. If you skipped those minigrammars or just "read them over," go back *now* and master them. If the book doesn't give you enough help, ask your instructor. You will not regret having made the extra effort, because afterwards you will find that your control of grammar and mechanics comes more easily.

But being understood is not the only issue involved here. Many people say things like, "Him and me went to the show," which are just as clearly understood as the "correct" "He and I went to the show." Why isn't "I be tired" just as understandable as "I am tired"? It is. At this point, the choice becomes a matter of social convention; perhaps in certain environments it is better to say "him and me went," or "I be tired." That is for you to decide. The fact is, however, that as educated Americans, you are expected to know the conventions of what is called *Standard English* or, more accurately, *Edited American English* (EAE). You very likely will encounter situations where your chances for a job, a promotion, or even a friendship are influenced by the words you choose. Some people's fetish for "correctness" is often annoying, limiting, and immature, but where it exists, you need the tools to deal with it. Always being "correct" is not necessarily essential; what is important is to know *when* you are being "correct" and when you are not. Then you have the choice; you are in control.

In this country, many people use dialects which depart in various ways from Standard English. Many of you use varieties of language that serve you well. A bilingual "mixing" of two or more languages can produce very effective expression, as can the various American dialects. Much attention has been given to black dialects in particular, and white society often has been criticized for demanding that blacks learn Edited American English. A freshman student, originally from Georgia but more recently from the Midwest, has expressed this point of view well:

> Through the years, the Black man has changed his life-style considerably, developing a style that is uniquely his own. This style may be characterized as being just plain cool. Blacks, having to adapt to a hostile environment, adopted this non-caring "cool" attitude as a protective covering.
>
> In every way we as Blacks try to show our uniqueness, like in the way we get clean (dress), strut (walk), and rap (talk). Our style is now our culture and

way of life, since we have no true culture to claim as our own. And as long as I remain black in mind, body, and soul, no one is going to deprive me of my culture. I am proud of my culture. I want to show the world.

I think personally that the standards of writing in the English manner are a threat to my culture. Black dialect in writing is not considered proper English. I, as well as other Blacks, have to write in a way completely different from the way we normally express ourselves. It's almost like translating in another language, and this is no fun. Neither is it a challenge. Examples of Black dialect are: The hawk is flying high today. (Translation: The wind is blowing very hard today.) I'll catch you in the wind, my friend. (Translation: I'll see you later, pal.)

Once I wrote a paper in high school with a slight dialect. The instructor told me I was using improper English and my paper made no sense. I was asked to rewrite the paper, but I refused. It wasn't my fault she didn't understand. The assignment as I recall was to write naturally and that was what I did. I don't understand it. Black people are the second largest race in the U.S.A., and I think Black dialect should be respected, not rejected. I mean, who can really say that the Black dialect is an improper form of English? As I see it, it's another way of expressing one's thoughts. In some ways, Black dialect can express what Standard English can't.

Who indeed can say black dialect is an improper form of English? But if this black girl had not been able to write Edited American English—and almost without a flaw at that, far better than many of her white classmates—she could not have communicated as well with a majority of whites. All black writers, no matter how they feel about being forced to talk "differently" on paper, used Edited American English to communicate with a white audience—*and they know how to do it!* At other times, when they want to communicate with speakers of black dialect, they use their special ways. They have a choice of which "language" they are going to use. People who have not learned to use Edited American English have no choice.

Dialect is only the extreme form of the problem. To some extent, everyone translates when writing. Even those brought up in environments where Standard English is used regularly do not speak in the same terms as they write. Nor do they always use their most colorful terms in writing; certain four-letter words, for instance—though they are beginning to crop up in some writing—are not accepted in a company report to the stockholders.

Your particular "dialect" may be the product of a number of factors: the environment you grew up in, the kind of schooling you have had, your own interest—or lack of interest—in language. But where choices are to be made—between A and B when grading an essay exam, between two applicants for a position, between two candidates for graduate school—your ability to frame sentences in Edited American English could be the deciding factor. You handicap yourself by not working hard to learn Edited American English well.

Keep in mind, however, that in all self-expression *the emphasis must always be on what you are saying,* and only secondarily on whether you use "correct" grammar, punctuation, and spelling. If what you say doesn't appeal to a reader—if, for instance, in your descriptions you let "Proud Peacock" language substitute for deeply observed facts—then a grammatically or mechanically perfect sentence will count for little. Don't think too much about your sentence structure and spelling *while you are first putting your ideas on paper.* The procedure presented in Chapters 2 and 3 should be continued as you work through later chapters: first your preliminary gathering of ideas, as in the fact sheets, then the writing itself, and *afterwards* a return to check the grammar, the spelling, and the mechanics. Few people can frame perfect sentences as they go, never changing a word afterwards. If you can do it, fine. Do whatever works for you. But most of us aren't that sure of ourselves and need to go at it the other way around.

On the other hand, total carelessness as you write your first drafts is dangerous, too. Taking the attitude that you can always catch mistakes later means you can run the risk of missing as many as you find, leaving a marred manuscript that may distract the reader's attention from what you are saying. You wouldn't expect perfect manners in public from children allowed to eat any way they want at home. Don't expect to end up with acceptable final drafts if the first one looks as if it has been written by an illiterate.

Ultimately what it all adds up to is that as you gain increasing control of the tools of grammar, vocabulary, and mechanics, you will free yourself for what is really important—expressing your own ideas and communicating more easily with others.

> **Principle 10** When communicating with others is important, control of language will help you win the attention—and respect—of your reader.

Activity 4-1   *Reviewing What You Already Know*

You need two tools: a good handbook and a good dictionary. Many excellent ones are available. A handbook deals with parts of speech, punctuation, language usage, and the mechanics of writing a term or research paper. The dictionary should be desk size, not a pocket dictionary. If you don't already have these two tools, obtain them. They will be indispensable for your college work.

✔   Right now, look through both the handbook and the dictionary to remind you of things you may have forgotten and to alert you to the types of information available in the two books. Educated people are characterized not only by what they know, but also by their knowledge of *where to look.* Jot down a few things from each book, points you think may be useful later. Does your dictionary, for instance, have a section on punctuation? Does the handbook show you how to use footnotes?

Make a list of terms from the table of contents or index of your handbook that you think you ought to study up on. In particular, do you need some work on the following?

1. Agreement between subjects and predicates
2. Verb forms and tense shifting
3. Sentence fragments and run-on sentences
4. Pronoun usage
5. Faulty sentence logic
6. Dull sentences

There are other language problems, but these are the ones that entering college students most frequently have trouble with. It would be nice if you knew all your parts of speech, every rule of punctuation and grammar, and every principle of spelling, but if you have control of the six listed problems, all of which are dealt with in the minigrammars of this text, others should be relatively easy to work out with a little help from your instructor.

Activity 4-2   *Playing with Sentences*

There is more to language control than simple "correctness." Sentences may be grammatically and mechanically perfect but still lack effectiveness and style. You are not stuck with a sentence once it is written. The same thing can often be said in a number of ways—sometimes more effectively, sometimes less. For now, don't worry about what is most effective; this activity is designed to help you become more flexible in your sentence patterns.

A. Adverbial Modifiers

Although, as we have noted, English grammar relies heavily on a rather rigid word order, some elements—notably adverbs and adverb phrases and clauses—are easy to shift around. (Adverbs are modifiers, usually of verbs—*ad* + *verb*—but also of other adverbs and of adjectives.) Sometimes only one word, like *however*, is involved:

Susan went to the store; *however*, I stayed home.
Susan went to the store; I, *however*, stayed home.
Susan went to the store; I stayed home *however*.

Other words of this type are *nevertheless*, *meanwhile*, and *therefore*. Short phrases can perform similarly: *on the other hand*, *for example*, and *in other words*.

✔ **1.** Choose one of the above words or phrases (or something similar) and write a sentence using it. Then move the word or phrase to as many positions in the sentence as feasible.

The above example deals with a special form of adverb, but other adverbs often give us opportunities for variety.

The bull turned *angrily* and charged.
Angrily, the bull turned and charged.
The bull *angrily* turned and charged.
The bull turned and charged *angrily*.

Note in this case that the shift in the adverb *angrily* changes the meaning somewhat. Did the bull turn angrily? Or charge angrily? Or did the angry bull turn and charge? When varying sentence patterns, you must of course be sure you are still saying what you *want* to say.

✔ **2.** Write a sentence in which an adverb ending in *-ly* describes the action. (Examples might be *happily, rapidly, strongly, smartly.* Not all adverbs end in *-ly* but many do.) Then vary the position of the adverb in as many ways as seem feasible.

Sometimes whole phrases or clauses that modify the main action—telling where, when, why, or how—can be shifted around.

The day passed slowly, *because it was warm and humid.*
Because it was warm and humid, the day passed slowly.
The day, *because it was warm and humid,* passed slowly.

The bird flew in a lazy circle, *spreading its wings effortlessly to catch the downdraft.*
Spreading its wings to catch the downdraft, the bird flew in a lazy circle.
The bird, *spreading its wings to catch the downdraft,* flew in a lazy circle.

✔ **3.** Write one or more sentences, using the above as models, in which the main action is modified by a phrase or clause. Then vary the pattern in as many ways as possible.

B. Active and Passive Voice

Not only can words be shifted around, but patterns can be changed in other ways. One is by changing the main verb from passive to active voice or vice versa. In the active voice, the subject of the sentence is *the doer of the action*, as in "The pale robber flourished the gun wildly." Here the subject of the sentence—the robber—performs the act of flourishing the gun. In the passive voice, the subject of the sentence is *acted upon by some other agent:* "The gun was flourished wildly *by the pale robber.*" Here the subject of the sentence—the gun—is acted *upon*; it "receives" the action performed by the robber. Both are good sentences and mean essentially the same thing, but the emphasis shifts. In the first sentence, the emphasis is on the *doer of the action,* the robber (active), while in the second sentence the emphasis is on *the receiver of the action,* the gun (passive). Which you choose is determined by which element you wish to emphasize.

The impression you convey is also affected by your choice of voice. Usually the active voice is stronger than the passive voice. In a sports column, where you wanted to stress hard-hitting action, you would probably want to use an active construction, as in "The quarterback threw the football straight down the field." The passive—"The football was thrown straight down the field by the quarterback"—seems weaker, less effective.

✔ **1.** The following sentences are all in the active voice (the subject is the doer of the action). Write a second sentence for each, changing the sentence into the passive voice (the subject is acted upon by some other agent).

a. The boy laid the book on the table.

b. The Governor granted a pardon to the condemned man.

c. The shipwrecked sailors left the island on a rickety raft.

✔   **2.** The next sentences are in the passive voice. Rewrite them so they are in the active voice.

a. In the first part of the variety show, a sword was swallowed by Andrew.

b. The school teacher was frightened by a face at the window.

c. Different moods can be created by using different lights.

Activity 4-3   *Combining Sentences into More Complex Patterns*

Very often when an English teacher says something is "poorly written," it turns out that the sentences are all short and are written in a uniform, simple pattern. The following paragraph is an example:

It was early morning. The first rays of sunshine peeped around the corner of my bedroom window. The window was slightly cracked open. The rays discovered this opening. They found it inviting. They crept stealthily under the window. They entered my room.

This passage is not only wordy, as you will discover if you try Revising Activity 2-1, circling all repeated words, but it sounds choppy; most of the sentences are short, all about the same length. In addition, every sentence is built on the same pattern: a simple sentence with subject, verb, and then a sentence completer of some sort. (*It was*—early morning; *rays peeped*—around the corner of my bedroom; *window was*—slightly cracked open, etc.) Now read the paragraph as it was actually written by a freshman student.

The first early rays of morning sunshine peeped around the corner of my bedroom window, which was slightly cracked open. Discovering this inviting opening, the rays crept stealthily under the window and entered my room.

Do you see how much more interesting this latter version sounds, how much more quickly it reads?

✔   Practice combining and varying sentences in the following paragraphs to make them smoother, more varied, less wordy. Try different patterns. There is no "correct" way, but you will find the original in the key on page 250. Is your best effort better? Or would you change some things in yours after reading the original?

The first rays danced around the room. They went in circles. They leaped from my bed onto the floor. They waltzed in time with my vanity stool. Then they tired of this slow-paced dance. They threw themselves at the wall. They climbed up and down. They raced all around the corners. The rays were beautiful and radiant. This gave a mystical glow to the room.

There was a sudden loud tremble. It was outside the room. A shadow appeared before the window. The shadow was mystical and dark. His angry face looked in. He scorned the gaity taking place. He blew through the open window. His breath was a sharp, bitter wind. It frightened my new friends. They saw his cold and unfriendly face. They scattered in all directions. Their lights whizzed by. They flew out the window. I was left in the darkened stillness once again.

Activity 4-4   *Punctuating a Passage*

like grammar vocabulary and spelling punctuation is essentially an aid to helping others understand what you are trying to communicate without it we would have to puzzle through apparently jumbled word groups like this one a paragraph follows transcribed without punctuation try to make it more understandable without changing any words or the word order.

Did you get all that? Probably—after thinking about it a bit. But why bother when it works so much better like this?

Like grammar, vocabulary, and spelling, punctuation is essentially an aid to helping others understand what you are trying to communicate. Without it, we would have to puzzle through apparently jumbled words groups like this one. A paragraph follows, transcribed without punctuation. Try to make it more understandable without changing any words or the word order. Compare your punctuated version with the original in the key on page 250.

paddles dipping quickly into the rushing waters trees and bushes flashing by the deep clean smell of the outdoors assailing ones senses and the bobwhites call are all part of that oncoming sport canoeing today everyone is canoeing causing a growth to twenty percent more canoers on american rivers each year senior citizens families and young people are discovering the need to get back to the earth and they are doing just that through canoeing there are many reasons for the increasing popularity of this sport the retiree and his wife after a hectic week of golf and teas arrive at the river with their starcraft canoe ready to get away and leave it all behind them there are also families hoping to increase their togetherness through the outdoors screaming and yelling at each other all the way down the river not to mention the many young people looking for the challenge involved in avoiding river obstacles but you say i thought canoeing was for the rugged and im not that type at all you dont have to be with two people to a canoe one guiding and the other steering the trip can be smooth and enjoyable.

ASSIGNMENT 4   Rewriting a Passage for More Variety and Understanding

✔   Now see if you can put all the foregoing together. Turn the following little story into good prose—rearranging, varying, combining, rephrasing, repunctuating: do whatever you think will make it flow more smoothly and gracefully. When you are finished, do Revising Activities 4-1 and 4-2, type a clean, double-spaced copy, and submit your version of the passage, *attaching to it all the activities from this chapter.*

A car that was the Most Beautiful in the world

It happened one night this summer. I saw the most Beautiful car in the world. I had taken my mother up to a local discount store. She had to do some last minute shopping for the weekend. It was a lazy Friday night. It was about 7:30 p.m. I decided to sit in the car. I would watch the sun go down. That was better than push a shopping cart through a maze of aisles.

It was about ten minutes before I noticed it the car two rows over the driver had carefully backed his 1974 corvette kittycorner across two parking spaces. This is a common practice among Vette drivers. It prevents a carelessly opened door from scratching the body. The body is fragile fiberglass. the position now though gave it more than protection. it seemed to show off it's long curvy body lines and low profile. A thought came to my mind. The car looked like a leopard or tiger. It was resting on its muscular haunches waiting for the return of its partner. Its partner being the driver.

The dusk slowly started to fall. The setting sun's rays were red. They bounced off the windshield. The car was glossy. Its color was a metallic brown. This color seemed to change. It became deeper and deeper. It was far away. I could still see the reflections of clouds on its finish. The finish was like a mirror. The Corvette looked out of place. All around it were dirty station wagons. There were also some dingy foreign cars. The Corvette seemed afloat in an ocean of Vega Pintos and Volkswagens. It was a ruby in a pile of rhinestones.

My mother came back and loaded a sack of groceries in the back of our Ford. I chuckled to myself as she did so. I imagined the driver of the Vette probably a chubby bald fellow in his late forties. He was probably going through second childhood. It doesn't really matter though I thought. I turned to get one last look. It didn't matter who the driver was. No one ever sees the driver of the most beautiful car in the world.

Revising Activity 4-1   *Wordiness*

✓   Before putting your version of the foregoing passage into final draft, check it for wordiness, using Revising Activities 2-1, 2-2, and 2-3.

Revising Activity 4-2   *Punctuation*

✓   Check your punctuation.

CHECKLIST   *Working with Language*

Preparations.   Check off each item when completed.

Activity 4-1   Reviewing What You Already Know . . . .
Activity 4-2   Playing with Sentences . . . .
Activity 4-3   Combining Sentences into More Complex Patterns. . .
Activity 4-4   Punctuating a Passage . . . .
Assignment 4   Rewriting a Passage for More Variety and Understanding . . . .
Revising Activity 4-1   Wordiness . . . .
Revising Activity 4-2   Punctuation . . . .

Goals to Be Achieved.   Write your answers on a separate sheet. Explain fully.

1. Do you feel you need extra time to review and strengthen your grasp on grammar principles?
2. Have you discovered some new ways to make language work better for you?

PART II:

The Bridge

When I write about personal ideas or experiences, I know when I'm done. I write as much as I want, about something I want, from my own feelings. It isn't all mechanics — though grammar and mechanics are needed to express ideas — or analyzing someone else's writing. It is my writing — about me, my ideas, and my feelings. I have discovered that I can enjoy writing. It can be fun and even exciting at times, trying to express myself on paper.

A STUDENT

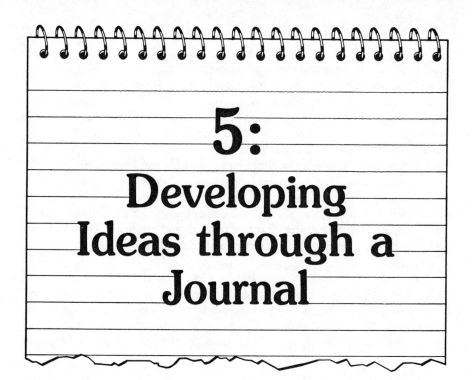

5:
Developing Ideas through a Journal

W ith the first part of the course completed, it is time to think about what has happened so far. Stopping once in a while to review is useful; it can help you get a better perspective and proceed with more purpose. To aid you in doing that now, write answers to the following questions:

1. What do I see as the purpose of the course to this point?
2. What specific things do I see as important to me?
3. In what areas, if any, should I have spent more time?

WHY "THE BRIDGE"?

This section is called "The Bridge" because it seeks to take you, in a real sense, from one bank of the river of writing to another, without your losing touch with either side. You have been writing from your own mind and feelings, and you should continue to do so; there is no real break as we now move from what seems like strictly personal experience to a more comprehensive embracing of the world around us. There is continuity between us and our world; we are separate individuals, but we are also a part of the whole. What we learn about ourselves through personal experience becomes a part of our individual endowment, but so does what we learn about the people and the world around us. There is such a thing as pure knowledge, pure research, but even that is merely held in abeyance until it can somehow be made relevant to human experience. Knowledge is important because it touches our individual lives, even if only remotely.

Let us try a metaphor. Think of yourself as an isolated village. In some ways, it is very nice, certainly more peaceful than if you were a big city. But you have no highways bringing information in, no radio, no television. You are limited in your understanding and growth to your own resources and those of the small area immediately around you. Then a highway is built through the village you are, and other kinds of communication follow. You begin to grow. You find yourself connected with other towns, other cities. What they are tells you more about what you are; you learn both what you have been missing and what you have gained by your previous isolation. If you are wise, you draw strength from what you already are and do not lose your identity even as you absorb the new elements of growth that come to you. *You* receive the information that flows in and *you* evaluate it and *you* make your own choices, and that way you retain your own identity even as you change.

Basically, unless everything is "personal" experience, it is useless to you. You must be alert to make connections between what you are now and the new material flowing in, so that your mind takes the new material and puts it through the deep well of your own experience, transforming it into something uniquely your own. It is to try to help you make the connections, to cross the bridge between you and the world around you, that this section is partly designed.

In another sense, the "bridge" is more immediate and practical; this section is intended to serve as a bridge between your writing about personal experience and your writing a "term paper." Although there have been a few hints along the way, you may still be uncertain about how the description of a place you love or the use of dialogue has relevance to the kind of writing you will be called on to do in college.

So far, this text has tried to help you develop skill in making your writing come *alive* for a reader. Telling a story well may seem at first little related to college writing, but you can use the concept of the *specific incident* in everything you write, even in answering an essay examination. Generalizations are just as vague and unsatisfactory in your college papers as in your narratives. The specific incident shows that you know what you are talking about and that what you are talking about makes sense.

Thinking of specific incidents may also help you examine and refine your own thinking. Often your general idea will change when you begin to cite a particular incident. Are you, for instance, unalterably opposed to abortion? You probably have a friend or acquaintance who has considered abortion or gone through the experience. When you begin to tell how the experience affected *her*, some new thoughts may come to you so that you take a less "hard line" in your paper. Or suppose you are opposed to off-shore oil explorations, and you begin to tell in detail what happened at Santa Barbara, California, a few years back. As you familiarize yourself with the events currently taking place there, you find a changing attitude in the town itself and you begin to recognize that both ecology and economy must be served. Generalizations seldom cause us to examine our ideas until they are put to the test of the specific incident.

Furthermore, a generalization often presents no challenge to a reader. Readers either agree or disagree, but they do not think twice. The specific incident that makes *you* "think twice" may have the same effect on them.

The other advantage of using specific incidents to illustrate your general ideas is that people like to read stories and will remember them. They like to have pictures formed in their minds through the use of *significant details*. Principle 1 in Chapter 1 warned you about boring a reader. You can create interest, as well as illustrate your point, with lively descriptions and little stories.

Skill in using significant details also is important because you need to learn to back up and support your generalizations with concrete evidence. There is no essential difference between the sharp visual details you use in describing a place and the sharp details in the form of facts, figures, and illustrations you use to support your opinion about some issue.

Finally, and perhaps most important, this section will attempt to bridge the gap between focusing a description or narrative on the peak moment and focusing a discussion of a general subject upon a central idea or thesis. There are really just two basic things to learn in order to write a good paper: (1) how to focus on a central idea or thesis and (2) how to develop the central idea or thesis in a thorough and interesting way. We have been working so far mostly with skills of developing ideas; now as we go forward the main emphasis will shift to the *central idea*.

THE JOURNAL

Some people welcome the opportunity to write a journal; they've either done it before and found it rewarding or they have always wanted to try it but never got around to it. Others, often those who have had to write journals for an English class in the past, respond to a suggestion to write a journal with something like "Yeck!" Usually this response rises from doing an extended journal, becoming bored, running out of ideas. The journal becomes nothing but a series of dutiful entries about nothing at all.

Whatever your response, a journal at this point is one of the most important things you will do in the course. If you take it seriously, try to understand its purpose, and do your best to respond, you will be far more ready for the assignments to follow in Part III. There is an almost one-to-one relationship between those who write good journals and those who do well on the subsequent work of the course.

WHAT IS MEANT BY A JOURNAL?

A journal is a sharing. When you write in a journal, you are writing something that brings pleasure and profit to you but it is *also* something that can please a reader. Students sometimes feel they don't have anything to say to anyone else. By this time in the course, you should have found you are writing in ways that no one but you could write. You have a unique background; there is no one quite like you. You therefore do have something to add to the understanding and experience of your reader, as long as you are being honest and true to yourself. It is when you try to imitate someone else that the reader becomes bored; we are interested in real things, not imitations. That goes for people and what they reveal of themselves in their writing as well as anything else.

A second but related consideration in writing your journal is that it *records the life of your mind.* People today rush madly from activity to activity without really thinking about what they are doing. Time passes without their being aware of what, if anything, they have to show for it. Having no overall image of what they want their lives to be, they don't know whether they are using their time well or poorly. Eventually lives become a meaningless muddle. Much could be saved if people would only "stop to think." That is basically what you are being asked to do in this journal—*stop to think, and share your thoughts with other people.* Form a habit of writing down what you think about, recording a problem, an idea, a feeling, a moment of pleasure or pain, something that counts for you and has significance for you. If something counts for you, it will count for other people too. We are all looking for new insights, new ways of looking at things. Out of your unique experience, you can supply something of that.

WHAT A JOURNAL IS NOT

A journal is not a diary. The difference is that in a diary you write only for yourself. Often a diary can be mere jottings meaningful only to you—the bare skeleton of a day. An example is the travel diary that reminds you of places you've been, but doesn't mean much to a reader.

A journal means something to a reader. Never forget you are writing something to be read.

WHAT DO YOU WRITE ABOUT?

Finding things to write about bothers some students. If you run into trouble, one possibility is to look back at your earlier writings, particularly your early free writings. The journal is a logical extension of the free writing you did in the first chapter, only now, rather than letting your thoughts wander, you should be able to direct them more purposefully, to *focus* on your subject or idea better. You should have learned better ways of *developing* your ideas: how to use more vivid descriptions, stories that explain or illustrate your point, bits of dialogue that make things clearer and more lively, metaphors that will add interest and punch. If you are having trouble, think specifically: Can I describe this more clearly? Is there a story I can tell? What is this *like*; can I think of a metaphor to help me out?

Some students write a series of journal entries on the same general subject, as it progressively opens out for them during the time they are working on their journals.

Or here are some suggestions—a baker's dozen!

1. Explore on paper some opinion that has been gnawing at you for a long time.
2. Describe or narrate an experience that has affected you deeply and try to deal with your response to it.
3. Describe a dream you remember vividly and try to analyze what it means.
4. Tell both what is good and what is bad about
   a. College classes
   b. The lowering of the age for legal drinking
   c. Home
   d. Abortion
   e. The legalization of marijuana
   f. Euthanasia
   g. Any other subject you are interested in
5. Explain some change of opinion you have experienced and analyze the reason for your changed ideas.
6. Tell someone else how to do something that you know a good deal about.
7. Explain in language a layman can understand some scientific or technical process.
8. Evaluate the differences between
   a. High school and college
   b. Dorm life and apartment living
   c. Going to college immediately after high school and working first for a time
   d. Two life-styles, both of which appeal to you in some way
9. Explore an idea that suddenly grips you in a way that is unexpected.
10. Speculate on
    a. Life in A.D. 2000 (coming pretty close now!)
    b. Your own future life
    c. The outcome of some current school, community, or national problem
11. Dream a bit on paper about how you would like things to be, or of things that have been lost that you would like to regain.
12. Observe things around you that you take for granted but probably shouldn't.
13. Air your pet gripe or, alternately, tell the world what is great about it.

WHAT SHOULD ENTRIES CONSIST OF?

Sometimes journal entries may be relatively short and not very focused, like the example that follows.

I'm listening to an album called "Four Way Street" by Crosby, Stills, Nash, and Young. Neil Young is singing "It's Only Castles Burning" right now. This song has a very deep meaning. It's about a blind man walking with his cane in the night. He trips and falls into the gutter and no one stops to help him. Neil Young must have gone through a lot of shit to write a song like this.

I've decided to put my roommate on my permanent shit list! I'm fed up with his lying! He tells lies to get in good with people, but he doesn't realize that he's alienating his real friends. It's gotten to the point where I don't even listen to him any more because I don't know if he's telling the truth or not.

Don't forget your personal experiences as sources of good journal entries. Experiences that remain vivid in your mind have special significance for you. Use a narrative of an experience to show the reader what that significance is, as in the following example.

I can think of nothing more exhilarating than losing myself to the wild, untamable world of nature. Last summer I had to work weekdays in Ann Arbor, and the monotony of traffic jams, horns honking, obscenities spewing out windows, police and ambulance sirens, and cold cement backyards were invading the intimacy of our love with nature. So every spare minute we had, Mary and I tried to get away from the city. We made it a point to be off every weekend to regain our sense of values and peace of mind. To Mary and me, nature provides the true humanism that allows one to breathe freely at peace in a world made of tar and cement. And one moment remains in my mind as if it were yesterday.

We were camping in Northern Michigan with another couple on a late August weekend. Pete and Loretta were ready for bed, so they climbed into their pup tent and were soon off in dreamland. Mary and I decided the fresh air would do us good, so we pulled out our sleeping gear and settled by the fire for a night under the stars. And what a night! To the crackling of the flames, we listened to the stillness of the night. I had never felt such closeness to God in all my life. It was as if he were saying, "See what I have made for you. Now drink it until you are intoxicated with the beauty of life." And I did become intoxicated. I drank in the freshness of the clean air until my lungs were ready to burst. I drank in the beauty of the scintillating stars which were like diamonds surrounding us at every angle. I drank in the sudden, yet calm wind which silently kept our fire glowing throughout the night.

Then two young college boys rode up next to our campgrounds on their Harley-Davidsons, and as the revving of the motors subsided, we could hear them bragging about the drugs and pills that they had taken that morning, and were about to take again. Their shouting, their language, their bright light shining into our faces . . . all of these things made me feel a hurt, the hurt for God who had to understand people and the ways they act. But once again, I looked around me, and the feeling of love came back to me, love for the world, love for Mary, love for God, and even love for our two invaders, who had yet to learn how to appreciate the beauty that was made just for them. Then I turned to Mary and smiled, knowing that she felt the same way, neither of us thinking of the city we would have to face again.

A good journal can be a delight to write and a delight to read. In the journal excerpt that follows, one student involved herself fully for the first time in the course and began to enjoy writing. Perhaps you can find the same sense of accomplishment she did.

In remembrance of my cousin
who died Friday, October 7

My cousin Mark died today. I was taking a nap when my mother called. It was a quarter past eleven. My roommate woke me up and said, "Your Mom's on the phone." I remember mumbling something like "Tell her I'll call back later." But she shook me and said that she'd throw water on me if I didn't get up and talk to my Mother. So I stumbled out of bed and tripped to the phone. "Hi, Mom."

"Deb, there's been a tragedy." (A tragedy? That's a strange word. Nobody uses that word unless they're writing a book or something.)

"What? What happened?"

"Mark was hunting with Joe Parson and Joe shot him." (Oh, relief, thank God, for a minute I thought something had happened.)

"Oh, no! How bad is it? Did they take him to the hospital? How is he?"

"He's dead." Dead Final.

DEAD, (from Webster's New College Dictionary) Adjective. 1. Not living; not existing; deceased. 2. Void, useless, forgotten. 3. Complete, as a DEAD STOP, exact. 4. Lacking feeling, lacking power to rebound; dull. 5. Lacking interest, appeal, or flavor. Adverb. Completely, exactly. Noun. 1. That or those which no longer exist. 2. An extreme or culminating point.

Mark, when he died, was only sixteen years old. He was not outstanding in school; in fact he flunked out in his seventh grade year. Mark had not excelled in sports, but he loved to hunt and fish, and drive his motorcycle and snowmobile. And brother, did he drive them! He got in one of his many accidents this summer because he popped a wheelie. After every accident, my mother would say, "Do you think it'll teach him anything?"

He drove my uncle's snowmobile just like he drove a cycle. He racked up the old snowmobile by running it into a tree last winter. One Christmas he gave me a ride and let me drive the thing and I rolled it while we were going around the curve (he forgot to tell me about driving slow and tipping around curves). He yelled at me but still gave me rides whenever he was in a good Samaritan mood.

We sat together last year on the bus riding home from school every day. We tried to gross each other out and we used every kind of sarcasm imaginable. He used to say that he wasn't related to me. I was so dumb. I didn't mind the sarcasm, because he was so funny and cute. He had no enemies, he was so easygoing, and everybody liked him. Too bad one of his friends had to kill him.

Last May Mark's older sister got married. His older brother was Best Man, and Mark ushered. They looked handsome in their tuxes, purple and ruffled shirts, and bow ties. It made them look taller, older. I realized that they were growing up. Everybody at the wedding kept teasing them: "Well, Mike and Mark, when are you guys going to get hitched up?" Everyone was so happy and proud.

So Mark is dead. Funny how dead people in the papers don't get to you the way dead people in the family do. Mark had so much life in him. Maybe too much. He was so crazy, and I loved him.

Everybody said he'd kill himself on his bike or his snowmobile someday. I think he'd have liked that, but it would have to be something fantastic, like riding his motorcycle across a high wire. He'd have gone the way he'd wanted to if he would've kicked off on the cycle, but instead he fell from a friend's irresponsibility. He wasn't ready for it. He had no choice, and had gone through only sixteen years. Boy, if he had lived another sixteen more, he would've turned the whole world upside down.

Damn you, Joe Parson.

Activity 5-1   *Writing a Journal*

✔   Begin a journal immediately. Do eight entries, each time writing *not less than one half hour*. That means *write*—keep your pen or pencil making words across a page—for at least a half hour. This does not include the times you let your attention wander. It does not include the time you spend wishing you were doing something else. It does not include the time you spend trying to think of something to write about. Contrary to the free writing practice, you can stop if you want to, but the total *writing* time should still be a half hour.

   Most of your journal entries should deal with ideas, as indicated by the topics suggested on page 69. *You* know what you think about various aspects of life; now try to convince others! Notice that the sample journal entries express definite points of view: getting out into nature is uplifting; youthful irresponsibility is potentially destructive. In each case, the conviction arose out of personal experience. Describe personal experiences of your own that have resulted in personal convictions; show a reader why you feel or think as you do. Or work through an idea, as suggested by numerous items in our "baker's dozen." As you do, use for evidence *specific incidents* that support your reasoning. Recall *significant details* to bring these incidents to life.

Occasionally you may want to spend a half hour describing the beautiful sunset outside your window or telling a funny but rather pointless story. Two or three entries, well done, can spice up your journal. But for the most part, concentrate on ideas and how you will communicate them effectively to a reader.

If your idea runs out in ten or fifteen minutes, consider whether you are developing it sufficiently. Remember the techniques from Part I. Are you generalizing without going into the specific incidents or the significant details that helped form your opinion? Ask yourself questions like "Why is what I have said true?" or "How would I support this statement if someone challenged me?"

If one entry totals about an hour's writing time, you may count it double. *Don't count one entry as two more than twice* during the assignment.

Date every entry! If you write two on the same day, indicate which you wrote first and which later. This will help both you and your instructor to tell whether you are increasing your ability to express yourself more efficiently, more vividly, more easily.

Activity 5-2   *Special Journal Entries*

✓   In addition to the eight entries done for Activity 5-1, do the two listed below. Label them "Special Entry 1" and "Special Entry 2." Keep in mind the purpose of the "bridge": to help you use techniques developed in Part I in dealing with ideas or opinions.

Special Entry 1: Try to sharpen your observation and your ability to relate small incidents of your daily life to something with greater significance. For example, one student found himself watching a single drop of water on a window one rainy day and then wrote about how people have a tendency to concentrate on insignificant details like the water drop while outside the window of their lives important events pass in a blur. Another student sat in a laundry room as clothes tumbled in the dryer: blue, red, yellow, all furiously whirling around with no identity. It was mass confusion — just like her first day on campus.

Use your eyes. Watch what is going on around you. Listen to what is being said. Think about something you have read. Concentrate on whatever it is until it *suggests an idea to you.* Then describe what you have seen, heard, or read, and explain the idea that it has brought to you.

It seems like everyday I hear about something happening to someone I know. Just recently I learned my tennis partner in doubles is engaged. Only the other day she was worried about a fight with her old boyfriend! Another friend of mine is pregnant. People grow up fast their first year after graduation from high school! I remember in the sixth grade the heartaches we suffered about who got to like who each week. We would write little notes back and forth, "Do you like me, circle yes or no." I had a really neat sixth-grade teacher,

named Mr. Howard. It was his first year of teaching. We did all kinds
of weird things with him. We used to make animal noises for the class
and have a record day once a week. When Mr. Howard got mad at the
boys he would stuff them in a wastepaper basket. What a time we used
to have. Now my youngest brother is already in seventh grade. I
didn't realize until recently he was growing up. I guess I've been
so wrapped up in my own life I forget there are others around me.
Sometimes people get wound up in themselves and forget the real joy
of sharing good times with others, like the time my cousin and I were
riding up on the T-bar at the ski slope and when we got to the top,
she got hooked on by her coat. She was just hanging there, her arms
and legs flying around in despair. I was a real big help. All I did
was fall down, I was laughing so hard. After she finally fell off, we
both laughed so hard we couldn't stand up. Those were the days.

Special Entry 2: Consciously explore two sides of an attitude, situation,
idea, or belief. Perhaps you can analyze a person you either like or dislike,
using a specific incident to show why; then turn around and show the
opposite side of that person's personality through a different incident. Or
explore a rather solid belief you take for granted, such as "football builds
character," and illustrate it with an incident, but then follow up with another
incident that challenges your belief in some way. Back up your opinions with
specifics: events and details. Whatever you do, try to look honestly and fairly
at both sides of the question. *If possible, arrive at some conclusion you have
not previously thought of or at least verbalized.*

My Summertime Experience

My first day at General Motors I was scared, I mean really
scared. I was eighteen, fresh out of high school. I asked myself,
"What am I doing here? My friends are out having a good time,
celebrating their graduation, and I'm stuck in here in this filth."
I worked seven days a week, putting in as much overtime as possible.
I wanted to say "Forget it" to college, if this was what it took to
get me there.

Every day I punched in at the same time: 4:12 p.m. I would go to
my spot on the line, pick up my hammer and chisel, and start
hammering on V-8 engine heads. It was so noisy I had to wear ear
plugs. Of course I had to wear safety glasses because hot chips of
steel were flying around. An apron, gloves, and steel-toed shoes
were also required. I looked as if I were ready for combat. The place
was so dirty from the cooling vents blowing dust onto my body that it
took at least two good showers a night before I was clean. I was
still trying to wash out dirt imbedded in my skin two months after I
stopped working.

I guess I can't complain about everything though. General
Motors has its good points. Working there taught me a lot about
responsibility, the value of money, and, now that I'm here at

school, the value of an education. In addition, I've seen more filth, bums, and dope than anyone knew existed. During lunch break, the place was filled with smoke from people smoking pot. When working on the line, if it was a fairly dark place, I could always smell pot. In the parking lots someone was always making a dope deal. I finally realized what problems many of my uncles and dad have put up with to earn enough money to support their families, problems of noise, dirt, long hours, and rotten shifts.

    I tell you, from what I've seen I'm glad I'm going to college. I know something my friends who were out having a good time may never learn: college is a better place to be working in than any General Motors factory. What kind of future is there standing on a line, hammering V-8 engine heads for ten hours a day seven days a week?

ASSIGNMENT 5   Ten Journal Entries and an Opinion Paper

✓   This assignment consists of two parts. The first you have completed: *hand in your entire ten-entry journal, just as it is, without revising or recopying.* It will be read for content, to see how interesting and well-developed your ideas are. It is important not to revise it, because sometimes you revise the life out of your writing; your unrevised journal may be the best thing you write the whole term.

✓   Part two of Assignment 5 is to write your first "opinion" paper. Look for an entry in your journal that contains an idea or opinion meaningful to you. It doesn't matter whether you have explored it at length, but *be sure you believe what you are saying and think it is worth communicating to others.* In addition, *you must have some personal experience* on which to base your idea or opinion. Under no circumstances try to write on "big" subjects about which you know little: subjects like capital punishment, the draft, the country's economic problems, peace in the Middle East. You cannot write well on these subjects without in-depth research; in this paper concentrate on your writing rather than on research. Be careful, too, about subjects about which you *think* you have strong opinions: legalization of marijuana, the drinking age, abortion, child abuse. Such subjects are overused; unless you have personal experience to add, you probably have nothing to say beyond what has been said many times. The key is *personal experience.* If, for instance, as a result of having a friend who was faced with whether to have an abortion, you have arrived at a valid conclusion, you may be able to write on abortion effectively and convincingly. Otherwise, avoid the subject; it is too complex, involving ethical and moral values difficult for even an experienced writer to handle well.

    Instead, choose opinions closer to home. What ideas, derived from experience, have you formed about standards of conduct among young people? What about family relationships, perhaps changes in your attitude since you came to college? What about the quality of the education you are receiving? You have all sorts of ideas and opinions, grounded in experience: choose from those. (If you have no journal entries that seem to apply, look back at your free writing; perhaps you expressed there an opinion you can now illustrate and expand. Or write a new journal entry, focusing on an idea or opinion that matters to you.)

When you have an entry that qualifies, revise it as instructed in the revising activities that follow, put it into final draft, and submit it along with *the original entry from which it was taken.*

Revising Activity 5-1   *Developing an Idea Fully*

Read the journal entry you have chosen to develop into a paper. Think about the sentences *one by one* and ask yourself *three* questions:

1. Is there anything in this sentence that needs explaining—terms I've used or an idea I've stated without explaining what it means to me?

2. Is there any way I can *illustrate* this statement with a *specific incident* which demonstrates what I have said is true? Is there something that happened to me or to someone I know that convinced me and might help convince a reader? (Consider the possibility of starting your paper with the incident and then drawing your conclusions.)

3. Is there any other type of supporting evidence or proof I can use to help drive my point home more forcefully—startling facts or figures, for instance?

Revise and expand your original entry as necessary. In the initial stages *do not radically change your original entry.* Use the supporting material as just that: support for what you have already said.

If, however, as you begin to expand your entry you find you have more than you can cover in a paper of perhaps five pages, consider the possibility of limiting your topic to some portion of it you can handle adequately in a short paper. Or, if you become convinced you must change your original idea or approach it in a different way, use your judgment.

It may be that one of your journal entries already meets the above criteria. If so, fine. Use it.

Original Journal Entry

Writing papers is something I've always hated to do. Whenever a teacher required a paper to be written I started devising ways to avoid doing much work. One way I did it was to paraphrase articles in magazines and encyclopedias, which I soon found invariably brought me good grades. When that didn't work, I would bribe someone else to write my paper for me. But when I got to college I knew I was going to have to pay for all my scheming. I did my own papers for a while until we got an assignment for a ten-day journal. When I mentioned that to a friend, she offered me some of her papers to use for entries. I thought I had it made until I read the papers. Then my enthusiasm died. They were really bad, not at all like what we'd been doing in class. So I decided to take my chances from here on in on writing my own papers. One thing I've learned in this composition class is to write my own papers, no matter how rotten they might be.

The Completed Paper

Ways to Avoid Writing

Writing papers is something I've always hated to do. Whenever a teacher required a paper written I started devising ways to avoid doing much work.

In seventh grade Mrs. Blair, my science teacher, assigned a term paper. It was to be four pages long covering any topic we had discussed in class. The paper was due in two weeks, and by the end of the first week I was still deciding what to write. Finally, five days before the due date, I decided to write about the planets in our solar system. Being short on time, I hauled out the World Book Encyclopedia. Changing a few words here and there, I copied what the encyclopedia had to say on the planets. Two hours later, the paper was done. I recopied it, feeling extremely proud of myself. The paper came back two days later with an "A" on it. "Very interesting paper, good work," was scrawled across the top. Feeling smug, I put the paper in my folder. The pattern for writing my term papers was set. Paraphrasing articles in magazines and encyclopedias became a habit.

In my senior year, composition was required to graduate. Mrs. McKay, the teacher, was a strange lady who liked anything written about death, witchcraft, or religion. The class was told to read Edgar Lee Masters' Spoon River Anthology and write a critical review. Mrs. McKay informed us that "A critical review consists of an introduction, thesis, and conclusion. Or, in words you can understand, tell 'em what you're gonna tell 'em, tell 'em, and tell 'em what you told 'em."

I walked out of class complaining about the assignment. Reaching my locker I saw my friend, Sherry. "What a drag!" I said. "You know what we have to do for comp?"

"What?"

"Write a critical review of this book." I showed her my copy of Spoon River Anthology.

"Hey, I read that book last year."

As I opened my locker, a thought came to me. Sherry had borrowed $5.00 that I never expected to get back. I could have her write my paper to pay off the debt! Shutting the locker door, I turned to her. "Hey, Sher, you know that five bucks you owe me?"

"Yeah." Her face turned red.

"If you write my critical review, I'll consider us even."

"Dammit, Kath. I knew you were up to something!"

"I'm sorry. I just thought it would be a good way for you to pay me back. I know you don't have the money."

She started laughing. "I think you just conned me into writing a damn paper."

"Great! I'm glad you'll do it."

The next weekend Sherry gave me the paper. Monday I handed it in, hoping for the best. Two days later the paper came back with an "A—" written in bright red ink. Walking out of class I muttered, "Well, so much for critical reviews."

Walking into Ms. Martin's English 101 class at college, I knew it was time to pay for the scheming done in school. I found myself writing my own papers until one day an assignment was made for a ten-day journal. When I mentioned it to Sally, a girl who lives next door, she said, "Kath, I've got five papers you could use for entries."

"Really?"

"Sure. Here take my notebook."

Grabbing the notebook I went to my room. But after reading the papers my enthusiasm died. Here's an excerpt from Sally's notebook:

Peanut brittle is a chewy, hard, sticky kind of candy. When I am eating it, I feel like I'm a giant jar of hard peanut butter. Jiffy maybe. When you're done eating it, you quickly run, or walk fast, to the nearest toothpick or chisel to indulge in an excavating demonstration.

After reading that paper, whicr was the best one, I decided to take my chances writing my own papers. I've finally learned to write my own papers, no matter how rotten they might be.

Revising Activity 5-2   *Grammar (Minigrammar C)*

✔   Review your paper for sentence fragments and run-on sentences. Avoid run-on sentences entirely. If you use a sentence fragment, be sure you are using it intentionally and for a special effect. (If you are not sure about sentence fragments and run-on sentences, work through Minigrammar C, starting on p. 193.)

Also check for problems of subject and predicate agreement and for instances of tense shifting. Have you used the proper verb form? Check particularly to be sure your past tense verbs have the final -d if regular or are correct if irregular. (Minigrammars A and B, pp. 171 and 183.)

Revising Activity 5-3   *Punctuation and Paragraphing Form*

✔   Check your paper carefully for punctuation, reviewing Revising Activity 3-2 (p. 46) if necessary. Also check your dialogue form if you have used dialogue (Revising Activity 3-1, p. 43). Be sure that all your paragraphs are indented sufficiently so that it is clear where you intend to paragraph. When typing, the conventional indentation for all paragraphs, *including* the first one, is *five* spaces. If you are still doing your final drafts in longhand, be sure your paragraph indentations are about equivalent to that.

Revising Activity 5-4   *Wordiness*

✔   Make a final check for wordiness before you put your paper into final draft (Revising Activities 2-1, 2-2, 2-3, pp. 29-30).

CHECKLIST   *Developing Ideas through a Journal*

Preparations.   Check off each item when completed.

Activity 5-1   Writing a Journal. . . . .
Activity 5-2   Special Journal Entries . . . .
Assignment 5   Ten Journal Entries and an Opinion Paper . . . .
Revising Activity 5-1   Developing an Idea Fully . . . .
Revising Activity 5-2   Grammar (Minigrammar C) . . . .
Revising Activity 5-3   Punctuation and Paragraphing Form . . . .
Revising Activity 5-4   Wordiness . . . .

Goals to Be Achieved.   Write your answers on a separate sheet. Explain fully.

1. Do your journal entries give a real picture of your mind at work, not only recording events but explaining and evaluating the significance of what has happened?
2. Have you made a sincere effort to use techniques learned from Part I in both your journal entries and your paper?
3. Have you left your journal just as you wrote it, but have you put your paper into neat and proper form, paying attention to grammar and mechanics?

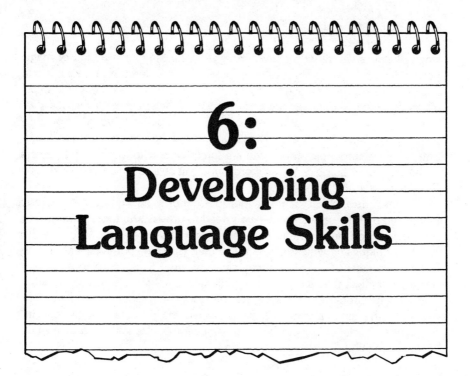

6:
Developing Language Skills

Until now, you have been trying to write naturally and then looking at what you've written in specific ways to make it more efficient and to avoid problems of grammar and mechanics. Now let's work on some new and interesting language skills that should *become* natural to you and help make your writing more effective.

Language is a mystery to many people, so much so that primitive cultures often see it as magical. Certain words become very powerful, and ordinary people are forbidden to use them. An obvious example is the word for God, which in some cultures is a sin to pronounce. One reason language exercises this strange power is that people with little language skill are awed by people who have an ability to use words well.

Although some people seem born with the "gift of gab," everyone, given reasonable intelligence and industriousness, can achieve fairly impressive language skills. In this chapter, you will be asked to experiment with some additional techniques that will introduce you to possibilities of manipulating language for your own purposes.

In a sense, language really is magical. Being able to put your thoughts and feelings into words can be personally liberating and powerful. Of course, language is limited and we must realize from the beginning that we can only approximate what we are thinking or feeling. But we can learn to come closer to total expression, as words progressively reveal in greater clarity our true thoughts and emotions.

Language is magical in another way too. People who can put ideas into words, who can use words to create new ideas, who can become masters instead of slaves where words are concerned, find they have a kind of magic power. You may not be interested in possessing that kind of power; it is one people have distrusted since the Greek days when Plato said he would expel all poets (probably meaning anyone especially skilled in words) from his ideal Republic. But consider that unless you can use a tool well, you do not completely understand its use and are at the mercy of the person who is skilled. If you can't use carpenter's tools, you are forced to bow to the superior powers of the carpenter. If you can't use words, you can be swayed and controlled by those who talk and write well.

To gain control of language—either to use it or to be sure not to be overly influenced by how others use it—you need to understand more than how to revise what you have written so it is efficient and error-free. You need to know techniques by which people make their language both efficient and effective in order not only to convey clear information but also to achieve a heightened effect that will appeal to a reader's emotions and love of beauty. The ancient Greeks—who were very language-conscious—classified techniques of this kind, and the Romans refined the process. For anyone interested in how language can be used persuasively, classical rhetoric, a study of these techniques, can be fascinating.

Activity 6-1   *Parallelism through Repetition of a Grammatical Element*

All the exercises in this chapter deal in one way or another with parallel structures in English. You probably associate the word *parallel* with mathematics, where parallel lines are always equidistant, extending in the same direction and never meeting. Another dictionary definition for *parallel* is "something equal or similar in all essential particulars," and this more nearly coincides with its use in writing.

By now, if you have mastered Minigrammars A, B, and C, you should be familiar with the principal parts of speech, such as nouns, pronouns, and verbs, and you should be able to recognize complete sentence structures. Once you recognize language features and their functions, you can *duplicate* those features; such duplication is the essence of parallelism. The ability to use parallel structure is perhaps the single most valuable skill in achieving effective, efficient sentences.

A. Verbs

Almost any grammatical element, when repeated, is a type of parallelism. A well-known example is Caesar's "I *came*, I *saw*, I *conquered*," in which different verbs are used in the same *construction*. Translation into English masks the true parallelism of this famous Latin phrase: *veni, vidi, vici.* Any string of verbs can be thought of as a form of parallelism, *provided they all perform equal functions in the sentence.* For example, suppose you have a character named Jim who, lost and exhausted, performs three acts: he *reaches* a lake; he *looks* across the water; he *wonders* how he will ever make it home. You can avoid wordiness by combining these actions in the sentence "Jim *reached* the lake half dead from exhaustion, *looked* out across the water, and *wondered* how he would ever make it home." Here all the verbs are the same part of speech; they *also* perform a similar function in the sentence — they are *predicates* for the *subject* "Jim."

Remember: the *function* in the sentence is crucial. In a sentence like "Jim, looking across the lake, *wondered* how he would ever make it home," only the verb *wondered* performs the *function* of a predicate for the subject *Jim*. The other "action" — *looking* — is contained in a participial phrase, which has a *different function* in the sentence structure; it is therefore *not* parallel with *wondered*.

✔ **1.** Write three sentences in which you use three or more verbs in a parallel structure as *predicates* of a single subject. Underline the verbs used as parallel predicates.

Example

While Susan and Bob were working on the farm, <u>they</u> <u>arose</u> at 5:00 every morning, <u>helped</u> with the milking, <u>ate</u> a big breakfast, and then <u>worked</u> all day in the fields.

Note that *were working*, although an action verb similar to *arose, helped, ate* and *worked,* is *not* one of the *parallel* elements, because it does not serve as a predicate for *they*.

B. Nouns

Just as verbs can be used in parallel structures, so can nouns. The principle is the same: the nouns must be used in *similar functions*. Multiple subjects can be in parallel form, like the italicized nouns in the following sentence: "All the *houses, apartments,* and *motels* were inspected for beetle infestation." Similarly, direct or indirect objects (the receivers of the action of the sentence) can be multiplied through parallel structure: "John viewed with regret the *spill* on his jacket, the *stain* on his best pants, and the *wrinkles* in his only tie." There are other possibilities, but these will suffice for illustration.

✔ **2.** Write three sentences in which you use nouns in parallel structures. For now, limit yourself to the use of nouns as subjects or objects in the sentence. Underline the parallel nouns.

Examples

Subject   <u>Men</u>, <u>women</u>, and <u>children</u> will benefit from this law.

Object   This summer, in search of peace, I visited the high <u>mountains</u>, the lonely <u>seashore</u>, the quiet <u>lakes</u>, and the deep <u>forests</u> of my native Pacific Northwest.

C. More Complex Patterns

Once you have grasped the basic principle, you can use parallelism in endless ways. Among the simpler are parallel adjectives (The *immense, heavy, overbalanced* platform sank into the sea) and adverbs (He kicked the horse *savagely, repeatedly, disgustingly*). On a slightly more sophisticated level, you can try parallel prepositional phrases (The girls walked *along the lakeshore, past tall buildings, through the park,* and *into the city center*).

Effects can be mixed and matched, as in the following piece written by a student.

     In the band there are prancing drums, blazing trumpets bounc-
ing and spinning their notes around and above them, woodwinds
quietly and gracefully doing their aerial acrobatics, French horns
boldly announcing themselves with a roar of sound, and clumsy-
looking tubas slowly moving along.

The most obvious parallelism is the series of nouns naming the instruments: *drums, trumpets, woodwinds, French horns, tubas.* But each of these nouns is also accompanied by one or more present participles ("-ing" forms of the verb) which add to the parallel effect: *prancing* drums, *blazing* trumpets *bouncing* and *spinning,* woodwinds *doing,* French horns *announcing,* clumsy-*looking* tubas *moving.*

The participles in the foregoing examples are handled with considerable variety so that you don't get bored by the repetition; in fact, you may hardly have noticed what the writer was doing. Most writers do routine things that you can do too, once you recognize them. A professional artist learns the routine techniques but then puts them together in new and unexpected patterns. You may not be able to create new patterns, which takes a special quality of mind able to see as others do not see and to combine elements in new ways. But you can learn the basic techniques and become a skilled crafts-man for your own purposes.

✓ **3.** Try writing a sentence or short paragraph, using varied forms of paral-lelism. If you wish, use the band description as a model. Experiment a little, not worrying too much whether you produce a work of art. Just begin to find out what *you* can do with language.

Activity 6-2   *Extended Forms of Parallelism*

Parallelism is not necessarily confined to a single sentence. It can run over a series of sentences. One student, trying to define loneliness, used a series of sentences starting with "It is" followed by a noun modified by a phrase or clause. This is just one of many patterns we can learn

---

     What is loneliness? Loneliness is an emotion we feel when there
is no one to talk to or share with. It is a feeling of being in-

secure, not knowing whether or not we are accepted. It is a realization that others are "out there" and we are "in here." It is a frustration of our deep desire to share our being with others. It is the knowledge that others do not fully understand us, that others can never understand us, that others can never come inside us to know and share our true selves.

Caution: Such obvious parallelism must not be carried to such extremes that it becomes monotonous and boring. This writer has stretched the pattern to its limits; the pattern may have been repeated once too often.

> **Principle 11** Economize with words, phrases, forms, even punctuation; use exactly what you need—no more and no less.

✔ As a preliminary to trying some extended forms of parallel structure, make a list of at least twenty items modeled on the following list developed by a student. Choose some abstraction such as Love, Freedom, Justice, Corruption, Loneliness, Alienation. Be sure that the verb *is* leads to a *noun* (Sadness is a *friend* . . .; Sadness is a *forest*, etc.), as this will help you maintain the parallel structure in the exercises that follow.

Sadness is a friend who needs help you can't give to him.
Sadness is a forest butchered by lumber companies.
Sadness is a man treated unjustly by a society that does not see itself as unjust.
Sadness is a farewell after a beautiful day.
Sadness is a proud buck lying dead in the snow.
Sadness is the last swig from a refreshing beer.
Sadness is a man who has no self-respect.
Sadness is a home left behind and the realization that a period of your life is over.
Sadness is a rapist who hurts people because he cannot accept himself.
Sadness is a girl who no longer needs you.
Sadness is a football game lost by a point when everyone recognized your team was a three-touchdown favorite.
Sadness is a cold when you want to kiss your girl friend.
Sadness is a misunderstanding on your part that hurts a friend deeply.
Sadness is your new suit being spilled on right before an important date.
Sadness is any person that has lived his life and toward the end cannot find meaning in it.
Sadness is a football player who loves the game but finds he is too small to play on the team.
Sadness is capital punishment.
Sadness is anything that makes you sad.

✔ **1.** Write a short paragraph modeled on the paragraph "What is loneliness?" Use the "It is" sentence structure—with discrimination.

✔ **2.** Write a sentence using parallel noun phrases, modeled on the following example. Note that each phrase starts with a *noun* used as a completer of the phrase "Things that make me sad are . . ." Underline the parallel nouns in your sentence.

Example
   Things that make me sad are the loss of a football game by a point when everyone recognized our team was a three-touchdown favorite, a cold when I want to kiss my girl friend, or a spill on a new suit right before an important date.

✔   **3.** Write a sentence based on each of the following models, in which the repeated (parallel) element is a clause introduced by a relative pronoun (such as *who* or *which*) or a subordinate conjunction (such as *that, when,* or *because*). Underline the repeated pronoun or conjunction. You may find it necessary in this and the succeeding exercise to do some rewording of your original items. This rephrasing is *part of the activity*, to help you learn to make language flexible enough to suit your purposes.

Examples
   A sad person is one who has lost his self-respect or who has been unjustly treated by a society that does not see itself as an unjust.

   I feel sad when a forest can be butchered by lumber companies, when a proud buck can lie dying in the blood-stained snow, and when a rapist hurts people because he cannot accept himself.

   It is sad that a misunderstanding on your part can hurt a friend deeply and that a person can live her life out and at the end find no meaning in it.

✔   **4.** Write a sentence in which the repeated (parallel) element is a series of present participles (the "-ing" form of a verb), as demonstrated in the example below. Underline the parallel participles.

Example
   Saying farewell after a beautiful day, taking a last swig of a refreshing beer, having a cold when you want to kiss your girl friend, and spilling coffee down the front of your suit before a big date are times of sadness.

Activity 6-3   *A Special Case: Repetition for Effect*

   Until now, you have been examining your writing for monotonous and ineffective repetition of words and phrases, and you should continue to do so. But not all repetition is dull; sometimes we can repeat for very good effect. For a good example, look again at the journal entry on p. 71, where repetition of *love* signals a series of phrases that balance or parallel one another in a recognizable and orderly way:

   But once again, I looked around me, and the feeling of love came back to me, love for the world, love for Mary, love for God, and even love for our two invaders.

As this passage shows, whole sentences or phrases can be parallel:

> love for the world
> love for Mary
> love for God
> love for our two invaders

Notice that each of these phrases begins with the same word, each is followed by the same preposition (*for*), and each is completed by an object of the preposition (*the world, Mary,* etc.).

✓   Write at least two sentences on your own, modeling them on the foregoing passage. Underline the repeated word that signals the beginning of each part of the parallel structure.

Activity 6-4   *Combining Parallel Elements*

✓   Now that you have experimented with numerous forms of parallelism, write a paragraph in which you try to explain or define the abstraction (Love, Freedom, etc.) you have been working with throughout these exercises. Try to use various types of parallelism. The following passage demonstrates the exercise (signals of parallelism are underlined to help you understand), but don't follow it slavishly. Invent your own ways of using parallel structures effectively.

> Wouldn't it be nice if we could always be happy? But only an insensitive person can help feeling sad sometimes. How can sadness be defined? Sadness is a feeling I get when I see a proud buck lying dead in the snow or a forest butchered by lumber companies or any person who has lived a long life and at the end can't find a meaning for it. I feel sad when through some misunderstanding I hurt a friend, when I find the girl I love no longer loves me, when I learn I'm too small to play varsity football, or when I leave home, realizing a part of my life is over. I feel sad for friends who need help, sad for men unjustly treated by society, sad for people with no self-respect. Of course, there is a less depressing kind of sadness: the sadness of taking the last swig of refreshing beer, of saying farewell after a beautiful day, of knowing that the happy times are often fleeting. As I think about it, I guess sadness is the difference between what life is and what one wants it to be: the difference between helping a friend and not being able to, between valuing every human being and not recognizing one's own injustice, between loving and wanting to be loved.

Activity 6-5   *The Extended Metaphor*

In Chapter 2, the idea of an extended metaphor was introduced with the student's description of how a crack in the sidewalk might seem like a great canyon to some microscopic organism. Introducing a metaphor in your writing can be effective in numerous ways. It can add a dash of seasoning to liven up your writing. It can help you make a reader visualize something unfamiliar by comparing it with something familiar. When it is extended, as in the description of the sidewalk crack, it can help organize a whole paragraph or even a whole paper.

An extended metaphor involves another kind of parallelism. It is like two sides of an equation; everything on one side must be equal to something on the other. For example, let us take an overused metaphor: Life is like a river flowing from small beginnings to the sea of death. We could list the parallel elements thus:

River	Life
Starts at a small spring	Begins as a small infant
When small, flows merrily	Plays and laughs as a small child
Grows larger, flows gracefully between its banks	Grows up, learns how to act and dress well
Joins another stream	Marries
Smaller tributaries branch off	Has children
Etc.	Etc.

To write a good extended metaphor, the two sides need to be balanced against one another, expanded of course with vivid details. Two examples follow, illustrating differents types of organization; perhaps you can think of other methods.

The Birth of a Project

When I hear a teacher announce that the class will have a project due at the end of the semester, I feel like an unprepared girl who has just been told she is pregnant. Although the prospect is intriguing, I feel apprehensive and scared about the final product. But since the hard work won't come for a while, I take things in stride. Time passes and the pressure begins to build, increasing to the point of sickness. As the big day nears, the weight becomes a terrible burden. Periodically, I check with my instructor to see how I'm coming along. With the "due date" upon me, I grow touchy and tense. Suddenly I feel sharp pains. Sweating heavily and pushing hard, I put forth all the effort I can, and my "baby" is born! I am relieved, and although I had misgivings at first, the results are a source of pleasure and pride.

On Adolescence

A scared mouse hurries through the maze, not knowing which way to turn. He keeps coming upon dead ends and circles, and is frustrated and confused. He wants to reach the end of the maze, for he knows that there will be a reward for him there to make all his efforts worthwhile. Each time the mouse takes a wrong turn, he learns not to go that way again, and in so doing gains another step of progress.

Adolescence seems to be much the same. As young adults, life appears to be nothing more than a maze to us. We don't know where each new turn will take us or what pitfalls may await us. We often find ourselves traveling in circles and gaining no ground. When we think that we have found an open door and are on the right path, we run into a dead end and must backtrack to start all over.

Adolescence is a time of trials and errors, trying to find the right way and failing to do so. It is a time of frustration when we can't seem to get ahead. Each time we do get off on the wrong foot and find we have done the wrong thing, we learn from it. We know not to go that way again. We gain from these experiences and our travels through life become more familiar, just as the mouse becomes familiar with the maze. We know which paths to take and which to stay away from. We move through life with gathering speed and purpose, going in a determined direction. We know what things lie ahead and what our goals and rewards are.

The mouse starts at the beginning of the maze and runs through it in record time, making no errors, and is unafraid. He now knows what his destination is and how to get there. At the end of the maze he nibbles his cheese, at peace with himself and his little world.

When writing extended metaphors *stick to the main image*; don't mix your metaphors! And *be sure every detail reinforces your analogy or comparison.* In any analogy there are elements on both sides that are not comparable. For instance, mice and adolescents can hardly be called intellectual equals, but mentioning such a discrepancy would weaken the author's central idea.

✔ Think up an extended metaphor. Let your search for an idea percolate in your mind. Perhaps one of the special journal entries done for Activity 5-2 will be applicable. If you cooperate, your mind has an almost miraculous way of supplying you with pertinent ideas. When the right one strikes, write your extended metaphor. Remember: stick to the main image and be sure *every detail reinforces your idea.*

ASSIGNMENT 6   Parallelism and Metaphor

✔ Revise the paragraph you wrote for Activity 6-4 and your extended metaphor (Activity 6-5) in accordance with Revising Activities 6-1 and 6-2 which follow. Put the *two* pieces of writing into neat final copy. Hand in *all* the work done for this chapter with your final copy on top.

Revising Activity 6-1   *Spelling*

For most students, spelling is not a major problem, though many think it is. Most of you spell most words right. On the other hand, most of you have some spelling problems. Some of these are particular to you; we all know certain words we can't remember how to spell no matter how often we look them up in the dictionary. You know what these words are for you, and you are just going to have to look them up *every time*.

A few students have special problems; for instance, they may not *see* a word in the usual way. But with few exceptions, if you have more than usual trouble with spelling, it's because you really don't want to spell well. Either you've let it get the better of you or you don't think it's important to spell well. Do you really want to go through life with people saying, "Well, you have good ideas, but you can't spell worth beans!" It's your choice.

One way to begin to control your spelling is to watch carefully which words are marked *sp* on your papers as they come back. *Make a list!* Choose about five that you know you use most often and concentrate on those. Write them over and over, or make up sentences using them. Resolve to become so familiar with those words that you will never misspell them again. Do whatever it takes to live up to that resolution. When you have the first five in hand, move on to another five.

One clue: many words fall into groups (entrance, substance, circumstance on the one hand; existence, persistence, subsistence on the other hand). If you watch your misspellings, you may find they fall into some sort of pattern. If so, concentrate on that pattern. Your handbook, if it is a good one, may deal with it. Or there are spelling handbooks and guides that group spelling problems by patterns.

Very often, you spell something wrong because you hear it wrong. Many words are pronounced differently from the way they are spelled. An obvious example is a word like *tonight*, often spelled *tonite* because that is how it sounds (or sometimes because of sheer laziness). *Through* is often spelled *thru*, for the same reasons. Even if words are spelled as they sound, the sounds may be nearly indistinguishable to the ear, as in words like *environment*, *government*, and *sophomore*. If you find yourself misspelling words such as these, concentrate for a while on the *sound*; train your ear to hear all the *n*'s in *environment*, for example, or the middle *o* in *sophomore*.

Another problem with sound occurs in words that sound much alike, such as *accept* and *except*, or *affect* and *effect*. Other words sound *exactly* alike (*hear, here; two, too, to*). These include such common spelling problems as the "there/their/they're" and "your/you're" puzzlers. You have to learn which is which.

This text, as usual, does not pretend to give you a complete guide to spelling. But here are a few basic aids to help you remember.

1. Whether to put the *i* before *e* when the combination sounds like *ee* is answered by probably the most-used formula in the English language: "*i* before *e* except after *c*." Almost everyone says this formula before *ie* or *ei* words (bel*ie*ve, rec*ei*ve). There are some exceptions, but no one can remember them. If you get this much in mind, you have control of most of the problems.

2. Whether to drop the final *e* (dare, daring) is a tough one. Ordinarily we think the *e* should be dropped when the next letter is a vowel (*a, e, i, o, u*, and sometimes *y*). But that doesn't always work. If you are in doubt, look it up in the dictionary, as everyone else does. One partial rule is that the final *e* changes the pronunciation of the word (*par, pare*), but that doesn't always hold either.

3. Another "sort-of" pronunciation rule is that doubling a consonant in the middle of a word makes the vowel ahead of it short (*planning* a trip, as opposed to *planing* a board). This may help you in some cases, but again, if you are in doubt, consult your dictionary.

4. As a general rule, *y* becomes *i* when it is preceded by a consonant and is followed by a vowel (*dry + ed = dried*). When the *y* is preceded by a vowel, it does not change (*play + ed = played*).

5. Literally thousands of words are formed by adding prefixes or suffixes to what is called the root. Sometimes the root is a word in itself, like *trust*. You can add prefixes such as *mis-, dis-*, and *en-* to form *mistrust, distrust,* and *entrust*, or you can add suffixes like *-ful* to make *trustful*. This is a simple matter of addition; if you know how to spell the root and you know how to spell the prefix or suffix, you can spell the word they combine to make. This will help you with such commonly misspelled words as *misspell*, which is the root *spell* with the prefix *mis-* in front of it. Some roots are not words in themselves. An example is *-mit*, which with prefixes can become *admit, commit, submit, transmit*. If you build yourself a fund of prefixes, suffixes, and roots you will reduce your spelling problems by leaps and bounds.

6. Another large problem area can disappear if you remember that many words are simply two words put together. Among college students, perhaps the most commonly misspelled word falling into this category is *roommate (room + mate)*. Watch for others.

7. Your problems with *there, their,* and *they're* and with *your* and *you're* can be lessened if you think a little. Take *there, their, they're;* how can you differentiate among them? If you recall Revising Activity 3-4 (7), you'll know *they're* means *they + are (They're* going with us). *Their* is related to *they:* the *y* of *they* changes to *i* to form the possessive *their* (It is *their* house). That leaves *there* to be used in expressions like "*There* are seven pears in the basket." Exactly the same reasoning applies to *your* and *you're*. *You're* means *you + are (You're* a college student now); *your* is the possessive of *you* (It's *your* life).

In addition, there are some words that are consistently misspelled. Watch out particularly for the following:

1. *whether*, as in "I didn't know whether you were coming or not." (Often confused with *weather*, as in "The weather was stormy.")

2. *writing*. People keep doubling the *t*. This is probably a confusion resulting from a double *t* in *written*. Notice this follows the "rule" mentioned just above in 3.

3. *too*, as in "too many" or "too much." *Too* sometimes means *also*, as in "I went too," but students don't have trouble with that. For the use of *too* in terms like "too far," try the following rule (which doesn't always

work, but does often enough to be useful): If you can substitute *very* for *too* and the resulting sentence makes sense, the spelling is *too,* i.e., I believe doctors are often *too* successful at extending a patient's life; I believe doctors are often *very* successful at extending a patient's life. Both sentences make sense, so *too* is the proper spelling. BUT: I wanted to go; I wanted very go. The second sentence doesn't make sense, so *to* is correct.

4. *existence.* Remember "Existence is tense" and maybe you will remember that *existence* is spelled with an *e* and not an *a.* (By the way, "Experience is also tense.")

5. *a lot,* as in "I saw a lot of people last week." There are *two* words here. If you remember that *lot* is sometimes a term for measuring (land is divided into "lots"), you may be able to keep this straight. Some people also write *alittle.* There is no such word as this either. Concentrate *a little,* and you should be able to remember.

6. *all right,* as in "She said it was all right." Although some dictionaries give *alright* as an alternate spelling, educated people still prefer the two-word form: *all right* (two words).

✓   Review your paragraphs for spelling problems and correct them.

Revising Activity 6-2   *Grammar and Mechanics*

✓   Review your paragraphs for the following problems and revise where necessary:

1. Subject and predicate agreement (Minigrammar A, p. 171)
2. Tense shifting and verb forms (Minigrammar B, p. 183)
3. Sentence fragments (Minigrammar C, p. 194)
4. Run-on sentences (Minigrammar C, p. 200)
5. Punctuation (Revising Activity 3-2), p. 46
6. Correct dialogue form, if applicable (Revising Activity 3-1, p. 43)
7. Conventional paragraph indentation (Revising Activity 5-3, p. 78)

CHECKLIST   *Developing Language Skills*

Preparations.   Check off each item when completed.

Goals to Be Achieved.   Write your answers on a separate sheet. Explain fully.

1. Do you feel you have a reasonable grasp of the principle of parallelism or does some major confusion still exist in your mind?
2. Does your metaphor bring out an analogy between two basically unlike things in such a way as to cast new light on one or the other (or both)?
3. Have you preserved an easy, natural voice in your paragraph using parallelisms and in your extended metaphor?
4. Have you performed the revising activities carefully? Can you pinpoint at least one spelling problem you should especially watch out for?

PART III:

Focusing Your Ideas

Two years ago if someone had told me I would like writing my thoughts and expressing my ideas on paper for a reader, I would have said they had to be kidding. Writing, I thought, was reserved for research papers, essays, and those few and far between letters I wrote to my relatives. I thought that to write anything I really felt was to betray my sense of privacy or to make my thoughts cheap.

Now I feel differently. I've learned that writing can be more than just drudgery—I can gain insight. I feel writing consists of thoughts and significant details worked out to some kind of conclusion. It's like being given a problem in math, and the only way to solve it is with paper and pencil.

A STUDENT

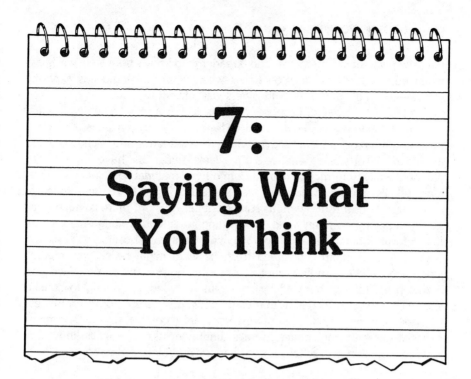

7:
Saying What You Think

Y ou have "crossed the bridge." At least, you should have by now. Through your journal you have begun to move from strictly personal experience to ideas, thoughts, opinions, and beliefs. In your opinion paper for Assignment 5, you have expressed an idea derived largely from your own experience and have tried to show a reader the evidence on which you base that idea. Part III continues that process, with more emphasis on looking thoughtfully at the great body of information that exists all around and on evaluating, interpreting, reacting to, and drawing conclusions about the world in which you live.

By now you have written a good deal, more perhaps than you would have dreamed you could in so short a time. You should have more understanding that writing, to be good, must be part of you, a getting what's inside outside, as we set out to do in the first chapter, and that even what starts outside—external facts and figures and happenings—must somehow become part of *your own mind and experience* if *you* are to write about them with conviction.

Remember always, as we move ahead, that *you* are doing the thinking and talking. *Writing is the product of your own mind.* The coming assignments are going to sound more like traditional "themes" or "term papers"; therefore, beware of slipping back into old patterns. Keep in mind what you've learned about how to be informative and interesting. Trust your own intelligence. Don't try to borrow someone else's brains or someone else's voice. Rely on good significant details, a bit of dialogue here and there, and specific incidents to make your writing lively and convincing. Otherwise you run the risk of sounding phony. Though you may not realize it, you have your own style, your own way of saying things, and a reader who knows your style will know when you depart from it. You know when what you write has a phony sound—when it's not *you*—and others will sense it too.

The title of this chapter proposes nothing new; from the beginning this text has urged you to use your own mind, to formulate your own ideas, and to express your own opinions, based on whatever experience and background are available. All sorts of experience are available: things that have happened to you personally, information gained from others, material contained in books, films, television, and magazines. As a student, you still have much to learn, either directly or through various sources of information; there is much to be said for keeping an open mind, suspending judgment, waiting until you are fully informed before making up your mind what your position will be.

On the other hand, you need to make what might be called "interim" judgments. The expanding mind is constantly grappling with new facts and experiences, testing them against previous knowledge, coming to conclusions. The secret is to realize that *every* conclusion is temporary, a process that does not miraculously cease when you finish college, for the best minds never stop expanding, never come to final conclusions, always know that whatever opinion is reached, it can change with additional facts.

> *Principle 12* **It is better to say: "This is what I think now, based on what I know. I reserve my right to change my opinion any time new information comes my way."**

Activity 7-1 *Formulating a Central Idea*

The main emphasis of Part III is on the *central idea. A central idea is an expression of an opinion or idea you have now, based on your knowledge at the present time.*

Many of you find it difficult to make a clear, concise statement of your opinions or ideas. There are a number of possible reasons for this. Perhaps you have seldom been asked to make a straightforward statement of ideas and you have little faith in your ability to do so. You may think your thoughts aren't important or perhaps you have been criticized when you have tried to express real opinions. Some of you may feel threatened in other ways; you don't want to be labeled aggressive and pushy. Maybe there is peer pressure against those who are "too smart."

Or perhaps you have so many ideas you can't focus on one. You may even feel active resistance to trying to "simplify" your ideas to a point where you can put one into a single sentence. The fabric of your thought seems to lose its richness; the fullness is lost if you start to pick it apart. A nineteenth-century poet, John Keats, may have captured your idea when he objected to attempts to "unweave the rainbow."

Ultimately, however, to function with any sense of purpose or direction, we must secure a solid bridgehead in the moving waters of our thoughts. We must risk taking a stand and fortifying it with the supporting details, incidents, and evidence that convince us. We must risk simplifying our ideas and focusing on one central idea long enough to begin to understand — not just to react to — the wholeness.

In a sense, that is what all writing is — what all thinking is: establishing a momentary bridgehead in the swirling waters before we jump back in. No matter how simple or complex the writing or thinking is, it is only one small piece of the total picture. It may not even be a very valid piece; the important thing is that for the moment it makes sense to us and we have evidence that seems to support it. When you have an idea, take your chances with it; it is something to build on. Otherwise, it is apt to remain so vague in your thoughts that you can't examine it carefully enough to make an informed decision about it.

How does one go about forming a central idea, establishing the momentary firm ground among the swirling thoughts? No one can do it for you; you are responsible for your own ideas. At this point, don't worry about coming up with something new and startling. Just be sure your ideas are *yours*. Too many students think they must be "original"; they often end up sounding affected, unlike themselves. Since you are unique, one of a kind, no one has exactly the same background and experiences you have. If you are yourself and write like yourself, you are far more likely to write in an original way than if you force an unnatural train of thought that momentarily seems more sophisticated or that you think would appeal more to your instructor.

A recurring question among students when no subject is assigned is "What can I write about?" Ask yourself, "What am I interested in?" No paper can succeed unless you are interested in what you are saying. Perhaps in earlier free writings or in your journal you have the germ of a paper. If not, start jotting down ideas that appeal to you. Don't stop too soon; the first few off the top of your head tend to be shopworn, overused, and stale, or they may be too general and vague to be productive. For instance, "sports" is too broad a subject and so is "football." But a topic like how to cut down football injuries in high school may catch your interest because, having played, you already have some ideas about it. Keep your list of possible subjects going until you experience a flash of recognition that says, "This is something I *know* about and might *enjoy* writing about." Then you are ready to start. Finding the right subject is important; don't short-cut this step.

Sometimes, of course, a topic is assigned and, as often as not, it is one you would never pick yourself. Your responsibility is such a case is the same, though sometimes harder to achieve. You must find a way to *make the subject interesting to yourself.* To do this, you first need to learn about it (which is equivalent to having experience with it) so you can *find* your own area of interest within it. You might consider this a voyage of discovery. Second, you need to be able to formulate an idea or opinion about it, based on your knowledge.

However you arrive at your angle of interest in a subject, the essential first step in writing well about it is to formulate your *central idea*—often called a *thesis*—carefully. No paper can succeed without being centered on *one idea*, either stated or implied, that *you* want the reader to understand.

Again, don't close in too soon. Write down the first central idea that occurs to you *in a complete sentence*, with subject and predicate. If your topic is "Cutting down on high school football injuries," what *particular* point do you want to make? What is your suggestion? Be as specific as possible. State it in a sentence: for instance, "Football injuries could be cut down in high school if there were better equipment and playing conditions." Now you have a sense of direction; you know exactly what point you want to make and you have an idea how to prove your point.

Don't stop with *one* central idea! Your first idea may be good, but give yourself a chance to find out. Write at least *three* central ideas, each of which would lead to a different paper. For the football paper, another might be "Football injuries could be cut down if there were less pressure on winning games and more on playing well and safely." A third possibility is "Parental and peer pressure often makes a player feel he must play even when he knows he is not physically fit." Or perhaps you might decide to limit your topic more: "Knee injuries are the single most damaging injury in high school football; more attention should be given to avoiding them."

Stretch your mind. Look at your subject from different angles. Talk about it with others who are interested; perhaps their ideas will help you arrive at new insights.

When you have listed several possible central ideas, choose the one you like best. You may go back to your first one, but at least by thinking through your topic you will be fairly sure you have a good idea, and you may have broadened and deepened your approach.

✔   For this activity, choose a topic—or, if one has been assigned, find an angle that interests you—and write at *least* three possible central ideas—*in complete sentences*—which would each lead to a *different* paper.

Activity 7-2   *Developing Your Central Idea*

A paper that seeks to develop a central idea, to explain and support an opinion you hold, is generally called an *expository* paper. Within this category, there are several ways to develop your idea. Always keep in mind, however, that *whatever* method you choose, the effectiveness of your writing will rest *largely* on *specifics:* the significant details and specific incidents by which you illustrate, support, and prove your general ideas. All of Part I was designed to help you understand the importance of specifics and to use them with increasing skill. This chapter will introduce you to several ways of organizing and using specifics; that is the only difference between Part I and Part III in developing ideas. No idea can be valid unless it is grounded in fact—good details and actual incidents or events that *prove* your point.

Keeping narrative and description as part of your repertoire, let's now add other useful methods of development, several of which are:

1. Classification
2. Definition
3. Comparison and/or contrast
4. Analysis of a process or method

Each of these represents a *way of thinking* we use all the time. There is nothing mysterious about developing a central idea; you simply approach the problem logically, choosing ways to help a reader understand your point, and supporting it with relevant, convincing, and interesting specifics.

✔ Read the following explanations before you try to do anything more with your central idea.

Classification (The Pigeonhole Method)

One useful way to approach your task is to make lists, similar to fact sheets, dividing your subject into various related subheadings. You can think of these subheadings as pigeonholes or slots in a desk into which you place your material in an orderly manner. For instance, in the football paper, suppose you have chosen the central idea "Football injuries could be cut down if there were better equipment and playing conditions." Already you have laid the foundation for a classification; in one section of your paper you will discuss equipment and in the other playing conditions. Under each subhead you will have others: under "equipment" you might take up, in order, helmets, padding, shoes, and the like. Under "playing conditions" you might discuss upkeep of the field, the pressure to win at all costs, and perhaps peer pressure among players.

Examples from student papers may help clarify the form. One student, entitling her paper "Where the Campus Jerk Lurks," tells how, while trying to concentrate on a lecture one day, she was annoyed by "the quiet but distinct undercurrent of mimicking and cunning remarks" made by the person sitting behind her. (Notice the use of *narrative* in choosing and detailing a *specific incident* to *show* the reader what she means). She identifies this person as a species of campus jerk, then goes on to classify and describe various kinds of jerks: the classroom jerk, the jerk who lurks in crowded halls, the jerk who sits in smoky bars, the dorm or apartment jerk. Each kind she explains or exemplifies with a *specific incident*. This development, a typical example of classification, can be outlined easily:

Central idea: Annoying campus jerks lurk everywhere.
  I. Some can be found in the classroom.
 II. Others lurk in crowded halls.
III. Some jerks sit in smoky bars.
IV. Dorm or apartment jerks are common.

This is a very "skeletony" skeleton, which needs fleshing out with significant details and specific incidents. Notice that a parallel form of expression is used in each item. Major headings like this are often expressed in complete sentences that can serve as topic sentences and should, when combined, *form a logical statement of how the whole paper will move from its beginning to its conclusion.* The central idea and four major headings above make a coherent statement when combined:

Annoying campus jerks lurk everywhere. Some can be found in the classroom. Others lurk in crowded halls. Some jerks sit in smoky bars. Dorm and apartment jerks are common.

Complete sentences help your logic to be clear and are usually helpful for major headings, but outlines can consist of fragments or even single words. *The important point is that within each level or sublevel the items must be parallel.*

    I. Some can be found in the classroom.
      A. Mimicking teacher
      B. Keeping up constant undercurrent of talk
      C. Packing up books five minutes before class is over
      D. Making rush for door, practically knocking over everyone else
   II. Others lurk in crowded halls.
      A. Stop to talk with friends and won't move out of way
      B. Race for door with no consideration of others
      C. Make snide comments as others pass by

In this example, items A through D under I are all introduced by present participles ("-ing" form of the verb) and items A through C under II are introduced by present tense verb forms. It is not necessary to carry a parallel pattern beyond the specific series in which it is featured.

Note on outlining: Outlines can be either good or bad. Not all good writers outline every paper *before* writing, but all have some effective method of keeping their thoughts in order. Outlines prepared before you write, according to a mechanical formula, can actually be harmful. Many student papers contain an introduction and a conclusion that echo one another, but between may be three or four points only loosely related to the introduction and conclusion, often not logically developing any central idea. An outline is not a mechanical formula that guarantees success; it is more like an organic plant that grows naturally in your mind as you decide how to develop your central idea.

Ask yourself: Can you outline your paper *after you have written it?* Does everything relate to the central idea you have set out to explain and prove? Is there an orderly, outlinable movement from one point to another? If you can answer these questions affirmatively, you have probably (1) formulated an identifiable central idea and (2) developed your central idea in clear, logical steps.

The pigeonhole method of classification exemplified by the campus jerks is fairly easy to understand. Other kinds of classification are less obvious. You are, for example, using essentially this method when you list three or four examples to support a proposition. Or when you give several reasons for making some statement. A student describing changes in her life since coming to college uses classification by allocating one section of her paper to each of the following: (1) changes in environment, (2) increased open-mindedness of the people she associates with, and (3) losses resulting from separation from people she loves. Another student tells how to construct a terrarium: the choice of container, the soil, the planting, the subsequent care. This too is a kind of classification, because each item is a step that can be listed and developed.

In the following example of organization by classification, the student, after using details nicely to orient a reader to her subject, develops her central idea—"Fear is no laughing matter to those who experience it"—by listing and illustrating some common phobias: fear of the dark, fear of the dentist, and so on.

The house is dark. From your bedroom, you hear the wind blow fiercely through the trees. The stairs leading to your bedroom creak; suddenly you hear a large crack of thunder. As the room lights up, you grab your pillow to hide your face. You are experiencing a terrible feeling—fear—as does everyone many times.

The most common fear, especially among children, is fear of the dark. Do you remember when those big, dark monsters and huge, black spiders seemed to crawl out of your closet when mom turned out the lights and left the room? Or when you were afraid to hang your arm over the edge of the bed for fear a man with hairy hands and long claws would seize you?

Another common fear is fear of a dentist. You lie back and try to remain calm as you see the long, terrifying needle coming towards you. Panic runs through your entire body, and your stomach feels tied into one big knot. You grip the arms of your chair and try, but fail, to focus on something more enjoyable.

Unexpected accidents and situations can create extreme fear and result in phobias. When I was younger, I was trapped in an elevator of a large department store. Though it was only for a short while, to my nine-year-old mind it seemed forever. I began to panic, wondering where my air supply would come from or whether the cable was going to break. Since then, I use the stairs. Others may have had an experience of nearly falling from a high place and so fear heights; they can sometimes develop a nervous twitch or even faint from one look off the top of a ladder.

Such fears may seem ridiculous to some people, but to others they are no laughing matter.

Outline

Central idea: Fear is no laughing matter to those who experience it.
III. Introduction: a frightening moment
    A. Dark house

B. Wind blowing through trees
C. The stairs creaking
D. Thunder and lightning
II. Common types of fear
A. Fear of the dark
1. Monsters and spiders in closets
2. Someone under the bed
B. Fear of dentist
1. Terrifying needle
2. Panic overwhelming you
3. Stomach tied in knots
4. Hands clutching arms of chair
5. Mind trying to focus on something else
III. Phobias created by accidents
A. My fear of elevators
B. Fear of heights
IV. Conclusion: Fears may seem ridiculous to some but are no
laughing matter to others.

With more development, perhaps in this case specific facts or illustrative incidents about each type of fear, a paper using classification can be quite satisfactory. Or the foregoing piece of writing might serve as an introduction to a more ambitious essay exploring causes of phobias and ways of dealing with them, or perhaps a paper dealing in depth with a particular fear such as agoraphobia, the fear of being in open spaces.

The following classification, for example, is only one of several strategies used by a student to develop his paper on writing a paper.

There are several things you can do to help find your central theme and stick to it. I have listed some that help me. First, I try to choose a central idea on a topic I know something about and that influences and interests me. This allows my paper to include personal experiences and feelings. It is important, too, to pick a limited subject that is not so general it's hard to cover. It's easier to write on one Congressman than all the legislators in Washington, D.C. Next, I know I must have information to back up my central theme or know where to find it. A central idea is useless unless I can show my reader evidence to prove my point. Finally, I wait until I hear others comment on my paper before I change my central theme. A central idea may sound corny to me, but my reader might find good thought and information in my paper.

Central idea: There are several ways to find a central theme and stick to it.

I. Choose a central idea on a topic I know about and am interested in
II. Pick a limited subject I can handle

III. Have sufficient information to back up my point
IV. Get response from readers

Definition (The "What It Is" Method)

A second way to develop central ideas is by trying to explain clearly what they are. Sometimes this involves only a small—but very important—part of what you are saying, but it must not be neglected. How many times have you had serious disagreements with someone, only to find afterward you were really saying the same thing in different words? You have not *defined your terms*. Watch yourself. Don't assume everyone else has the same mental image as yours of abstract terms like *justice, education,* or *student government.* Explain what you mean by your terms. Your reader may not agree with your definition, but at least he knows what you are talking about. For instance, one student, in an effort to define writing, started off very well:

In grade school, writing was a composition that made the class laugh. One of the funniest papers I ever wrote was during sixth grade. My teacher asked us to write a composition starting with the phrase "My hair stood on end." I thought for a couple of minutes and then gave it my best shot. "My hair stood on end when I saw President Johnson standing in the IGA store eating a tootsie roll." When I finished reading, the whole class including my teacher burst out in laughter. It was five minutes before they stopped. I really didn't think it was that good.

Here the student has communicated with a specific example of what a composition meant to him in grade school. But he goes on:

All through high school I didn't have a good definition of writing. The term papers, essays, and reports all came from books. I didn't have to write; the books did it for me. Compositions came the closest to real writing, as they were the imagination in action.

What does he mean by "compositions" in the last sentence? What does he mean by "imagination in action"? What is the difference between "compositions" and "term papers" or "essays"? He simply hasn't defined his terms.

In his closing paragraph, the student succeeds better:

As I was writing this paper I asked my ten-year-old sister what writing was. She gave me a simple definition: "Writing is using a pencil to write the alphabet down on paper." Now that's as simple as you can get.

The excerpts from this definition illustrate a useful technique to be aware of—defining something by what it is *not*. Ultimately this student is saying that writing is *not* a sentence that makes others laugh, *not* term papers, essays, and reports from books, and *not* "using a pencil to write the alphabet down on paper." While he doesn't say what writing *is*, he has still given us some good insights.

Although, as the excerpts show, definition can form the basis of an entire paper, often it is limited to short explanations of terms, as in the following passage from a paper devoted to methods of effective learning. Notice that the term defined—"putting something into a class"—appears on the surface reasonably understandable. By specifying his own definition, however, the student writer has assured that the reader knows exactly what he means before going on to his next point.

The only way a student will get anything out of a class is by putting something into it. By "putting something into" a class, I mean more than just listening to the instructor and taking notes. The student should select a topic interesting to him that is related to the subject being taught. He can then go about his learning in whatever creative way he wishes and at his own pace. He needs also to recognize that certain basic skills and knowledge are necessary to understand a subject, such as the ability to read proficiently, and he should on his own take whatever steps are needed to develop such skills. With this approach, a student will develop self-reliance, responsibility, and initiative.

Definition is particularly important in scientific writing or other subjects where the vocabulary may be unfamiliar to the reader, as in the following example.

The blades of both simple and compound leaves contain the epidermis cells. Since epidermis means "skin," it is easy to understand these cells form the outer layer of the leaf and protect it. Another cell, the stomata, is one that regulates the water pressure in the leaf by opening and closing. Chlorophyll, the chemical responsible for transforming sun energy into plant energy, is also found in the blade.

Whether you are briefly defining technical terms, as in this example, or writing an extended definition of a more complex concept, you need constantly to ask yourself whether your audience will understand the words or concepts you are working with, especially if they are abstract and subject to numerous interpretations.

> *Principle 13* **It is not enough to know a reader can understand you; you must say exactly what you mean so that the reader cannot possibly *misunderstand* you.**

An effort to probe the meaning of abstract words may become very extended; Plato, trying to define justice, wrote a ten-volume book, *The Republic*, outlining his concept of an ideal, just society. For the best results, you too need to translate abstract terms into concrete images, using specific incidents and significant details, as does the writer of the following piece.

I'm Free!

When I think of freedom, two kinds come to me: physical freedom and freedom of the mind.

Physical freedom is more than not being behind bars or in a locked room. To have physical freedom is to be able to go anywhere and do anything whenever you want to. I had an opportunity to experience a degree of physical freedom last summer. My parents and brother went away for the weekend, leaving me with two whole days by myself. It was great! I was free to get up as late as I wanted and run around the house in my underwear if I felt like it. I could sit and do nothing. I went to a party Saturday night and didn't have to worry about what time I got home or how drunk I was. I was able to call up my girl friends and talk about anything without worrying about being overheard or told to get off the phone. It was as though I had the whole world on a string to do with whatever I wanted.

Freedom of mind is easier to accomplish, for brief periods anyway. If I am feeling depressed and trapped, all I have to do is go in my room, put on some soothing music like the Lettermen or the Carpenters, and stare at one of the two paintings on my walls. One is of an ocean tide churning up, about to crash against some rocks on the shore. There are dark clouds scattered about the sky, which is a brilliant mixture of red, orange, and yellow as the sun begins to set. The sky casts multicolored shimmers on the water, except for the tip of the wave which is a violent grayish-white color.

The other painting is also of water. In the background is a huge mountain with the buildings of a small village at the foot on the shoreline. Unlike the first painting, this water is calm, with only slight ripples here and there. On the water, which has a greenish orange tint from sky of the same color, are three Chinese junks. Two have sails that are reddish orange from the sun, and the other is propelled by a man with a pole.

Water—lakes and oceans—has always had meaning for me. I find it a great escape. It is so vast, it seems to go on forever, never ending.

A couple of years ago I experienced firsthand the same kind of freedom I get from my pictures. I was camping with my family on Lake Michigan. One day, toward dusk, I went down to the beach. There was no one else in sight. A gentle warm breeze was blowing, causing small waves to crash lightly on shore. As I looked down the beach in both directions, there was nothing but golden tan sand as far as I could see. The bright blue water began to take on a slight reddish tint from the brilliant red-orange sky as the sun began to set. The

```
only sounds to be heard, besides the crashing of the tide, were the
squeals of two seagulls flying around an abandoned dock that extend-
ed out into the empty water.
       It was so peaceful and quiet, I felt like I was the only person
on earth. I just wanted to stand up, run down the beach and scream,
"I'm free!"
```

Comparison and/or Contrast (The "This Is Like This/Not Like That" Method)

Sometimes you can best develop your idea by comparing it to something else and pointing out the similarities and differences between the two. If you are discussing a subject with which your readers are unfamiliar, comparison with something better known will help them understand. For instance, one student, explaining floor exercise, a gymnastic event for women in the Olympics, compared it with dancing. Another use of comparison and/or contrast is as an extended metaphor, exemplified by a student paper in which the United States was characterized throughout as "a newborn infant, thinking herself the most important nation in the world" and indulging over the years in temper tantrums when she could not get her way. In the final paragraph the United States was urged to cultivate a more "grown-up" image.

Finally, comparison and contrast may be used as an end in itself: discussing the advantages and disadvantages, the pros and cons, of two related situations or things, or simply setting side by side two related instances that somehow inform or clarify one another.

Caution: Remember this method is a way to *develop your central idea.* Sometimes, because comparison and contrast, like classification, is taught as an entity in itself, students think the only goal is to produce a valid comparison and contrast. But comparison and/or contrast *by itself* has little purpose. Suppose you compare an airplane with a horse. A horse is a four-legged animal, while an airplane is a mechanical vehicle with wings; both are used for transportation. So what? You need a *purpose* for the comparison, a *central idea.* Perhaps you want to promote horseback riding as a form of transportation that brings you close to nature, is less polluting, and conserves our resources. Or perhaps the comparison will help explain why airplanes have supplanted most other forms of transportation. In either case, focus on a central idea will direct your development and cause you to construct the comparison with different *significant details. The central idea must come first.*

In addition, *be sure your points in each half of the comparison correspond.* Sticking to our farfetched example of the plane and the horse, no purpose is served by outlining points of beauty in the horse and points of speed in the airplane. Let us say the horse is beautiful and the plane is fast. Again, so what? Depending on your purpose, or central idea, you must compare the beauty of the horse to the beauty of the airplane, or the speed of the horse to the speed of the airplane. You may, on the other hand, *contrast* dissimilar attributes if that serves your purpose. Thus, you could implement a central idea that each form of transportation has its unique advantages, and one must make a choice between the beauty of the horse and the speed of the airplane.

As an example, one student used comparison and contrast in a paper with the central idea "Volleyball is an excellent way to achieve physical fitness—but only if you play the type suited to you." She compared recreational volleyball and power volleyball, pointing out that the average player should probably stay with the recreational form, as power volleyball demands superior knowledge, skill, and stamina. In one section of her comparison, she characterized recreational volleyball as a more casual game, which can be enjoyed by almost anyone.

One basic difference between recreational and power volleyball is that there are no referees at recreational matches. The players officiate themselves; only violations easy to call are enforced. In power volleyball, where up to six officials watch the net, lines, and hits, violations are called on many more things, such as touching the net, stepping over the centerline under the net or outside the court boundaries, or touching the sideline when the ball is served. In recreational ball, teams aren't usually well organized and games often involve a good deal of haphazard hitting at the ball. Power volleyball, on the other hand, is clearly a game of skill. Coaches stress the importance of the three-hit strategy, for instance: a bump to the player at the net, who passes the ball up high for a spiker to slam it down at the opponents.

Notice the balancing of point against point in the comparison.

Recreational volleyball	Power volleyball
No referee	Up to six referees
Only violations easy to call are enforced	A wide variety of violations are enforced
Hitting may be haphazard	Definite strategies followed

Comparison is only a small part of this paper on volleyball, which contains other information useful to a person taking up the game for physical fitness: an explanation of rules and procedures, types of clothing, and levels of competition. But comparison and contrast can lend itself well to forming the foundation of an entire paper, *providing it is used to illustrate a central idea.*

Equality in Sports?

In 1975, the Title IX law was passed assuring women equal rights to sports in school. The law states that women have to be given the same number of sports as men, equal facilities, and the same quality of equipment. Overall, it is supposed to guarantee equal opportunity for all.

This law is constantly abused. Discrimination on the basis of sex occurs often in sports, as I have reason to know. During my high school years, the girls were saddled with the raw end of the deal. The boys took advantage of fine equipment and beautiful facilities. They had three locker rooms, brand new uniforms every year, and finer equipment than many colleges have. They were given cheerleaders and all the school support they could ask for. The girls, on the other hand, were happy to have any organized teams at all. I was a member of the girls' basketball team at my high school and we enjoyed a four-year period that was matched by no other team in our school's history. During this time, we were State Finalists three years in a row, won thirteen titles and trophies, and compiled an overall record of 87 wins and 6 losses. We gained much recognition for our school and were respected throughout the various leagues.

Yet even with our outstanding record and long list of accomplishments, we never knew the luxury the boys had. We took a back seat to them in every instance. They were given first priority over the gym. They practiced at the convenient hour of 3:00 p.m., while we were left with the before school and late night practices. The boys' referees were always the cream of the crop, while we were umpired by unqualified, inexperienced judges. Free meals at nice restaurants were awarded to the boys after many games. We never enjoyed any free meals, even at the State tournament level. Our record was far better, but they still got the best, including extensive coverage in the media and the support of their school and community.

Girls today show just as much interest and enthusiasm in athletics as boys. They have the desire to keep themselves physically fit and the will to compete. They want to develop their strength to its fullest and to be great. They are held back, though, because it's a man's world. Women have come a long way in athletics, but still have a long way to go. I hope someday women are able to overcome this barrier and take their rightful place in the sports world!

Analysis of a Method or Process (The "How to Do It" Method)

Often part of your paper will call for analyzing or explaining steps in a process with which your reader is not familiar. In a paper on snowmobiles you might need to explain what to do if the machine stalls while you are far afield from expert advice. Perhaps you will want to describe a process for mellowing the sound of a guitar or preparing a room for painting. As with the other techniques discussed, you may devote an entire paper to analyzing a method or process, moving step by step through your explanation. The crucial consideration in this form of development is to include all essential information, so that a reader doesn't become lost.

There are numerous ways to explain a method or process. Most involve strategies we have already worked with or discussed, such as use of a specific incident to clarify your points. Writing strategies are not mutually exclusive and you will often use several in developing any given idea. A common way to analyze a process is through classification, listing steps or techniques. In a paper entitled "Between the Chicken and the Frying Pan," one student who grew up on a chicken farm described the process of preparing eggs for market, explaining each step in detail and defining terms: (1) the eggs are graded; (2) they are washed; (3) they are candled and the "bloods," "cracks," and "dirties" are removed; (4) they are sorted by weight; (5) they are packed. Her central idea was that there's a great deal of work "between the chicken and the frying pan."

Sometimes explaining a process or method is facilitated by comparison or contrast; repairing a snowmobile might be more understandable if compared to the more familiar process of repairing a car. A refinement of the comparison method might be to use an analogy or extended metaphor, rather neatly accomplished in the following piece.

It is important to know how to write a sentence correctly. I look at a sentence as if it were a football play. A football play is diagrammed on a board showing the job of each position. Some positions help others in making the play successful. For instance, a guard and center might both block the same person to help the fullback break free for a large gain. A sentence is the same. It can be diagrammed on a board, breaking it down into each part of speech. The parts of a sentence—subject, predicate, adjectives, prepositional phrases—have each a certain job to do. A preposition shows the relationship of a noun or pronoun in a sentence. Verbs express action or help to make a statement, and adjectives modify a noun or pronoun. When these parts of speech are put together with skill, they blend to create a sentence that will work successfully.

Like the other strategies discussed, explaining a method or process may be only part of a larger paper, or it can form the organization for an entire essay, as in the following paper. This student writer skillfully interweaves several types of development. Can you identify the various strategies?

The Important Difference

Revising is an important step in writing papers and many mistakes could be avoided if more time were spent on it. I, for one, never used to revise what I'd written; I'd write a paper and hand it in without even proofreading it, then be embarrassed when I got it back. One paper was particularly terrible, with so many mistakes on the first page my instructor gave up. She handed the paper back and said she wouldn't look at it again until I had corrected my errors. I'd get comments on my papers like "Good content, but you must do something about your grammatical errors, paragraphing, and spelling." Finally I realized this wouldn't happen if I'd revise my papers. I was tired of getting them back filled with corrections caused by my own stubborness and stupidity.

Revising involves rereading my paper several times. My first draft contains my ideas in whatever order I think of them. It's a collection of thoughts, ideas, and facts that I try to put into paragraph form. I then go through and make notes on the copy, maybe telling myself that a certain part belongs somewhere else. If I'm not sure of a spelling, I check a dictionary. I try to fix my sentence structures the best I can. Sometimes I omit several sentences because I find they don't belong.

After the first draft has been edited, I write the second draft and revise that carefully, just as I did the first one. My roommate often reads my second draft, pointing out any mistakes or problems she finds. A second person helps quite a bit in finding errors and making sure I am getting my point across clearly. Sometimes my roommate and I discuss words or phrases endlessly, trying to figure out how they should be written. She once asked me if I knew the three uses of the words to, too, and two. When I said, "Yes," she said, "You never use the right one."

As I'm typing the final draft of the paper, I read ahead a few lines to make sure everything sounds all right. After I type each page, I check for typographical errors before removing the sheet from the typewriter, because once the paper is out of the machine it's hard to line it back up if I find errors. When the paper is all typed, I read it through one more time, then hand it in.

These steps may seem to some like a lot of work, but now I feel confident I'm handing in a fairly good paper. My writing has improved and so have my grades. The extra time revising takes is worth it; it can really make the difference between a good and a bad paper.

Classification, definition, comparison and/or contrast, and analysis are not the only strategies available for developing a central idea, but if you make a conscientious effort to use them, you will find it easier to communicate effectively with your reader.

✓   Return now to the central idea you chose in Activity 7-1. Do you still find it interesting? If not, rethink your central idea. *Always be prepared to modify or change your central idea if a better one occurs to you.* (But remember the advice of the student about not abandoning your idea too soon!)

Once you feel reasonably comfortable with your central idea, go *systematically* through the various kinds of development discussed in this chapter, beginning with classification. Name the method and then list ways to use that method in developing your particular idea. If the method is not applicable as the *chief* method of development, could you use it as part of your paper?

Go through *all* the methods, and jot down at least one way you *might* use each. An example follows.

Let us say I have been asked to write a paper on mental retardation. I find my own point of interest in this general subject from the fact that I have a mentally retarded niece. Also, recently while at the university center watching a group of mentally retarded people, I saw a college student stop to talk with one of the retarded women; I was impressed by her happiness that someone, a stranger, had taken time to notice her.

I have formulated three central idea I think I could write on:

1. Retarded children and adults often suffer from unintentional neglect not only by the general public but even within their families, especially if there are other children.

2. People are often dismayed at the birth of a retarded child, but the experience of caring for and loving one can be remarkably rewarding.

3. The mentally retarded should be educated as fully as possible in order to permit them to lead active and productive lives.

I have decided to choose the third central idea and I have written it at the top of a blank sheet of paper: *The mentally retarded should be educated as fully as possible in order to permit them to lead active and productive lives.*

I now proceed with the following ideas for development.

Classification:

1. I could list various ways of educating the mentally retarded, and discuss the advantages or disadvantages of each.
2. I could classify types or degrees of retardation and discuss methods of educating each.
3. I could focus on three or four specific cases and discuss the problems involved in educating each one.

Definition:

1. I should define what I mean by "educating" the mentally retarded.
2. The term "mentally retarded" needs defining.
3. What is meant by "an active and productive life" when applied to the mentally retarded?

Comparison and/or Contrast:

1. I could compare the life of a mentally retarded person with and without productive education.
2. I could compare possible results, depending on the amount of retardation present.
3. I could compare the lives of mentally retarded persons with those of other people.

Analysis of a Method or Process:

1. I could set up a sample program for educating the mentally retarded.
2. I could analyze a typical day in the life a retarded person.

Having completed my consideration of the methods outlined in this chapter, I will not forget that description and narrative, learned in Part I, are also available methods of development.

Description:

1. I could describe some mentally retarded people, especially those to be used as illustrations in the paper.
2. I could describe a school for the mentally retarded.
3. I could describe the changes in mentally retarded people who receive proper education.

Narration:

1. I could tell the story of the incident at the university center that initially sparked my interest in doing this paper (perhaps as an effective introduction).
2. I could tell the story of my brother, crushed by the birth of his mentally retarded child, later coming to recognize how much richer the family life has been because the child was a part of it.
3. I could tell the story of a particular child who has benefited from special education.

Activity 7-3 *Plotting Your Paper*

By now you should have a good fund of possible material for developing your central idea effectively. In fact, you should have more ideas than you can use, in which case the problem becomes one of limiting the possibilities to what can be handled in the time and space available.

✔ Write your chosen central idea on another sheet of clean paper. If you want to modify the central idea as the result of thinking more carefully about your topic, do so. Always be alert to recognize upon further examination where your first ideas need refining, remolding, expanding, or clarifying.

Now look carefully at the possible kinds of development you have discovered. Does one particularly lend itself to structuring the essay as a whole? Would a classification of various aspects of your idea work well? Or would a comparison (or contrast) be more useful? Does an analysis lend itself well to your overall development?

Once you have chosen your major method of development, determine whether other methods might be used in a minor way. For instance, would a vivid description or a short narrative make an effective introduction — or conclusion? *Concentrate on the introduction and conclusion: these are the most important parts of anything you write,* as they are points where the reader's attention is most focused. A reader decides whether to continue after reading the introduction; the conclusion gives the final impression of your writing. As you plan your essay, learn to begin strongly and always leave something important or striking for the end.

Keep in mind certain organizing principles. First, *be sure everything you use relates clearly to your central idea* and somehow helps to clarify or explain it in a manner that interests or convinces your reader. Resist temptations to wander off into only marginally related areas, however interesting; you can confuse your reader—and perhaps yourself as well.

> *Principle 14* **In the best writing, every element—every incident, detail, phrase, even every word—relates to the central idea underlying the whole work.**

Once you are sure everything relates to your central idea, *group similar materials together,* so that as you take up each aspect of your subject, you exhaust that part before going to another. Returning to our example about improving the safety of high school football, all the material on equipment should be covered before the writing moves on to playing conditions. If there seems to be some overlapping, make a decision about where the material fits most logically. Such an overlap might well come at the end of the first section and serve as a good transition into the second.

✔ When you are reasonably sure how your material relates to your central idea, write either a paragraph explaining the order of the points you will make as you go along, or, if you like outlining as a way to visualize your organization, make an outline. If you write the paragraph, think of it as a *plot*—like the plot of a story: first this, then that, then something else. Or you may explain your plan: First I will do this and from there I will go on to such and such, etc. And I will end with . . .

If you outline, review the principles discussed under "Classification" in this chapter. Are the ideas at each level of your outline parallel? If you were writing a paper on college pressures, for instance, do items I, II, and III express similar aspects of your subject? An example might be this:

 I. Pressures caused by too much homework.
 II. Pressures caused by a change in environment.
 III. Pressures resulting from changes in my values

These headings are parallel, but if you then add "IV. Ways to reduce pressure," you are sliding off into a related but not parallel area. To be more certain of developing a useful outline, *first* formulate your central idea; for example, "Pressure is a fact of life in college; to cope with it, one must understand its causes." Second: divide your main idea into major subheadings, such as "Causes of pressure," and "Ways of coping with pressure." Then arrange your supporting material under the appropriate subheading. You might come up with something like the following outline. (Possible specifics to support the general ideas are included in parenthesis.)

Central idea: Pressure is a fact of life in college; to cope with it, one must understand its causes.
 I. Introduction (a vivid picture of a student breaking under pressure)
 II. Causes of pressure
   A. Too much homework

---

    1. Heavy assignments (description of a typical day or week)
    2. Tests pile up at midterm (list of exams)
  B. Change in environment
    1. Study habits at high school not sufficient for college (specific case history)
    2. Responsibilities at college distracting and disorienting (specific incident)
    3. Too much priority on social life
      a. Studies slide (example)
      b. Students find new relationships difficult to handle (example)
III. Methods of coping
  A. Learn to set priorities
    1. Make lists of what needs doing
    2. Budget time for various activities on engagement calendar
    3. Start assignments before last minute
  B. Consult with knowledgeable persons
    1. Roommates or friends
    2. Instructors
    3. Academic or religious counselors
IV. Conclusion: With careful planning, you can find room for everything: studying and fun. You may still feel rushed many times, but you'll know you can handle it.

There is usually more than one way to organize your material; your responsibility is to consider alternatives and choose which works best for you. For instance, the paper on college pressure might take up one kind of pressure, then discuss ways of coping with it before going on to another kind. A skeleton outline might look like this.

Central idea
  I. Introduction
 II. Academic pressures
    A. Causes
    B. Methods of coping
III. Personal pressures
    A. Causes
    B. Methods of coping
IV. Conclusion

The importance of your knowing how everything relates to your central idea, what material belongs together, and how you will move from beginning to end cannot be overemphasized. Take time *now* to think your paper through carefully; it will save time when you start to write.

ASSIGNMENT 7   An Expository Paper

You are ready to write your paper. You know what your central idea—or point—is. You know what material you will use to support and develop that central idea and you have the material grouped into logical sections. Now write your paper *as fast as possible*. As you are doing so, remember *specifics*.

Tie every important point to details or events that illustrate, clarify, or support it. Don't worry during the first draft about sentence structures or mechanics; get the *ideas* down while they are still fresh in your mind.

Let your paper sit for at least four hours, preferably overnight. Then revise it according to Revising Activities 7-1 through 7-5. Put it in neat, final form, then *proofread carefully* for errors in spelling and punctuation. These may be corrected neatly in ink on your final draft if you are not accomplished enough to make corrections on the typewriter.

Give your essay a title. *All self-respecting essays have titles.* A title gives your readers the first clue about what to expect and helps them decide whether to read what you have written. Furthermore, if you cannot write a good title, perhaps you don't know what your central idea is. In that case, rethink your paper. What exact point are you trying to make?

Revising Activity 7-1   *Central Idea and Development*

✔   Once again, write your central idea in a sentence. Then, check your paper for complete development. Are there any terms that still need defining? Will an example or illustration help make your ideas clearer? Have you developed your examples with significant details so they "come alive" and are meaningful to a reader? Does your introduction catch the reader's interest? Is your conclusion strong, striking, and satisfying?

> *Principle 15* **Never assume a reader's knowledge. Learn to give enough information about your subject to help a reader who knows little about it to understand, while not going into so much detail you bore or insult a knowledgeable reader.**

Revising Activity 7-2   *Checking for Unity*

✔   A unified paper is achieved when everything relates to your central idea. Ask yourself again: "Does *everything*—every subpoint, every illustration, every paragraph, every sentence—relate to my central point?" Will that relationship be clear to your reader? If you have doubts, have someone read your paper. If there are points whose relationship to your central idea might not be understood by a reader, what can you do to clarify them?

Revising Activity 7-3   *Checking for Coherence*

✔   A coherent paper is one in which every element relates clearly to the one preceding it and leads clearly to the one following it. Try to read your draft as if you were a stranger to it, preferably after letting it cool for some time. Reading aloud might be helpful. Do you recognize places where the connection from one paragraph to another is not quite clear? Is there any spot where one sentence doesn't clearly relate to the previous one? Can you reword so as to make the connections solid and clear?

> *Principle 16* **Every sentence and paragraph must be a link in the chain of your idea, clearly joined to the ones that precede and follow it.**

Revising Activity 7-4   *Grammar (Minigrammar D)*

✔ Check yourself for sentence fragments and run-on sentences (Minigrammar C, p. 193) and for agreement and verb forms (Minigrammars A and B, pp. 171 and 183). In addition review your paper for correct pronoun usage, taken up in Minigrammar D, p. 205. Proper pronoun usage is a problem shared by almost everyone, so be especially careful with Minigrammar D. You are rare if you don't sometimes shift pronouns or occasionally use a pronoun with no clear antecedent or referent.

Revising Activity 7-5   *Review*

✔ Check yourself for the following:

1. Wordiness (Revising Activities 2-1, 2-2, 2-3, pp. 29-30)
2. Spelling (Revising Activity 6-1, p. 90)
3. Punctuation and Dialogue Forms (Revising Activities 3-1, 3-2, pp. 43-50)

SAMPLE PAPERS FOR ASSIGNMENT 7

Lost: A Way of Life

Farming over the years has changed remarkably. I can remember looking across an open field five years ago and seeing a small tractor surrounded by a cloud of dust whirling its way across the field. Today, looking across this same field, I see huge funnel-like clouds of dust, with many of the same features as a tornado, coming from a giant tractor.

Besides the size of tractors, many factors have caused farming to become a different way of life from what it used to be. In the last ten years, the farming industry has become a corporate business, with accountants, lawyers, and plenty of employees to help with the crop. Corporate farming has affected almost every farmer in some way, making it hard for the small farm to survive.

Growing up on a farm, I became aware of the hardships, problems, and hassles small-time farmers go through. An example is Earl Johannson, a friend of ours, who had a beautiful small farm

located among scenic streams and rolling hills. Now about fifty
years old, Earl had been renting the same ground for years. It
wasn't a very big farm, but it gave him enough income to support his
family. One spring day as I approached him, I could tell something
was wrong. He just didn't have the same zest, cheerfulness, or
enthusiasm he usually had.

"What's the matter?" I asked cautiously.

"Oh, nothing. It's just a small matter with the Hansen
Brothers."

A dead silence followed, so thick I could feel it pushing down
on my shoulders. I wanted badly to hear what had happened, but not a
word did he say. Then abruptly he let the whole story out. "Those
crooked, no-good bums have taken over my land. They went to the
people I rented my land from and overbid me. Now, at the age of 50, I
have to look for work."

Corporate farming is taking over. Farmers are beginning to buy
not one farm but two or three, making their farms bigger and
stronger. The farming industry has become like General Motors, with
only a few landowners owning all the land and hiring local farmers
to do the work. A small-time farmer can't even get started any more
because of rising costs of equipment, buildings, and ground. A
tractor without any luxuries costs anywhere from fifty to one
hundred thousand dollars, and the rest of the equipment, such as
plows, disks, and and cultivators, is expensive too. Land isn't
cheap either! One acre of land with a good soil base will cost $1500.
Multiply this by an average farm of 150 acres, and you have $225,000
invested. These figures are just the beginning of farming costs. I
haven't mentioned things like fertilizer, seed, and gasoline, all
of which need to be figured into the price of farming.

In the past, small-time farmers have often had two jobs, one to
provide for family needs and the other, you might say, for extras
such as vacations, road trips, or a new car. As the cost of farming
keeps rising, these part-time farmers will have to quit farming and
devote more time to their everyday jobs. The larger, more
experienced farmer will take over the land, making the trend toward
corporate farming even greater.

The way it looks now, the small-time farmers are sunk. They are
being caught up like flies on flypaper, leaving their land to the
larger farmer to control and run. If something isn't done to hold
down the increases in corporate farming, we as citizens will pay for
it in the end, as prices skyrocket right out of control.

Stereo Hunting

When buying a sound system people often become confused
because of the complexity of choosing the right receiver, turntable,
and speakers. A few easy steps will help you alleviate the problems.

Remember, anyone can tell you how to buy a sound system, but in the end, you're the one who has to live with it. Before you commit yourself, you should answer the following questions. "How much do I wish to spend? Should I buy a compact system or separates? Is my listening area large or small?"

You can save yourself a lot of grief if you first determine how much you are willing to sink into a sound system. If you establish a budget price, you're in a better position to decide where to shop and how much to spend on each item in the system. For example, you wouldn't spend $350 on a receiver if you only want to spend $450 altogether. It would be more realistic to spend about $150 on a receiver, $200 on speakers, and $100 on a turntable. A budget price also gives you bargaining power if you buy the whole system from one store, because you are more apt to get a deal from the salesman if you purchase a complete stereo from him.

Once you've set your budget price, you should determine whether you want a compact system or "separates." A compact system is one in which the receiver (tuner, preamplifer, and amplifier) and the turntable are mounted in a single cabinet. This is a relatively less expensive and simpler system, because there are only a few wires to hook up. A compact system may also be indicated where space is a problem. "Separates" are individual components that make up a sound system, including the tuner, preamplifier, and amplifier. An advantage to separates is that you can gradually build your system by adding and upgrading components. But it is complex, and you should first do a lot of reading up on separates.

The most popular type of sound system is a combination of a compact system and separates, consisting of a compact receiver and a separate turntable. This combination provides a better sound than a compact system but is less expensive than separates.

The size of your listening area is important in deciding the type of receiver and speakers you should use. For an average-sized room, say 10 feet by 10 feet, a receiver which pushes out about 15 or 20 watts per channel is adequate. If your listening area is large, say 40 by 40, you would need a relatively high power receiver, 50 watts or more, and some good speakers. The size of your speakers goes hand in hand with the size of your listening area and the output of your receiver. A good rule to keep in mind is to put half of your total expenditure into speakers, because your speakers are the most important part of your sound system. In choosing a pair of speakers, have the dealer play several of your favorite albums on a variety of speakers. Let your ears be the judge.

After you decide on the sound system you want, call around to different dealers to find the one with the lowest price, then check to see if he's reputable and what kind of warranty he offers. Have your dealer set up your system for you before you take it home to make sure it's working properly. When you get it home, read all the instructions carefully before hooking it up. Then sit back, relax, and have the time of your life!

CHECKLIST   *Saying What You Think*

Preparations. Check off each item when completed.

Activity 7-1   Formulating a Central Idea . . . .
Activity 7-2   Developing Your Central Idea . . . .
Activity 7-3   Plotting Your Paper . . . .
Assignment 7   An Expository Paper . . . .
Revising Activity 7-1   Central Idea and Development . . . .
Revising Activity 7-2   Checking for Unity . . . .
Revising Activity 7-3   Checking for Coherence . . . .
Revising Activity 7-4   Grammar (Minigrammar D) . . . .
Revising Activity 7-5   Review. . . . .

Goals to Be Achieved. Write your answers on a separate sheet.
Explain fully.

1. Do you have a strong central idea to which everything relates? Is there logical progression from sentence to sentence, and paragraph to paragraph?
2. Have you used specific incidents and illustrations, significant details, and, where appropriate, bits of dialogue to support your central idea and make your paper come alive for a reader?
3. Have you preserved a nice, easy natural tone?
4. Have you revised carefully for grammar, spelling, punctuation, and mechanics? Have you carefully proofread your final draft?
5. Would you like to have your high school composition teacher see this paper as an example of your present writing skill?

8:
Knowing Your Audience

Often, throughout this text, references have been made to your reader. Several of the "principles" scattered through the book and collected inside the back cover stress the importance of considering your audience. Principle 1 is "If what you're writing about doesn't interest you, it will bore your reader to death. It isn't good to bore a reader." Principle 3 is similarly oriented: "A primary criterion of good writing is the ability to communicate with a reader. Anything that interferes with that communication is poor writing strategy."

Ultimately, the purpose of all writing, except personal notes and diaries, is to communicate with a reader: to delight and inform, and perhaps to persuade your reader of the truth of your ideas or the necessity of doing something you think is important. Ideally, any writing—letters, journals, term papers, stories and poems, even essay examinations—is an attempt to share some part of your thought, experience, or knowledge. One way or another, you are trying to communicate with a reader.

The more you can visualize and "know" your reader, and the more you attempt in your writing to interest and convince a reader, the better writer you will become. We learn to write well when—and only when—we *want* to write well; with few exceptions, wanting to write well grows out of wanting a reader to respond affirmatively to what we say.

In college writing, you are often faced with a dilemma. You know for whom you are writing: the teacher. That knowledge can be a trap. You assume the teacher "knows everything" and therefore you don't need to explain fully. Not so. Sometimes teachers *don't* know everything, strange as that may seem. At other times, they may not quite grasp the particular evidence on which you base your general statements; as with any other reader, you must make sure you have explained fully. (See Principles 13 and 15.) Suppose, for instance, you are assigned to write a paper on Robert Frost's poetry for your American Literature class, and, assuming your professor "knows everything," you state, without supporting evidence, " 'Stopping by Woods on a Snowy Evening' is closely related in theme and mood to the earlier 'The Road Not Taken.' " Your professor may not have thought about the two poems that way and may be puzzled; if your entire paper hinges on the similarity you have pointed out, she or he may have difficulty following the rest of your paper. You end up with a poor grade, though your idea may be perfectly clear to *you*.

Even if you know the professor understands your statement—perhaps he or she has pointed out the similarity in class—you need to explain *your* understanding of it, or it may seem that you are simply regurgitating without thinking the poem through. For all your professor knows, you may not have the slightest idea what the similarity is or why it is significant. Your professor is not the usual reader, looking for information or even new insights into the material—though she or he welcomes unexpected, well-documented insights and gives A's to those students who provide them. What your professor wants to find out is *what you know* and how deeply and clearly you have thought about the subject at hand. Only by using supporting details as evidence can you demonstrate your knowledge and understanding.

Writing for teachers is a special case, and by studying your instructors and learning to be flexible in your responses, given their particular requirements and idiosyncracies, you are building valuable skills. The same is true no matter who the reader is. In all writing—as in all human relationships—we must subtly change our approach for each person we encounter. We find ourselves making constant adjustments as we learn to visualize our readers clearly. The permutations are endless; only by understanding our reader *each time we write* can we hope to communicate successfully.

Activity 8-1   *Understanding Your Reader*

✔   Consider your classmates as a potential audience. Do a fact sheet, jotting down as many of their characteristics as you can think of. Include what you know of their age, sex, education, environmental background, and potential attitudes. Then add factors that particularly characterize them *as an audience*.

Do a similar fact sheet, considering your instructor as your audience. Be as thorough and specific as possible.

Next choose a subject that interests you and about which you know a good deal. Answer the following questions first with reference to your classmates and second with reference to your instructor. Write down your answers.

1. What about my subject can I assume will interest my audience?

2. How much information can I assume my audience already has about my subject?
3. If my subject is controversial, in what ways can I assume my audience will agree with me? What points of disagreement can I anticipate?
4. What tone will be most effective for this particular audience?
5. What about vocabulary? Will this audience understand and react well to my word choices? Are there unfamiliar terms I must explain?

Finally, imagine writing a paper for *both* audiences, as may well be true of your paper for Assignment 8. Ask yourself the same questions. Do your answers change when you shift from an audience of your peers to an audience consisting of your instructor? Are the answers somewhat different again when you write for both audiences simultaneously? They should be.

Activity 8-2   *Analyzing Cause and Effect*

Any writing benefits from sensitivity to one's audience, but certain types of thinking and writing demand particularly careful analysis and understanding of a reader's response. One is *cause and effect*, a term used to describe our efforts to understand the causes of situations, events, and problems we perceive around us. We do this constantly: we find our roommates aggravating and try to figure out why; we can't make deadlines and wonder why; we see our favorite fishing stream fouled, covered with green slime, and look for the source of the pollution.

This may sound personal, not "reader-oriented." But typically, after thinking through a problem, we want to share our discoveries and insights with others who have similar problems. The question of how to approach those others may be delicate; often, in essence, we point out their errors and mistakes, something none of us like to hear. How do we go about it tactfully yet forcefully enough to convince our listeners or readers? How do we persuade our readers without antagonizing them?

✔   Assuming that your classmates are your audience (but not forgetting the instructor lurking in the background), choose a problem—a real problem of your own. Don't try to figure out the world's problems; start with the roommate who won't pick up after himself, the 8:00 class you have trouble making, a family conflict, a falling-out with a friend, a decision whether to continue in college or what curriculum to follow. Base your choice in part on a conviction that other people in the class may encounter similar difficulties. This problem is the "effect" for which you will later try to ascertain the "causes." Of course, not all "effects" are problems; you might sometime try to decide what causes your times of happiness, for instance. But for this activity, we will limit ourselves to problems, of which we all have plenty.

First, describe the problem as graphically as you can, perhaps with vivid, relevant details, perhaps with a little story or incident that illustrates it. Although not all cause-and-effect papers start with a description of the problem, it is the logical point to begin thinking about it; we *first* perceive the effect and *then* try to find its causes. And somewhere in a cause-and-effect paper, the situation must be described vividly enough to capture your reader's interest and attention. Develop details you think will appeal to your classmates.

When I walk into a store, I want to buy everything in sight, whether or not I need it. There is always something to buy: a coat, a pair of boots, a new hat, jewelry, sweaters, skirts. If I hear a song I like on the radio, I immediately go out and buy the album. When wearing knee socks with skirts became popular, I bought ten pair in assorted colors and then I "needed" more skirts to match the socks. Last Sunday, I saw a lady in church wearing a hat, so I drove over to the mall that afternoon and bought a hat. Once I got it home, I wasn't sure I liked it. Shoes are probably the most tempting items. I'm always buying new shoes to match an outfit or coat. My problem: I'm an impulsive buyer of the first degree.

Next, analyze as clearly as you can the causes of the problem, as you see them. The impulse buyer decided on three main reasons for her compulsion: (1) in her affluent family, everyone always received anything they desired; (2) she was fad conscious; (3) there was always a gift to buy: for a birthday, a new baby, a wedding. If it helps, use the following formula to begin your analysis, but don't feel bound by it: "Why does this problem occur? Because _____." (Note the root word *cause* in the word *because*.) Make a fact sheet of every reason that occurs to you. Don't be satisfied with *one* reason. Go beyond generalities. Keep asking yourself "Why?" *Why* is my roommate an inconsiderate slob? Because he is lazy. *Why* is he lazy? Because he never had to clean up after himself at home. *Why* didn't he have to clean his room at home? Because he was spoiled. *Why* was he spoiled? Because he was the only boy in a big family of girls.

Eventually you will come to some new insights about your problem. Incidentally, you may have outlined the body of a paper, as each answer is set forth and developed, using significant details and illustrative incidents. Following the course of your own probing is one way of organizing a paper. Or you may decide to skip the intermediate steps and go directly to what you consider the root cause. Another effective presentation is by the *inductive* method, starting with the causes and leading up to the effects, as in "Where Riots Rage" on p. 137. This employs a different kind of logic; instead of starting at the problem—*your* first perception—you start where the problem started: at the root cause or causes. Then you move step by step toward the problem, or effect.

When writing about causes and effects, you need not supply a solution, though certainly you may do so if one occurs to you. The cause-and-effect paper should not be confused with a problem/solution paper, though the two are logically related; how can you suggest a solution without knowing the causes? You may, if you wish, suggest a solution, but for this activity concentrate on *causes* and how to present them convincingly to your classmates.

Audience: Students who share apartments

The Case of the Vanishing Peanut Butter

One day, coming back from class, I saw my roommate Karen eating my bread. Normally this wouldn't bother me, but recently I'd noticed my food slowly disappearing. I talked it out with my other roommates and we all agreed it was definitely Karen who was eating everybody's food but her own.

I confronted her about it the next time I saw her in the kitchen looking for something to eat. "Karen," I said, "I have to talk to you about the food situation. You see, one of my pet peeves is when someone eats my food without asking."

"Oh, I'm sorry," she said.

"I feel bad about having to say this, but it does bother me."

"It's all right," she replied. "I'm glad you told me."

A week went by and everything seemed to be going well. But the following Sunday when I returned from a trip home, I noticed someone had been at my food again. My almost full jar of peanut butter was gone except for a little stuck on the bottom and sides of the jar. My cheese and half a loaf of bread had disappeared. I was furious. How could Karen do this after I had talked to her? I thought maybe I should start eating her food so she would know how I felt. Unfortunately, she's a vegetarian and all she had was cans of beans and spinach. Her mother had sent those; she hadn't done any shopping since we started school.

I began to wonder why Karen eats everyone else's food and decided she thinks that since we share an apartment, we share everything else. She goes through our refrigerator and cupboards as if she were at home with her family, feeling no guilt or embarrassment, ignoring our attempts to solve the problem. Besides, she hoards her money and doesn't want to spend it on food that will only be consumed. During a year between high school and college, when she worked at a good job, her parents let her live at home without paying board and room. That was fine for saving money for college, but it didn't help her realize she was to carry her fair share of our apartment expenses. She is basically selfish and inconsiderate, and there is no way around it, no matter how much we talk to her.

My roommates and I finally came to a conclusion. I made separate shelves in the refrigerator and cupboards for each of us, and of course Karen's were empty except for her beans and spinach. I think she caught the hint. We also started to buy food she didn't like, such as meat. I keep my bread in the freezer and my peanut butter, along with other vegetarian foods, hidden far back in my cupboard. Karen seems to think we don't have any food she likes, and sometimes she even goes to the grocery store.

Activity 8-3   *Persuading Your Reader*

A type of paper that depends almost totally on your perception of your audience is the *persuasion* (or *argument*) paper. Obviously, if you are trying to persuade a reader, you must consider how he or she will react to your ideas, to the supporting evidence you produce, even to the words you choose.

Trying to persuade someone else to think as you do or to act in a way you think beneficial is challenging. Every writing skill you possess comes into play. You must be logical and clear, appealing to the reader's intelligence and common sense. In explaining yourself convincingly, you may use any or all of the strategies we have studied so far: classification, definition, comparison and contrast, or an analysis of some sort. Cause-and-effect considerations often play an important part. An appeal to your reader's intelligence, however, is often not enough; you need also appeal to the emotions, forcefully enough to convince the reader but without overdoing it. Often some vivid description or a "telling" story to illustrate your point helps accomplish this purpose.

Basically, you have some belief you want your readers to adopt or some act you want them to perform. For instance, you may want to persuade your readers to be more considerate in their dealings with others or to cease taking for granted the benefits they receive from their parents or from the country they live in. Perhaps you have had—or you know someone who has had—a "bad trip" with drugs and want to convince others not to go the same route. Maybe in your town a school millage is coming up and you want to convince voters to support it.

Convincing others is not easy. There are basically three types of readers: those who already agree with you, those who will not agree with you under any circumstances, and—fortunately the majority—those who can see both sides and haven't made up their minds. It is a waste of time to write for the first two groups; those who haven't made up their minds are the ones you need to reach.

To persuade the undecided, you need first to develop as many good arguments as you can, along with concrete, specific evidence to support them. Say you are writing about the school millage; one strong argument might be that if it isn't passed the athletic program will be cut back. You interview the school principal or the athletic director—or both—to obtain specific information about exactly what cuts will be made, and you use this information to back up your argument. Then you might investigate another probable cut: the art, drama, or music program. Or if you stick to the athletic program, you could try to convince voters of its value by basing your arguments on your own experience participating in athletics. Perhaps you could compare your experience with that of a friend whose school temporarily abandoned its athletic program as a result of losing a millage vote.

Simply advancing your own arguments is not enough, however; you must also anticipate the arguments of your opponents. "Let's go back to basics," some may say. "I want my children learning to read and write well; never mind the athletics." Others may say, "I haven't any children in school; why should I pay?" Such people must be shown that, while they may have valid objections, your position is the stronger one. This, of course, takes tact and sensitivity toward your reader's point of view, which you must recognize and deal with respectfully.

Finally it is helpful to think of points that you and your opponent can agree upon. No citizen wants high school students roaming the streets after school, taking out their high spirits in possibly destructive ways instead of on a basketball court. People in your city don't want industries hesitating to locate there because voters refuse to support good schools. They want to be proud of their town, not have to apologize because it doesn't meet its responsibilities toward young people. Points like this can be turned into powerful arguments to convince the doubters.

To begin preparing for an argument paper, the most important element is, of course, your central idea. Though this seems self-evident, many inexperienced writers have difficulty with it. This problem may be partly attributed to high school exercises in which the emphasis is placed on developing "pro" and "con" arguments for their own sake, rather than on arriving at a conclusion. More often, however, it rises from a lack of confidence in the validity and worth of one's own concerns and opinions. The time has come to take a stand. Dare to say "This is what I think," and then prove you are right with solid supporting evidence!

Once again, don't try to solve the world's problems. Avoid overused, complex topics such as legalization of marijuana, capital punishment, child abuse, abortion, and euthanasia — *unless you have personal experience on which to base your opinion!* Concentrate on subjects within your own sphere of activity: your family, your school, your town, your state. As in all the writing so far — and all that follows — *your personal experience and knowledge is a vital factor.* You may expand your personal experience, drawing on knowledge gained from the experience of others, from the media (newspapers, magazines, or films), or by interviewing knowledgeable persons. But unless the subject *counts* for you, unless it has engaged your personal interest and you are actively involved in what you are saying, your writing is apt to be stiff, wooden, and boring.

✔   For this activity, *carefully* choose a topic of concern to you, about which you have a firm conviction you would like others to adopt, perhaps one that would lead to some kind of action. Before coming to a decision, jot down *many* topics — five at least. Cross off those that only marginally interest you. Cross off the overused ones and those with which you have had little or no personal experience. Cross off those that you would need to research in depth before you could write knowledgeably about them. From the remainder, choose one that you find interesting and for which you think you can assemble good supporting arguments.

Write out your central idea in a complete sentence. This is essential.

Think equally carefully about your reader. Directly under your central idea, identify your reader or readers: a single friend, a teacher, the people in your town. As in Activity 8-1, make a fact sheet of your readers' characteristics. In all that follows, *keep your reader in mind*.

Next, make yourself a chart with three sections as illustrated below. Head the sections "I. Arguments For," "II. Arguments Against," and "III. Common Ground." Subdivide each section, with a column on the left for "Points" and a column on the right for "Supporting Evidence."

I. Arguments For		II. Arguments Against		III. Common Ground	
Points	Supporting Evidence	Points	Supporting Evidence	Points	Supporting Evidence

In column I, list on the left-hand side all the arguments for your central idea. On the right-hand side, jot down possible supporting evidence for each point, including information you may need to research. Do the same for arguments against your position (column II) and points on which you and your opponent might agree (column III). Stretch your imagination. Ask others, *especially those who don't agree with you*, for points you may have missed.

When you begin to organize your ideas, first be sure *you* know how they fit together logically to prove your point. As in all writing, concentrate on your central idea. If you're sure everything relates to it and you have your materials grouped logically together, you've taken a large step in the right direction.

Never feel constrained by a preconceived form for a paper. Many texts suggest formulas, especially for argument paper, e.g., "State and develop your first argument; then write a paragraph discussing and disposing of possible objections to it. State your second argument . . ." and so on. This advice sometimes works well for experienced writers, and may for you, but more often it results in stiff, awkward essays if it is not handled well. Use your own judgment and common sense.

In a persuasion paper, your introduction is especially important, as you can easily lose a reader in your first sentence (or even in your title). Blurting out a controversial statement at the beginning is not always good strategy, whatever you've been taught. Think how to lead your reader tactfully to your point of view. Can you capture his or her interest with a little story that will strengthen your case? Can you start by talking about the common ground (column III) you perceive between you and your reader?

Start your argument with a strong point, preferably one that is not too controversial. Be sure as you bring up your points (column I) that you recognize and deal with possible objections. You don't need to use all the positive points you've thought of; choose the most convincing. A shaky argument can weaken your paper. But be *extremely* careful about ignoring *objections* to your arguments; your reader could be quite justified in saying, "Since you haven't considered my objections, you haven't thought the situation through carefully, and I'm not convinced."

Leave a strong point for the conclusion; if you end weakly, perhaps with only a restatement of your position, your reader will feel let down and less convinced. Plan a "clincher" for the conclusion, but don't worry about the exact phrasing until you're ready for it.

There are many ways to present a convincing argument; one is illustrated in the following example. Notice that the writer starts on common ground, admitting to his opponent (who perhaps is thinking of dropping out of college) that he too has doubts. He himself has been convinced, however, by his brother's experience, which he uses as evidence. In the course of telling the story, he brings up various arguments for and against going to college. Can you isolate them?

Audience: My college roommate

Only Fools Quit College

Is college really worth it? Often this thought crosses my mind, as I'm sure it does yours, but each time I just think how bad things can be out in the real world today without a college education. Working in a factory or doing backbreaking manual labor are about all that is left these days for anyone who doesn't finish school.

My brother Rob's experience exemplifies the life of a college dropout. Rob graduated from high school in 1976 and started college that fall. His college career was brief, lasting only one year. In high school he was a big partier and never had to study to get good grades. He thought college was going to be one constant party and that he could get by in classes the same as he did in high school. His grades were consistently poor his entire freshman year.

During summer break Rob got a job in a factory for almost eight dollars an hour. His job was the excuse he was looking for to quit school. Now he could party and fool around as much as he wanted. He said college was for eggheads. My parents spent hours trying to convince him to return to college because they knew his real problem was that he was young and immature, lacking in self-discipline. But he ignored my parents and stayed with what he felt was a good life: big money and good times.

Close to three years passed before Rob's good life came to a screeching halt. Thousands of blue collar workers, including Rob, were laid off indefinitely when the country entered a recession. Months passed before the economy picked up enough so that most workers were called back, but Rob was not among them. The party was over. He was forced to take a job driving a bread truck just to survive. What a loser.

Whenever I have doubts about school, I think of my brother, the bread truck driver, who knew everything and couldn't give up the good life long enough to get a college degree.

ASSIGNMENT 8 A Reader-Oriented Expository Paper

✔ You now have completed preliminary groundwork for two papers, one cause and effect and the other persuasive. Choose the one you feel more comfortable with, or, if neither pleases you, find another topic that fits one of these types and go through the preparatory exercises again.

Once you have the preliminary work for a paper that suits you, follow the development process introduced in Chapter 7 (Activities 7-1, 7-2, and 7-3). Be sure your central idea is expressed in a clear, well-formulated sentence. (Ask your instructor if you aren't sure.) Go through the various methods of development systematically: classification, definition, comparison and contrast, analysis, description, narration. You should already have decided on your overall plan in Activity 8-1 or 8-2, but be alert for effective ways to develop your subpoints. *At all times,* think about your readers: what will interest them; what they can be expected to know; what points they will agree with; what tone they will respond to; what terms you need to define.

Review the plot of your paper to be sure the points follow one another logically and are well developed, and that related material is grouped together. Does everything add up to support your central idea?

Write the paper quickly; put it aside until it "cools." Revise it according to the revising activities that follow. Try to look at your paper constantly through the eyes of your reader as you revise.

In the upper left-hand corner of the first page of your final draft, indicate your chosen reader or readers. Your paper will be partly evaluated on how well you take such readers into consideration. Attach *all* activities for Chapter 8, regardless of which type of paper you have chosen to write.

Revising Activity 8-1 *Focus and Organization*

✔ Reconsider your central idea. (Repetition will help you maintain a strong, clear focus.) Does everything in the paper relate to it? Is there anywhere you've strayed off into a somewhat different line of thought that may confuse your reader? Have you gathered related material together in one paragraph or section of the paper? Does each paragraph follow clearly from the one preceding it and lead clearly to the one following it?

Revising Activity 8-2 *Logical and Coherent Transitions*

We have considered how to achieve coherence before, but the art of developing good, logical transitions is important enough to rate additional concentration. Sometimes, although you have a clear and logical order, your reader has difficulty following; in such a case, your transitions may be at fault.

Read the following sample paper.

The Right to Die

In recent years medical science has made spectacular gains in its ability to save lives. Advances of medicine and technology have, however, spurred a growing conviction that life may not always be worth fighting for. I believe that doctors are often too successful at extending a patient's life. In many cases, using the wonders of modern medicine to keep a dying person alive is needlessly cruel, putting a tremendous financial burden on his family, but most of all adding an emotional burden.

What of the terrible power of medicine in its ability to prolong life? Take a patient whose spontaneous activities are limited to breathing and circulation. Such a creature can be kept alive with stimulants and nourishment for a long time. Cases have been known where an autopsy later revealed that the brain had even liquified. A California doctor reports such a case. Tubes for feeding and releasing wastes kept the body going in a state where there was no mental response for eight years. "You could have taken a lighted match and held it against his eyes and he still wouldn't have known you were there."[1] The cost of the patient's care over those eight years came to $300,000. If the tubes had been taken away, he would have died within seventy-two hours.

What could justify life when the body was being sustained, yet there was no hope for recovery or progress? To me this seems more cruel than humane. It reminds me of a movie I once saw entitled The Night of the Living Dead. The characters were the dead who rose from their graves because of a freak accident. These people walked around without any feeling or emotions. Keeping dying people alive when they have no chance of recovery or progress is just as freaky and even more cruel. In my mind, these people are the living dead.

Euthanasia (from the Greek, meaning "easy death") seems a more humane solution. It is, in fact, practiced in hospitals every day.

A survey taken in 1969 by the Association of American Physicians revealed that 87 percent of the doctors polled approved of euthanasia, and 80 percent admitted having practiced it.[2] When a person is going to die and there is no hope, the drugs and techniques (so-called "heroic measures") are simply withheld and the person is allowed to die.[3]

Who next to God is the most qualified to say when a person should die? I strongly believe the answer is the individual and his doctor. If the patient wants his life sustained by medication or machines, then if at all possible, let it be done. But what of the people who want to die because they are suffering great pain with no hope of recovery? Or perhaps they don't want to die in humiliating circumstances. Should these people be forced to live and suffer because the law says a doctor must do all in his power to preserve life?

Poets have called death such things as "gentle night,"
"untimely death," or "the great destroyer." A stanza from the poem
of one writer seems to me to be full of truth:

Of old when men lay sick and sorely tried
The doctors gave them physic and they died
But here's a happier age, for now we know
Both how to make men sick and keep them so.

Hilaire Belloc[4]

When I die I have only one request. Let me die naturally; I
don't want to have some machine or medication keeping me alive. When
my body can no longer function on its own, then let me die, for it
must be God's will.

FOOTNOTES

[1]Daniel C. Maguire, "Death by Choice, Death by Chance,"
Atlantic, January, 1974, p. 62.
[2]John Walker, "Euthanasia," Life, January 28, 1974, p. 45
[3]Paul Wilkes, "When Do We Have the Right to Die?" Life,
January 14, 1972, p. 48
[4]Quoted by Daniel C. Maguire, in "The Freedom to Die,"
Commonweal, August 11, 1972, p. 61.

BIBLIOGRAPHY

Maguire, Daniel C. "Death by Choice, Death by Chance." Atlantic,
    January, 1974, pp. 56-65.
_____. "The Freedom to Die." Commonweal, August 11, 1972, pp. 423-
    427.
Walker, John. "Euthanasia." Life, January 28, 1974, p. 45.
Wilkes, Paul. "When Do We Have the Right to Die?" Life, January
    14, 1972, p. 484.

The transitions in this paper are generally good, making it easy to follow.
Suppose, however, the student had worded his third paragraph as follows:

What could justify life when the body was being sustained, yet there was no hope
for recovery or progress? To me this seems more cruel than humane. Once I saw a
movie entitled *The Night of the Living Dead*.

Here the intrusion of the writer's seeing a movie is momentarily puzzling,
there being no obvious link between it and the cruelty of sustaining life
beyond hope of recovery. Rewording the last sentence to what the student
actually wrote removes this confusion: "It reminds me of a movie I once
saw . . ."

Certain other language techniques can help. Some words are specifically designed to indicate transitions. Words such as *furthermore, in addition,* and *also* indicate a continuation of the same trend of thought. Words like *nevertheless, however, on the other hand,* and *but* signal a shift of thought. An example occurs in the first two sentences of "The Right to Die." Here is what the student originally wrote:

In recent years medical science has made spectacular gains in its ability to save lives. Advances of medicine and technology have spurred a growing conviction that life. . .

How do you expect this sentence to end? From what goes before, probably something like ". . . can be prolonged indefinitely." The writer, however, having a different idea, wrote, ". . . may not always be worth fighting for." Be careful about the anticipations you set up, as an unexpected shift may confuse your reader. By the addition of one transition word—*however*—the writer clears up the problem.

In recent years medical science has made spectacular gains in its ability to save lives. Advances of medicine and technology have, *however*, spurred a growing conviction that life may not always be worth fighting for.

Repetitions of words can often be helpful. In the third paragraph, the last two sentences are held together by repetition of the word *people.*

Keeping dying *people* alive when they have no chance of recovery or progress is just as freaky and even more cruel. In my mind, *these people* are the living dead.

In the same paragraph, the coherence is helped by repetition of the phrase "the living dead."

Synonyms (words or phrases that have the same or similar meanings) can carry an idea forward. In the first two paragraphs of "The Right to Die" are several such phrases, referring to medicine's keeping people alive: "spectacular gains in its ability to save lives," "extending a patient's life," and "ability to prolong life." Two sentences in the second paragraph illustrate another example of phrases that help a reader understand the connection between sentences: "*Take a patient* whose spontaneous activities are limited to breathing and circulation. *Such a creature* can be kept alive . . ."

Relationships of space and time can also be kept clear with certain specific words: *first/later, here/there,* etc. Logical relationships can be indicated with words like *first/second/finally.*

Use judgment in employing these techniques too obviously or mechanically. Repetition of the same word over and over gets monotonous; attempts to find synonyms become artificial and belabored; *first, second, third* sounds stiff and formal. Vary your techniques.

✔ Review your paper carefully. Can you increase a reader's ability to follow your thought by rewording a sentence here and there, adding a transition, or using some kind of synonym, especially where you have a vague pronoun reference? Revise accordingly.

Revising Activity 8-3 *Paragraphing*

Your paragraphing is another important element in achieving coherence. Not only is it important to make clear transitions from paragraph to paragraph, but you must know *when* to paragraph. The usual rule, the one that will cover most of your problems, is "Develop one aspect—*and only one aspect*—of your idea in each paragraph." As you know, there are exceptions (e.g., paragraphing for dialogue). But as a general rule, a reader expects a new idea in each new paragraph.

Choppy paragraphing can make your paper difficult to follow. A series of short paragraphs usually means you either haven't developed your idea sufficiently or you haven't combined related ideas into sufficiently large units. Read the following example.

Unlike on other Monday mornings, today I was anxious to hear the loud alarm. I knew exactly what I was going to wear, too.

My grandpa and grandma had taken me shopping the Saturday before, and Grandpa Anderson, whom I was very close to, had picked out an outfit in the downtown Gantos.

When he first suggested the shopping spree, I took it for granted he'd give my grandma the money and she would take me to Grand Rapids. But surprisingly, Grandpa even went into the store and picked out the clothes I was going to wear: a dark green and beige tweed gaucho outfit.

Today something told me to wear my gauchos.

This series of short paragraphs is the introduction to a paper telling about the day the writer's grandfather died. Combined into one paragraph, it reads more smoothly and quickly, bringing the reader more effortlessly to the real beginning of the narrative—a call to the telphone during a mid-morning class.

Unlike on other Monday mornings, today I was anxious to hear the loud alarm. I knew exactly what I was going to wear, too. My grandpa and grandma had taken me shopping the Saturday before, and Grandpa Anderson, whom I was very close to, had picked out an outfit in the downtown Gantos. When he first suggested the shopping spree, I took it for granted he'd give my grandma the money and she would take me to Grand Rapids. But surprisingly, Grandpa even went into the store and picked out the clothes I was going to wear: a dark green and beige tweed gaucho outfit. Today something told me to wear my gauchos.

The other extreme, of course, is the paper with no paragraphs or only very long paragraphs. Paragraphing must occur at logical points, but it has a second function: to provide a break or resting point for the reader. Today's readers, unlike those of earlier times, are not used to wading through long paragraphs. If your paragraphs seem consistently long, look for places where there is a significant shift of idea or direction. Start a new paragraph there.

Variety is a key word. When all your paragraphs are short, your writing seems choppy; if all your paragraphs are long, your paper may seem dull and boring. Use your common sense. Think about what you are saying, keeping in mind the few principles discussed here.

✔ Review your paragraphing. Are all the ideas within each paragraph related? Are the lengths varied? Can you combine some choppy paragraphs under a larger topic heading? Can you break up paragraphs that seem too long—more than a typewritten page?

Revising Activity 8-4 *Development*

✔ Is your paper interesting? Have you included relevant specifics and details that make it enjoyable as well as informative? Have you clearly defined unfamiliar terms or abstract words to which you and your reader may attach different meanings? Will some description or little story clarify a point you've merely mentioned or that sounds dull as you reread your paper? Will your introduction catch a reader's attention so he or she will want to read the next paragraph and the next and so on? Is your conclusion strong, striking, and satisfying?

Revising Activity 8-5 *Grammar (Minigrammar E)*

✔ Check yourself for:

1. Verb forms and usage (Minigrammars A and B, pp. 171-183)
2. Sentence fragments and run-on sentences (Minigrammar C, p. 193)
3. Pronoun usage (Minigrammar D, p. 205)

In addition, check each individual sentence for sentence logic. Have you said exactly what you intended? Can your sentence be read *only one way?* Work through Minigrammar E (p. 213) to help ascertain what you are looking for. Often people get their wording twisted up somehow. Are you sure this has not happened anywhere in your paper?

Revising Activity 8-6 *Review*

✔ Check yourself for:

1. Wordiness (Revising Activities 2-1, 2-2, 2-3, pp. 29-30)
2. Spelling (Revising Activity 6-1, p. 90)
3. Punctuation (Revising Activity 3-2, p. 46)

SAMPLE PAPERS FOR ASSIGNMENT 8

<u>Audience</u>: My black friends

Where Riots Rage

Riots occur in poverty-stricken communities and leave scars on them that never heal. These spontaneous events occur most often in black ghetto areas where population is dense and employment is down, resulting in grinding poverty that produces tension among individuals that is nearly unbearable.

As a small boy, I lived in conditions that reflected a life of poverty. On many days our family had nothing to eat except bread and butter. My brother, my two sisters, and I went to school hungry and with no money for lunch. At the end of the school day, we would come home and be greeted by an empty table, empty cupboards, and an empty refrigerator. We couldn't wait until mama got her social security check and went shopping. But we kept food for only two weeks; after that, we were hungry again.

Our family had other problems. The house was infested with roaches. They crawled up the walls, in the refrigerator, and on top of the kitchen table. I would get up during the middle of the night to use the bathroom; as soon as the lights came on, thousands of roaches would run for hiding places. Hundreds would scamper into the furnace vents. They gave me chills every time I saw or thought about them.

To see the gorgeous homes of the wealthy white kids enflamed me more than anything else. The houses were sparkling clean and in sparkling clean neighborhoods. Naturally, I was jealous and hated everyone who had more than I did. But luckily enough, our family was able to escape. Many families weren't as fortunate as we were and remain in poverty-stricken conditions today. Tension rages in them, tension that causes violent uprisings in communities.

Between the years 1967 and 1971, riots erupted in many black communities: places like Washington, D.C., Baltimore, Chicago, Pittsburgh, Detroit, and even my hometown, River Rouge. In Detroit, where a massive riot broke out in 1967, the street where the most damage was done was Twelfth Street, an all-black neighborhood, where there were overcrowded conditions, few people owned their own homes, and most of the housing was below good living standards. Many people in the area were unemployed. In uprisings such as the one that occurred there, thousands of dollars in damages resulted. A great number of buildings have not been replaced yet, and once busy streets are now deserted.

The last time I was on the street where our riot occurred, it was still a deserted place where hoodlums hung out. Boarded-up buildings and vacant lots were present everywhere. Trash along the road provided food for hungry dogs and rats. Men and women sat on curbs outside filthy pool rooms and restaurants. The dope clinic was filled with people who needed help, guidance, and medication.

The horrible riots in the 1960's left many people jobless, homeless, and lifeless. Many of the cities hit by riots are in worse condition than before. These senseless uprisings are obviously not the solution for obtaining better living conditions. One day black people will become aware of this, and the violent uprisings will cease.

Audience: People advocating zero population growth

This Is Not the Cure

Over the past few decades overpopulation has been a major
concern for the people of the world. At the rate the population is
growing, the world will soon be overcrowded, causing more hunger and
starvation, and the natural resources of the world will diminish to
nothing. We need some type of population control. All of the
governments of the world would have to agree that something must be
done and enact some type of legislation to reduce population growth.
But I do not think that the government should pass laws making it
illegal for an individual family to have no more than two children,
which would result in zero population growth. There would be many
problems that would make it almost impossible to pass laws which
would successfully restrict families to no more than two children.
One problem would be that of an effective means of birth control.
    If all the governments passed laws restricting more than two
births per family, some systems would have to be created to
effectively prevent unwanted births. Clinics could be set up and it
could be made mandatory for hospitals to provide a birth control
program, but what means of anti-birth protection would they use? At
the present, the only one hundred percent sure, one hundred percent
safe, inexpensive way to avoid pregnancy is to refrain from
intercourse; and the only other one hundred percent effective way to
prevent pregnancy is through sterilization. Both these solutions
have drawbacks: one is idiotic because it denies human physical
needs; the other may very easily create psychological disorders. It
is a known fact, for example, that many women who have had
hysterectomies have become psychologically disturbed because they
fear loss of femininity.
    The "pill," which has proved to be the most effective birth
control device, is now used by many women, but it is still not one
hundred percent effective. One reason for this is that many women
forget or neglect to take their daily tablet.
    In addition, not all women can take the pill. A woman who has
had trouble with veins or blood clots or certain types of cancer
would become ill if she took it. This woman would still be
restricted by law to keep the number of her children to two, but it
would be almost impossible to guarantee successful obedience. Also,
there is the speculation that the pill might lead to formation of
cancer after many years of use. This device also has a number of
unwanted side effects: nausea, weight gain, depression, and crying
spells.
    There are other means of birth control such as condoms,
chemical contraceptives, IUD's, and douching, but their percentage
of effectiveness is not sufficient to warrant government adoption.
The governments of the world would still be faced with finding an

effective means of controlling births in order to enact laws restricting them.

The absence of a sufficiently effective and commonly accepted means of birth control makes it almost impossible for governments to enact legislation restricting the number of births per family. I have heard speculation that in the future everyone can be made sterile by drinking chemically treated water. And if you want a child, having fewer than two, you simply go to the government and get a pill, which would reduce the effect of the chemical. If something one hundred percent safe and sure like this should be made available, then, and only then, would government intervention in personal lives begin to seem plausible.

CHECKLIST   *Knowing Your Audience*

Preparations.   Check off each item when completed.

Activity 8-1   Understanding Your Reader . . . .
Activity 8-2   Analyzing Cause and Effect . . . .
Activity 8-3   Persuading Your Reader . . . .
Assignment 8   A Reader-Oriented Expository Paper . . . .
Revising Activity 8-1   Focus and Organization . . . .
Revising Activity 8-2   Logical and Clear Transitions . . . .
Revising Activity 8-3   Paragraphing . . . .
Revising Activity 8-4   Development . . . .
Revising Activity 8-5   Grammar (Minigrammar E) . . . .
Revising Activity 8-6   Review . . . .

Goals to Be Achieved.   Write your answers on a separate sheet. Explain fully.

1. Will your reader like this paper? Do you?
2. Does the paper hang together well?
3. Have you developed your ideas fully in a manner both informative and entertaining to your reader?
4. Have you performed all the revising activities carefully?
5. Have you proofread your paper carefully?

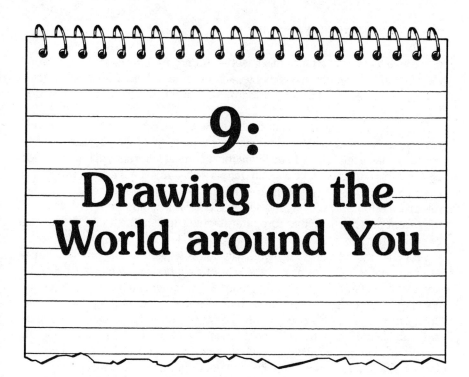

9:
Drawing on the World around You

By stages we have arrived at the *term paper* (or *research paper*) that most students are confronted with sooner or later in their college career. *Read the next sentence carefully!* There is *no essential difference* between the paper you are about to write and those you wrote for Chapters 7 and 8. More emphasis is now placed on information gained from reading and from experts on your subject; that is all. You will still rely on your own intellectual resources, *not* on a set formula delivered to you by someone besides yourself. You will learn what you need to know about your subject, partly through the vast storehouse of knowledge "out there somewhere" and you will explain what *you know* to a reader.

> *Principle 17* **The only real purpose of a research paper is to reach out and tap the knowledge that the world puts at your disposal.**

Do not, under any circumstances, assume you know how to write a research paper just because you've written them in the past. Read on to be sure you know what we are dealing with in this chapter.

WHAT IS A RESEARCH PAPER?

Many students think that all that is needed for a research paper is to assemble relevant material on a topic, arrange it in some logical manner, put in the required number of footnotes, attach a bibliography, type everything in a prescribed form, add a fancy title sheet—and *presto! A research paper!* Proficiency at this kind of thing is valuable, and in some college courses it is exactly what you will be asked to do. Furthermore, you may learn something by doing it.

It is not what we are talking about now, because what you will *not* necessarily learn from such an exercise is how to think for yourself, how to come to conclusions, how to evaluate the incoming information. If you do not perform this added step, you are in danger of becoming a mere automaton, a robot creature that takes input, files it, processes it in prescribed ways, and releases it as output. What I have just described is a computer. A nightmare of the recent past has been that computers would supplant the human brain: out of such a fear are spawned artistic endeavors like *2001: A Space Odyssey.*

Probably the human brain works in some ways like a computer, but a human brain is so sophisticated there is little chance that a mechanical creation can match it. How can any mechanical computer equal the possibilities of creating new thoughts and new patterns that exist among the human creatures of this earth? You may think you have nothing new to contribute, but with such an attitude you cheat yourself and, potentially, you cheat the world. Who knows where you will go, once you begin? Did the boy Einstein foresee the theory of relativity? Did the youthful Martin Luther King, Jr., see Birmingham ahead? Do ordinary people know what is ahead? Do you?

Stopping to take note of incoming information and to fashion your own ideas is a first requisite both for productive learning and for writing a good research paper. Every "research" project should be a step forward, however small, into your own future.

In this chapter, you choose your own area of interest, your own central idea, your own kind of development. At other times in your college career you will have to follow a more prescribed course. You will be given a topic and perhaps even an approach to take, along with a method of development. Confronted with such an assignment, you can mechanically follow instructions or you can make the assignment into a learning experience, drawing conclusions and making judgments. The choice is yours.

Activity 9-1   *Finding a Subject*

✔   List five topics that interest you and about which you would like to know more. Under each, jot down what about the topic stirred your interest in the first place; this may be a good place to begin a potential paper on the subject.

Also jot down possible sources of information. Your own personal experience is a good one that should not be overlooked. For example, if you are a motor bike enthusiast and decide to write on bike safety, an accident that involved you or a friend would help show a reader the need for more precaution. Or you may have some special knowledge that is both informative and interesting. Books and magazine articles are another obvious source. Is there specialized knowledge you can obtain from friends and/or experts in the field? One student, writing on agencies offering help to child abusers, talked with a county welfare agent and received both up-to-date information and referrals to other good sources of information. Material can be gained from film documentaries and TV. You may conduct a survey, as one student did of residents of his apartment house on their attitudes toward the smoking of marijuana. All of these—and others—are good sources of information. Be as broad as you can in trying to imagine such sources.

As part of your preliminary survey of possible sources, go to your college library and ask for information about how best to research a given topic. Do you know the most efficient way to locate books, magazine or newspaper articles, specialized facts and figures? Are you acquainted with the library's microfilm procedures? Do you understand the potential value of government documents? Does the library have special files, such as collections of material on popular topics? The librarians want to help you. Start with the questions above. Learn all you can about your library. The benefit now and in future years is inestimable.

✓   From your list of possible topics, choose the one that (1) interests you most and (2) seems capable of being developed in a full and interesting way (without padding) into a 750-1000-word essay.

In choosing your topic, go through much the same procedure as you did in Chapter 8, rejecting topics that are too broad and complex to research in the amount of time you have, those that have been done too often, those with which you have no personal experience and therefore no way to test the validity of the information you gather. Look for topics that somehow touch your own life: various kinds of college grants, a disease that runs in your family, problems facing handicapped people if you know and care for such a person, the dangers of using too much sugar or salt or of eating an unbalanced diet. Not only will you write more convincingly on a subject of vital interest to yourself, but you will, through your research, learn a great deal that will be personally valuable. Furthermore, researching a topic takes considerable time; if you are not interested enough to spend that time willingly, you may be constructing an insurmountable barrier for yourself. *Take time to consider* before you decide on your topic. It may be the most valuable time you spend during the whole project.

> *Principle 18* **A sure way to kill a paper is to choose a subject simply because you can find plenty of material.**

If you have been assigned a topic, the time you take in finding an *angle* is especially important. There is some way of approaching every topic that should appeal to you. Suppose you have been asked to write about the poetry of John Donne and your initial reaction is, "What? Somebody who's been dead for more than three hundred years?" Does it make it more interesting to reflect that Donne, a priest of the Anglican church, wrote both intensely passionate religious poetry and some of the most erotic love poetry ever to burn upon a page? If that doesn't spark your interest, find your own angle.

Activity 9-2   *Collecting Resource Material*

✔   When you have decided on a topic, look for background material, using as many different sources of information as possible. At the beginning, keep a relatively broad base of inquiry. By the time you choose your topic, you may think you know what angle of approach you will take. For instance, if you were to decide to write on crippling arthritis, which has struck your grandmother and mother and may later afflict you, you may want to concentrate on current research in the care and cure of the disease. Or you might want to emphasize preventative measures. Even so, read widely about your subject first and perhaps interview an expert for general background information. More study may convince you to adopt a different approach. Don't narrow down too soon; be sure you have found the best approach for your purpose.

On the other hand, look constantly for a good angle. The sooner you can focus on an area that you are sure is the right one, the better, because then you can narrow your search for materials to that one area. Reading up on arthritis may produce various kinds of information: facts about its prevalence, the types of arthritis, current research, its effects on its victims. You need such in-depth background, but you also need to arrive before too long at a central idea, such as "A massive effort should be undertaken to discover a cure for arthritis, a disease affecting almost everyone over fifty, as well as many younger people." Once you've decided you want to concentrate on research for possible cures, your field of inquiry narrows to that one aspect, allowing you to make more efficient use of your time.

In looking for material, concentrate first on magazine articles. Magazines of general circulation are indexed in the *Reader's Guide to Periodical Literature*. Despite sentiment to the contrary, many of these contain solid, well-researched articles. Use good judgment; an article in *Glamour* carries less weight than one on the same subject in *Consumer Reports*. Move on then to other treasures your library contains. Many subjects are discussed in scholarly journals, indexes to which are also available; such material is usually more solid and authoritative. Consult your librarian for help in using the indexes and locating the articles. If your library has government documents you may find a wealth of information there, since government now affects nearly every facet of our lives.

Books can be useful, but consider them second. Because it takes a long time to write and publish a book, many are already out of date when they reach the library shelves. Besides, a book takes longer to read and usually gives you only one point of view. Time limitations prevent the reading of numerous books on a subject. You can skim dozens of articles in the same amount of time.

Newspapers are another source of information that should not be over-looked. The *London Times*, the *New York Times*, and numerous other publications have been indexed, and most college libraries have back issues available on microfilm.

Lastly, don't forget *people*. Your college is crammed with experts on nearly every subject; seek them out. Most are happy to share their expertise with you. Other possibilities abound: local doctors, lawyers, social workers, master craftsmen, and mechanics. If you interview an expert, plan ahead, writing down questions you will ask. At the interview, *take notes*; don't rely on your memory. Be sure you can spell the interviewee's name correctly, and record the date. If the person you interview can't answer your questions, ask for suggestions on who else can or where the information may be found in articles and books.

Students run into serious problems when seeking background information, especially when relying on printed material, such as books and articles. If you have chosen a popular topic, the best resource material may have been checked out of the college library. Don't despair; try the public library. Or consider other places where the information might be available: the library of a major university near where you live, or the collection of a department around campus, even of an individual instructor. If you're doing something on employment of college seniors, ask the college placement bureau what it has to offer. Be inventive; don't give up the first time.

College libraries are not easy to use. Faced with their hundreds of thousands of items, you will inevitably run into some frustration. Persevere. The night you go home swearing you'll never enter a library again may be the eve of discovering a treasure chest of material only determined effort could uncover. Eventually it works out; either you find what you need or you decide what you need isn't available and change your approach. Don't consume precious time however, if it becomes apparent you are in real trouble. One student, for instance, who decided to write on the influence of Northwest artists on American art, simply couldn't find anything that had been done on the subject. In such a case, change your subject. There should be other possibilities on your list. If not, think again.

Be thorough in collecting your material, especially after you have decided on your angle of concentration. A paper derived from a single source cannot succeed, even if it "contains all you want to say" (a frequent student refrain). You will simply be regurgitating; a reader may as well go to the source, which is probably more fully documented and convincing. Read several articles on the subject, even if they seem quite similar. You may find new supporting evidence, a slightly different attitude, or even some doubts cast on your original source. If there is anything controversial in your subject, be sure to study points of view that contradict yours. Don't forget that in this assignment, *your teacher is your reader*. He or she is likely to know a good deal about your subject. Omitting important aspects through ignorance of their existence won't win you many points with such a knowledgeable reader.

Once you've chosen your special angle of approach, keep digging. Be *sure* you know as much as possible about that particular aspect.

> *Principle 19* **Failure to research your subject in depth is one sure way to lessen your reader's respect for what you have to say.**

In choosing sources, be cautious about general encyclopedias, such as *The World Book, Encyclopedia Americana,* or even the more thorough *Encyclopedia Britannica.* Though occasionally you may find information of value in encyclopedias, for the most part they are too superficial and too outdated to be useful. Sometimes their articles may help you orient yourself toward your subject, but no college paper should be drawn mainly from general encyclopedias. *Make it a practice neither to quote from them nor to include them in your bibliography.* Special encyclopedias, devoted to single subjects such as art, economics, medicine, history, or law, are different; they may contain considerable in-depth information.

As you take notes, keep a few guidelines in mind. Look for the following types of information:

1. Any facts you don't already know.
2. Statistics that apply.
3. Specific examples or incidents that illustrate your points.
4. Quotations that state points particularly well or in a striking manner.
5. Statements that either contradict or support a point you want to make.

Never plan to provide information essential to your paper in a quotation. You are the one making the points; use quoted material *only as support or confirmation of what you have already said or are about to say.* This is very important, since readers often merely skim or even skip quoted material, particularly long passages. Avoid long quotes as a general rule. If a long passage makes your point exactly, paraphrase the bulk of the material, *giving credit to your source,* and use only the most striking short passages as direct quotations.

Try to organize your paraphrase of long passages to avoid "peppering" your writing with footnote numbers. Instead of placing a number after every borrowed statement, indicate at the beginning of the material that what follows is from a single source. Present the material in essentially the same *order* as it appeared in the original and place a single footnote number at the end.

Norm Nelson, in a recent article for <u>The American Hunter</u>, counters the argument of non-hunters that animals are killed viciously or are wounded and left to die lingering deaths. He points out that the implication is that natural deaths are more humane and that if hunting were eliminated, animal suffering would be greatly reduced or ended. This argument, he says, is wrong. A natural death

usually is death by starvation. Regardless of age, deer in a
crowded, overbrowsed area take weeks to die, a process horrible to
see. Less hunting would mean more starvation. Animal suffering
would increase, not decrease. Nelson also graphically describes
another type of "natural" death: death by predators, who often
begin to devour a deer's "hot, steaming guts and quivering
haunches while the helpless animal is still very much alive and
conscious." (footnote number)

If the material thus covered is a summary of several pages, include a
reference to them all (e.g., pp. 13-15) in your footnotes; the purpose of indicating to your reader where you obtained the material is thereby adequately
served.

Do not "pile up" quoted material. If you are merely pasting together
passage after passage of source material, it's time to rethink your paper. Are
you reiterating the ideas of others instead of coming to your own conclusions
and then using quoted material for confirmation and support?

If you do have a series of quoted passages, separate them from one
another with transitional words.

In his book, Beyond the Ural Mountains, Ivan Aramilev illustrates one reason for hunting other than to make a kill. "How pleasant it would be not to grow old," he writes, "to roam through the
forest with a gun, discover new regions, swim in foaming rivers and
sleep at night near the camp fire in the cool dewy grass—for cen-
turies." Writer Kenneth Anderson, a lifelong hunter, reveals
another pleasure of hunting. "It lies in pitting your skill, wood-
craft, endurance and cunning against that of these animals and
beating them at their own game, rather than in merely killing
them." Anderson reminds his readers, "Remember always that a good,
cleverly taken photograph is a far more meritorious and commendable
achievement than any stuffed trophy."

A note on plagiarism: You plagiarize whenever you use another person's
words or ideas without giving credit to that person. Always give credit to your
source! Lean over backwards to be sure you are not plagiarizing. Take careful
notes. Whenever you copy down the *exact words* of your source, put them in
quotation marks *in your notes,* so later you will be sure which were the
author's words. Jot down the page number not only of exact quotations but
also of any significant body of materials you take notes on. *Even if you
paraphrase the material rather than copy it exactly, you must give credit as
long as the ideas or information come from someone else.* The only excep-
tion occurs when the source is universally known and available; you don't
generally footnote a dictionary, for instance, or general information known to
your reader and repeated in numerous sources.

Make a conscientious effort to give credit at all times. Until you are sure of
yourself, try not to give even the appearance of borrowing material and

pretending it is your own. Err on the side of too much accreditation when in doubt. The suspicion of plagiarism hangs heavy over researched papers, and even if a slip on your part is unintentional, your instructor may not see it that way. As a guide for freshman writers used some years ago at the University of Washington put it:

> An instructor may very well feel that there is, morally, little to choose between the student who is dishonest because he didn't take the trouble to be honest—to distinguish his work from the author's—and the student who is dishonest deliberately.[1]

Caution: Some students become overly fascinated with collecting material or use it as an escape from actually beginning to write. Many a thesis or dissertation goes unwritten while the student follows the trail of "one more book." *Be realistic.* You know how much time you have and how long your paper is going to be. Don't spend so much time looking for source material that you have none left to plan, write, and revise your paper.

Do, however, take time *before* you get into your research to check footnote and bibliography forms. As you collect material, put it in a form that is usable later, should you need it. Many students fail to copy down page numbers, for instance, which they find they need after returning the book or article to the library, but in the meantime the material has been checked out and isn't due until after the paper must be submitted. Don't let that happen to you. Find out *now* what information you need, and be sure you have it *written* down.

There is no set way to keep all this information, though handbooks tell you to make cards. Cards are undoubtedly the most efficient method, but use whatever ways suit you best.

This text does not give you detailed rules or techniques for doing research, such as how to find bibliographical sources or take notes. A good handbook will contain the basic forms you need, and college bookstores carry detailed guides devoted entirely to researching and writing term papers.

Activity 9-3   *Organizing Your Material*

A central idea is crucial to the organizing and writing of a successful research paper. This point cannot be emphasized too strongly. The deadliest paper for both writer and reader is the one that has no point to make. A typical example might be a paper on the aged, beginning with a long history of treatment of the elderly from primitive times to the present, followed by a section on problems facing today's old people, followed by a section on retirement homes, followed by a section on health care, one on research into psychological and physical problems, one on . . . . The writer doesn't know

[1]*Manual of Freshman English: University of Washington* (Palo Alto, Cal.: Pacific Books, 1967) p. 8.

when to stop or how to organize everything into a coherent paper. The instructor is faced with a formless mass, which is probably only one of many similar papers he or she must wade through. Boredom sets in; the paper is skimmed and a largely subjective grade is attached. No one is happy with the result.

Most college instructors *want you to think about the material and arrive at a conclusion.* The conclusion *is* your central idea, and the body of the paper includes whatever material is needed to explain and justify your conclusion — exactly the sort of thing we have been doing since the beginning of the term.

✔   In organizing your paper, first do a fact sheet characterizing your reader: in this case your instructor. Then follow exactly the procedure outlined in Activities 7-1, 7-2, and 7-3 (pp. 98-116). Write out your central idea. Go through the various methods of development to decide which you can best use. Gather related material together. Plot your paper carefully, being sure the points follow one another logically and add up to prove your central idea.

You may find as you work that you have more material than you can handle convincingly and thoroughly in the prescribed length for this paper (750-1000 words). Don't hesitate to *limit your topic* to a smaller portion you can cover in depth. Rewrite your central idea to suit the less extensive coverage and rework the plotting of the paper. For instance, the paper on the aged might be limited to discussion of *one* new development, such as group homes for the elderly. Save the rest of your material; it may come in handy for another paper sometime.

> **Principle 20** You don't need to tell all you know in one paper; choose an important aspect — and cover it thoroughly!

Activity 9-4   *Introductions and Conclusions*

You are ready to start writing. How do you begin? An old formula for writing research papers goes: "Tell your reader what you are going to say, say it, and then tell your reader what you have said." *Forget this formula.* The usual interpretation of it has led to incredibly dull, repetitious papers. Often a student gets off to a good start, making strong points rapidly and impressively, but suddenly seems to start over, making the *same points* again. It finally dawns on the bored reader that the *first* statement was the "introduction," a mere listing of subheadings to be developed later. This kind of paper usually concludes with another listing, mercifully shorter, of the points made.

In a relatively short paper, such repetition is not only boring but also insulting to the reader's intelligence, since he or she presumably has to be told three times before anything sinks in. This very old idea may be true of speeches; it does not necessarily apply to writing. In a long article or book, providing the reader at the beginning with a general overview of the material may be useful. But give your readers credit; most have an attention span that can encompass a paper of a thousand words.

What a good introduction does is attract the interest of a reader and give a *clue* to the general direction the paper is to take. If it includes your central idea, both you and your reader know what to expect, but stating your conclusion in the first paragraph may take away any sense of suspense. If you shoot off your big gun immediately, what follows may seem anticlimactic.

Think how you can start off to attract a reader. Can you use a bit of vivid description to put the reader there? Can you tell a short, effective story—a case history—that illustrates the problem or situation you are dealing with? Can you pose a question that piques the interest of your reader? Or in some other way engage his active involvement in your idea? Can you offer interesting background information *relevant to your central idea?* The following examples may help you decide how to begin effectively.

As the snow gently falls from a gray sky, a powerful cougar, perhaps the most majestic creature in all of North America, strides smoothly through the snow-filled forest. A coat of short tawny and white fur covers his sleek, muscular body. His yellow eyes, deep and piercing, see all. The rest of the cat's senses are as well developed as his sight; nothing escapes his superior sense of smell and hearing. This magnificent creature is now facing extinction.

Nine-year-old Donna died last May 1. She had been severely beaten, and fifty percent of her body was covered with second and third degree burns. Donna's father and mother were charged with first-degree murder. Her fifteen-year-old stepsister testified, "Mamma used to whip her with a belt or paddle. When she got the whippings, it was either red or purple or black . . . it was different colors."

Nancie refuses to buy anything purple. Michelle loves pink; Dave hates yellow. Does this tell anything about them? Yes, it does. It is as natural for different persons to like different colors as it is for them to be happy or depressed, active or passive, outgoing or quiet. Personality traits and color preferences are closely related.

We Americans have an innate need and right to expect privacy, claiming it as one of our inalienable rights. Unfortunately, however, the right of privacy does not extend to individuals in the public eye. Edward M. Kennedy is one such individual. Will the skeletons rattling in his closet keep this Presidential hopeful out of office?

In 1931 when the Welland Canal was opened between Lake Erie and Lake Ontario, two fish, the alewife and the sea lamprey, were able to migrate into the Great Lakes. The alewife population remained low until the late 1950's when sea lampreys greatly reduced the numbers of trout and turbot, which had preyed on the alewives. With no predators to keep them in check, the alewife population exploded and by 1967 accounted for 95 percent of the total fish tonnage in Lake Michigan. Fish biologists have succeeded in reducing the threat of the sea lamprey by the use of rotenone, a poison toxic to the lamprey but harmless to other fish. The large alewife population, however, remains a threat to the Great Lakes.

One word of caution: a good introduction sets up an anticipation in the mind of the reader. *This anticipation must be satisfied by the rest of your paper.* A purple patch of florid description (say, of an emergency room in a hospital after a four-car accident) followed by a primarily factual paper (facts and figures showing the overloading and understaffing of hospital emergency rooms) isn't going to work. You will be expected to continue in the same hyped-up style in which you began. Don't create an introduction *just* to attract a reader, like a dinner speaker starting off with a joke totally unrelated to the rest of his talk.

✓   For this activity, write an *effective* introduction. Remember it *is* an introduction and should be as concise as possible, while still creating the effect and serving the purpose you have in mind. If the first one doesn't work well, try a different one. If the introduction runs on and on, stop. Cut it somewhere or express it in a way that will pack a swifter punch.

Do *not*, for this activity, plan or write a conclusion ahead of time. If you know what you want to say, and how you are going to develop it, you know when you are through. Stop when you are through. Don't repeat yourself; don't tack on a few additional thoughts that don't amount to much; don't reach for fancy words; above all, don't raise a *new* question at the end of the paper.

Since the conclusion is what the reader is most likely to carry away from the paper, save a strong point for the end. The conclusion should contain some kind of clincher, something that draws the whole paper together and leaves a reader feeling enlightened and satisfied.

Leave writing your conclusion for the place where it belongs: the end. The writing of the paper may change the way you originally thought about concluding. Sometimes—the best times—a conclusion writes itself. Sometimes you find, as you try to think how to end, that you have *already* concluded, that the paragraph you have just written brings everything to a satisfying point. Or a single sentence may wrap it all up neatly.

However your conclusion comes about, its essential quality is a sense of satisfaction, of anticipation gratified, of something worthwhile completed.

Here are the conclusions to match the introductions above.

Time is what endangered species lack. The once plentiful passenger pigeon went from darkening the skies to being stuffed in museums, becoming extinct in less than a century. The cougar might be saved from this plight because of the publicity it has received. But "might" isn't good enough. Only the collective actions of many people can save these beautiful animals from extinction.

Child abusers have been described as immature, impulse-ridden, demanding, suspicious, and defensive people. What should these people do when they realize they are emotionally sick? Temporary foster care is one answer, providing relief for the parents and a safety factor for the children. When outside people are involved with the family, feelings of anger can be handled in a better way.

Color preference exposes emotions more readily and fully than any other simple method of personality analysis. Research is now being conducted and in the near future color preference may play an even more important part in the practice of psychology. Soon everyone will realize there is more to color than meets the eye.

We Americans need heroes and in each election we try to pick a man who fulfills our qualifications, someone who is above and beyond the average American, someone who can supply good answers to nasty questions. Kennedy, though seeming confident of himself, may be taking the American voting public too much for granted. Cheating in college may be forgiveable. Cheating on one's wife is understandable. Having opponents taunting one as a "murderer" may be dirty politics. But in combination, these issues, sure to rise, could be lethal to any Presidential hopeful.

Summing up the alewife problem, Senator Scott Baugh from Illinois stated before a Senate subcommittee looking into the issue, "The future lies in returning the natural predator-prey relationship to the Great Lakes, but for now the alewife problem isn't just an old wives' tale."

ASSIGNMENT 9   A Research Paper

✔   Write your research paper. Revise it according to the revising activities that follow. Use footnotes where needed and attach a bibliography. When you finish, give your paper a title that will attract a reader. Attach all preliminary work, including notes, outlines, and drafts, unless instructed otherwise.

Revising Activity 9-1   *General Organization and Development*

✔   Follow the procedure outlined in Revising Activities 8-1 through 8-4 (pp. 132-137). Is your central idea clear? Does everything in your paper relate to it? Is the material logically presented, with each paragraph clearly following the preceding one and with coherent transitions from sentence to sentence? Have you paragraphed at logical places? Are the paragraph lengths varied, neither all short and choppy nor overly long? Have you developed your central idea thoroughly and in as interesting a manner as you can? Are there any general statements left unexplained? Have you included specifics to prove your statements and/or illustrate your points in a convincing and effective way?

Revising Activity 9-2   *Quoted Material*

✔   Review your use of quoted material. Quotations must, first of all, preserve the general coherence of your paper, integrating with both your thought and your sentence patterns. For an illustration of how quotations may be misused, consider a paper with the central idea that hunters are among the best conservationists, in which the student writer started a paragraph as follows:

The longer you hunt the more you realize that the greatest pleasure is being with nature and enjoying it. A hunter can view nature in a way different from that of many people.

A quotation follows, beginning:

But killing one's limit is not the criterion of a successful hunt. In fact, getting any game at all is not essential. What is essential is an attitude, a state of mind, or a philosophy . . .

This quotation is weakly handled because of the initially puzzling way it is presented, with a sudden jump from "viewing nature" to "killing one's limit." The writer could prevent his problem with a more careful transition.

The longer you hunt the more you realize that the greatest pleasure is being with nature and enjoying it. A hunter can view nature in a way different from that of many people. *Gaining a greater appreciation of nature, not killing one's limit, often marks a successful hunt.* "In fact, getting any game at all is not essential. What is essential is an attitude, a state of mind, or a philosophy . . ."

In checking for coherence, follow essentially the procedure suggested in Revising Activity 8-2, providing careful transitions from your own sentences to the quoted material and back again.

In addition, watch your pronoun use, taking care to be consistent throughout. The paper on hunting illustrates the pronoun problem in the following passage.

> Hunters hunt for many reasons. Most pass through three stages. In the first, getting game is most important. In the second *they* become more selective, often enjoying good dog work more than killing a limit of birds. "And, finally, *we* reach a state of mind where the hunting itself, particularly with a congenial companion in surroundings *we* enjoy, is the most important part."

The pronoun shift from third person plural *(they)* in the writer's own prose to first person plural *(we)* in the quoted passage is jarring. One remedy is to change *we* in the quoted material to *they*. If you do something like this, substituting your own words or perhaps adding some to make the passage flow more coherently, enclose the substitution or addition in brackets ([ ]), e.g., "And finally, [they] reach a state of mind . . ." Another remedy is to change your own pronouns to fit the quoted material, but this probably wouldn't work in the example in question, since the whole paper is consistently in third person plural. A third solution—and usually the best—is to revamp your use of the quoted material to avoid the pronoun problem:

> Hunters hunt for many reasons. Most pass through three stages. In the first, getting game is most important. In the second, they become more selective, often enjoying good dog work more than killing a limit of birds. *In the third, they* "reach a state of mind where the hunting itself, particularly with a congenial companion . . ., is the most important part."

(The three dots, called *elision marks* or *ellipses,* are used when for some reason a part of the quoted material is omitted. The reason for omitting words here is to avoid the second *we.*)

How to give credit for sources is sometimes tricky. If at all possible, give initial credit *in the body of your paper.* Don't make a reader look at the footnotes to ascertain the reliability and authority of your source. Footnotes have only one purpose: to provide *additional* information beyond that directly pertinent to the point you are making. *The principal purpose of footnotes is to allow your reader to look up your source if that seems desirable.* As a general rule, provide as gracefully as possible in the body of your paper the name and title of your authority. Certain phrases are useful, such as "According to _____(name)_____, director of the hospital" or "As explained by _____(name)_____." Often effective is an inclusion of accreditation in the middle of your quotation, similar to a dialogue attribution, as in the following passage:

> According to license sales figures released by the Fish and Wildlife Service in 1976, a record 60 million Americans spent close to $318 million on state hunting and fishing licenses. "Both figures are record highs, and they show that Americans continue to find hunting and fishing major pastimes," *said Director Lynn A. Greenwalt.* "One out of every five Americans enjoys the outdoors this way."·

You will find other methods of giving credit among the examples in this text; consult your handbook for more suggestions.

In deciding how to set up a quoted passage, follow this rule of thumb: Incorporate short quotations of five lines or fewer into your own paragraph and surround them by quotation marks, as in the above example. If the quotation is more than five lines long, indent five spaces on both sides and single space.

Do not surround indented, single-spaced material with quotation marks unless the source contains them. The indentation indicates that you are quoting.

Example

Even though Leary and Alpert experienced a good trip, not all trips on LSD are filled with pleasant feelings and beautiful images. For example, one psychiatrist told a woman patient that the way to find God was through LSD.

> Once she had taken the so-called wonder drug, she lay down on the bed and felt a quivering in her stomach. When she tried to imagine what it might mean she found she could see inside her stomach. In it were thousands of worms gnawing at its lining--voracious, evil-eyed worms that chewed at the flesh while the dark blood oozed about them.

Revising Activity 9-3   *Footnote and Bibliography Forms*

Make it a habit to consult a good handbook for footnote and bibliography forms. No serious student tries to remember the forms or uses them without checking the guides. Find the form that applies to your particular source and *follow it exactly, down to the last period and comma;* each section of the form and every piece of punctuation has significance for the experienced reader. For this paper, follow the common standard form found in most handbooks. Some disciplines, such as social sciences, economics, and the sciences, prefer different forms; when appropriate, follow these—*exactly!*

Keep in mind that the chief function of footnotes and bibliographies is to allow the reader to locate your source material; be sure you have supplied all the necessary information. In collecting your bibliography, include all sources you found helpful, *whether or not you used material from them,* but keep in mind that general encyclopedias should not be used as serious sources. Do *not* include general dictionaries, even if you have quoted from them, or the King James version of the Bible, since everyone has easy access to these and needs no publication data to locate them.

The question of where to place footnotes may depend on your instructor's preference. If your instructor states no preference, place the footnotes at the end of your paper under a heading "FOOTNOTES" or "SOURCES CONSULTED"; follow that with your bibliography headed "BIBLIOGRAPHY." Putting footnotes at the end of the paper is preferred by scholarly journals and makes your typing job easier.

In consulting your handbook, note carefully the following differences in form between footnotes and bibliographies.

1. In a footnote, all information is given in its natural order; note in particular the name of the author (e.g., John Smith). (If there is no author, the first item in your citation will be the name of the article.) In a

bibliography, on the other hand, *put the author's last name first* (i.e., Smith, John) and alphabetize the entries. Note also that if you have several works by the same author, you include the name in the bibliography *only for the first work.* Subsequent items by the same author begin with a dashed line (------) the length of the author's name, followed by a period.

2. Indentations are different: in footnotes you indent five spaces for the first line and bring subsequent lines back to the margin. For the bibliography, the opposite is true: place the first line flush with the margin and indent subsequent lines.
3. Punctuation is also different. Commas separate items in footnotes. Major items in the bibliography are separated by periods.
4. Number footnotes consecutively throughout your paper, placing numbers *in both the body of the paper and in the footnotes* slightly *above* the line. In the body of the paper, the numbers *follow* the quotation; in the footnotes, the number *precedes* all other information. In neither case is there a space between the number and the other material. *Do not number items in a bibliography;* alphabetize them.

Note also that after the first reference in your footnotes, you do not repeat publication data; see your handbook for guidance on how to handle subsequent references to the same work. Confusion often arises about the use of *ibid.* in such subsequent references. Most Latin terms, such as *op. cit.*, are now out of favor; modern authorities suggest the use of the author's last name, or if there is no author, a shortened form of the title of the article or book. Sometimes, however, awkwardness results from such a practice, and *ibid.* seems the most sensible reference. Since it means "in the same place," ibid. can be used *only* if it refers to the item immediately preceding it. If you do use ibid., remember it is an abbreviation (for *ibidem*) and so must be followed by a period.

You will find some forms for footnotes and bibliographies illustrated in the research papers reproduced in this text, but *make your handbook your primary authority.* Learn to use it *now* so you will know how later.

✔ Check your footnote and bibliography forms carefully before you type the final draft of your paper.

Revising Activity 9-4   *Grammar (Minigrammar F)*

✔ Check your paper for:

1. Verb usage (Minigrammars A and B, pp. 171-183)
2. Sentence fragments and run-on sentences (Minigrammar C, p. 193)
3. Pronoun usage (Minigrammar D, p. 205)
4. Sentence logic (Minigrammar E, p. 213)

In addition, are your sentence structures dull and monotonous, all perhaps about the same length and the same structure (usually consisting of a subject and predicate followed by a completer of some kind)? Sentences, like paragraphs, need to be varied in both length and and structure. Minigrammar

F (p. 221) discusses the problem of dull sentences and suggests some methods for gaining variety. Revise your sentences, if necessary, for more variety.

Revising Activity 9-5   *Review*

✔   Check your paper for wordiness, spelling, and punctuation. Proofread your final draft with care.

SAMPLE PAPERS FOR ASSIGNMENT 9

Vegetarianism: The Healthful Way

Introduction uses question anticipating possibly negative reader response. Central idea stated. Good use of statistic.

Why try vegetarianism? Though moral, economic, and religious concerns are often cited, the most common reason named by the seven million vegetarians in the United States is that it is a healthful way to eat.[1] No longer looked upon as a fad or starvation regimen, vegetarianism, a common practice in most of the world, tracing its origins back as far as early Biblical times, is now recognized in this country as an alternative method of achieving a good diet.

A popular misconception exploded. Definition and classification.

Vegetarians don't necessarily limit themselves to natural or organic foods. Most of those who describe themselves as vegetarians eat everything but "red meat," such as beef, pork, and lamb, citing the fact that elimination of these meats results in a lower intake of saturated fat. The total vegetarian, very rare in the United States, consumes no animal products at all. Then there are the "ovo" and "lacto" vegetarians, who use either eggs or milk products along with their fruits, vegetables, and grains.[2] Whatever the regimen, vegetarians are convinced their way of eating is more healthful than that of most Americans.

Further possible objections dealt with. Minor arguments briefly disposed of. Information, available from many sources, not footnoted.

Some people, however, especially parents of young people who adopt vegetarianism, worry over possible nutritional problems. Since eggs often play a significant part in a vegetarian diet, some worry about cholesterol, but its intake can easily be reduced by using skim milk and limiting oneself to four eggs a week. Reported deficiencies of iron, iodine, and vitamins B_{12} and D can all be eliminated by use of vitamin and mineral sup-

Positive arguments advanced.

plements. On the positive side, plenty of carbohydrates can be obtained from foods such as whole wheat bread, pasta, rice, whole wheat breakfast cereals, and other grains. In addition, the diet includes fruits and vegetables, which are full of natural fiber.

Major problem acknowledged. Authority cited.

Most commonly, people worry about protein deficiency in a meatless diet. But, according to Ellen Laurence, writing for Cosmopolitan, the average vegetarian diet comes closer than does the typical American diet to meeting the distributions recommended by the U.S. Department of Agriculture: 15 percent protein, 30 percent fats, and 55 percent carbohydrates. Even though red meats are excluded, Laurence claims, daily requirements are met by including protein-rich sources such as eggs, lentils, peanut butter, dried beans, nuts, and milk products.[3]

Refutation of major objection strengthened by further evidence from sources.

Statistics.

Writer's knowledge used to supply specifics.

Protein deficiency diseases are rare in the United States, where the average American meat-eater consumes roughly twice the protein needed by the body. The Recommended Daily Allowance (RDA) is currently estimated at an average of 44 grams for women and 56 grams for men.[4] Consider a few dishes consumed by the average American vegetarian, each of which contains from 12 to 37 grams: whole grain cereals with milk; peanut butter or egg salad on whole wheat bread; oriental dishes with rice; macaroni and cheese; pasta with milk or cheese-based sauce; or a chef's salad with cheese, eggs, garbanzo beans, and plenty of fresh vegetables.

More support from sources.

In 1974, a committee of the National Academy of Sciences-National Research Council, which publishes the RDA, evaluated vegetarian diets and reached the conclusion that all but the most restricted are nutritionally sound.[5] In a similar vein, Consumer Reports asked three of its staffers, two ovolacterian vegetarians and one total vegetarian, to keep track of their food intake for one week; their daily protein averaged from 125 to 150 percent of their RDA.[6]

Positive argument to further refute principal objection

Technical term defined.

Specifics given.

The vegetarian diet not only provides enough protein; it concentrates on high-quality protein. A protein's quality is measured in terms of "net-protein utilization" (NPU). A NPU of 100 percent means that one gram of food protein produces one gram of body protein to be utilized by the body for energy and for tissue repair and creation. Eggs, with a NPU of 94, rank highest. They are followed by milk, 82; fish, 80; cheese, 70; meat and fowl, 67. Nuts, legumes, and grains range from 40 to

60.[7] Animal proteins are high-quality or "complete" proteins, while most plant proteins are low-quality or "incomplete" proteins. By combining "incomplete" proteins with other plant or animal proteins, vegetarian dishes can provide higher-quality protein than that supplied by

Specific example.

animal proteins alone. For example, when served in combination, grains such as rice, oats, wheat, and corn, together with legumes such as beans, lentils, and peas, equal the NPU of milk.

New positive arguments introduced. Point I: weight control.

Besides being nutritionally sound, the vegetarian way offers other health advantages. Since plant proteins are more filling and usually lower in calories than animal proteins, vegetarians have less tendency to overeat and thus

Brief reference to writer's experience shows interest and special knowledge.

find controlling their weight easier. Personally, I've found I can control my weight better and also trim off excess fat painlessly, since there is no strict diet to adhere to. Benefits from a lower percentage of body fat include not only a feeling of zest, vigor and vitality, but also a reduction in the risk of cardiovascular disease and adult-

Supporting evidence from source

onset diabetes. Statistics compiled by The New York Metropolitan Life Insurance Company, based on a study of 50,000 policy owners, show that the general mortality rate from cardiovascular disease, high blood pressure, and diabetes among obese men and women increases significantly with each 10 percent above their ideal weight.[8]

Positive point II: fewer digestive problems.

Along with increased health resulting from fewer weight problems, vegetarians reap the benefits of fewer digestive disturbances. Since the diet is high in fiber, it easily supplies the roughage essential for healthy intestinal flora, reducing constipation, hemorrhoids, and colon

Sources used as supporting evidence. Authority's name and title given.

cancer. Between 1958 and 1965, Dr. Frank R. Lemon, Director of Continuing Medical Education at the University of Kentucky, and a colleague, Dr. R. T. Walden, carefully followed the dietary habits of

Good statistic strengthens validity of example

35,460 Seventh-Day Adventists in California, mostly ovolacterian vegetarians, and found 28 to 50 percent fewer digestive and gastrointestinal diseases than among the rest of the California population.[9] The reduction of saturated fat in a vegetarian diet is also beneficial from the standpoint of digestion. Vegetarian basketball star Bill Walton advises vegetarianism for athletes "because it provides the essential nutrients, without bogging down your digestive system."[10]

Positive point III: lower incidence of heart disease, nation's number one killer.

Source material well integrated.

Besides overloading the digestive system, high levels of saturated fats in the diet cause an excess of fat in the blood. This excess may lead to atherosclerosis, a forerunner to coronary heart disease (CHD), cited by the American Dietetic Association as the number one cause of death in the United States.[11] CHD is a diet-related, chronic, degenerative disease. However, when saturated fats and cholesterol intake are reduced, as in the vegetarian diet, the incidence of CHD decreases.

Additional source material.

Various studies have been conducted of the Seventh-Day Adventists in California, and there is clear evidence that among the vegetarian men the first heart attack comes a full decade later than among other Californian males and that they suffer only 60 percent of the incidence of atherosclerosis and CHD as do non-vegetarians.[12]

Conclusion: a brief summary of positive points, with direct appeal to reader.

If personal health is one of your top priorities, vegetarianism offers benefits you won't want to miss. You may not choose to give up meat altogether, but no one says you have to. Unlike other diets, the vegetarian method doesn't tell you what or how much to eat; you make the decision. If you decide to give it a try, the ovolacterian regimen is probably the best choice, since it's actually very similar to the diet most people are used to. You have nothing to lose except a few unwanted pounds and a great deal to gain.

FOOTNOTES

1 "Vegetarianism: Can You Get By Without Meat?" Consumer Reports, 45 (June, 1980), 357.

2 Ellen Laurence, "Food for Thought: Is Vegetarianism the Better Way?" Cosmopolitan, April, 1979, p. 98.

3 Laurence, p. 98.

4 "Vegetarianism," Consumer Reports, p. 358.

5 Ibid., p. 361.

6 Ibid., p. 358.

7 Gary Sheldon, "The Virtues of Vegetarianism," Cosmopolitan, May, 1980, p. 137.

8 Dennis Craddock, Obesity and Its Management (New York: Churchill Livingstone, 1978), p. 6.

9 L. M. Sonnenburg, "The Vegetarian Diet: Scientific and Practical Considerations," Journal of the American Dietetic Association, 62 (January, 1973), 66.

10 Amby Burfoot, "The Meatless Runner," Runner's World, February, 1978, p. 48.

11 Sonnenburg, p. 66.

[12] Jeanne Goldberg, "Vegetarianism," Family Health, 10 (April, 1978), 31. See also Roland L. Phillips, Frank R. Lemon, et al., "Coronary Heart Disease Mortality Among Seventh-Day Adventists with Differing Dietary Habits: A Preliminary Report," The American Journal of Clinical Nutrition, 31 (October, 1978), S198.

BIBLIOGRAPHY

Burfoot, Amby. "The Meatless Runner." Runner's World, February, 1978, p. 48.

Craddock, Dennis. Obesity and Its Management. New York: Churchill Livingstone, 1978.

Goldberg, Jeanne. "Vegetarianism." Family Health, 10 (April, 1978), 30-31.

Laurence, Ellen. "Food for Thought: Is Vegetarianism the Better Way?" Cosmopolitan, April, 1979, p. 98.

Phillips, Ronald L., Frank R. Lemon, et al. "Coronary Heart Disease Mortality Among Seventh-Day Adventists with Differing Dietary Habits: A Preliminary Report." The American Journal of Clinical Nutrition, 31 (October, 1978), S191-S198.

Roddick, Cherry. "New Look at an Old Diet." Glamour, October, 1977, p. 164.

Sheldon, Gary. "The Virtues of Vegetarianism." Cosmopolitan, May, 1980, pp. 136-137.

Sonnenburg, L. M. "The Vegetarian Diet: Scientific and Practical Considerations." Journal of the American Dietetic Association, 62 (January, 1973), 66.

Life with Diabetes

My grandmother rises each day to find her first task waiting for her: giving herself an injection of insulin. Her meals are close to normal but are devoid of foods with concentrated sugars, such as cakes or candies. Before dinner she takes another injection. For her, missing a meal is serious and dangerous, making insulin shock a harsh reality. My grandmother is a diabetic.

What is diabetes? The full term is diabetes mellitus. Diabetes is Greek for "siphon" and mellitus is Latin for "honey," referring to frequent urination full of sugar, a symptom of diabetes, which is a metabolic disorder with no known cure.[1] Metabolism is a body function made up of two separate processes: anabolism and catabolism. Anabolism concerns the use of chemicals from the food we eat and the build-up of new cells and bone. Catabolism is the breakdown of worn-out or damaged cells into simple chemicals to be used again or eliminated. In diabetes, the metabolic process breaks down and a condition similar to starvation occurs. A starving person can use carbohydrates, a chief source of energy to the brain, but doesn't have them; a diabetic has the carbohydrates but can't use them.[2] A diabetic won't actually die from starvation, but as inefficient energy production goes on, it forms dangerous by-products of fat known as ketones or acetone. Large doses of these substances are poisonous. If the diabetic goes untreated, build-up of ketones will result in a coma and eventual death.

More specifically, diabetes is the absence or shortage of insulin, a hormone secreted by the pancreas and a vital part of our digestive system. Without insulin, glucose, the simple sugar made from the food we eat and the brain's chief source of energy, cannot enter the body cells.

According to the National Commission on Diabetes, "diabetes ranks third on our list of killer diseases, outranked only by cardiovascular disease and cancer. An estimated seven to eleven million Americans and Canadians have it."[3] Diabetes can be hereditary, and its occurrence also involves certain racial and ethnic factors. A study by the National Commission on Diabetes found that "women are fifteen percent more likely than men to have diabetes, non-whites are one-fifth more likely than whites to have it, and poor persons ($5000 or less per year) are three times as likely as middle income and wealthy individuals to have the disorder."[4] The Commission also found that between 1965 and 1974, the prevalence of diabetes in the United States had increased more than 50 percent and that in 1974 there were 600,000 new cases. Diabetics are twenty-five times more prone to blindness than non-diabetics, seventeen times more prone to kidney disease, five times more prone to gangrene, which often leads to amputation, and twice as prone to heart disease. The chance of being diabetic doubles for every 20 percent of excess weight and for every decade of life.[5]

At this time, not nearly enough is known about the causes and treatment of diabetes. Causes have not been pinpointed. Insulin deficiency is not the whole answer. Studies have shown that some adult diabetics have normal amounts of insulin; one theory contends excess calorie intake may overload insulin "receptors" in the cells. It has also been theorized that an abnormal immune response may destroy pancreatic insulin-producing cells or that, rather than a decreased insulin output, there may be an increase of another hormone, glucagon, which normally cooperates with insulin to balance the production of glucose and ketones in the liver.[6] In juvenile diabetes, a link between diabetes and viral infections such as mumps and chicken pox has recently been isolated. A ten-year-old boy suffering from a flu-like virus later died from severe juvenile diabetes. After an autopsy, a common virus found in the child's pancreas was injected into laboratory mice, which developed the same type of diabetes the child had.[7] Though experimenters are virtually certain this child's diabetes was caused by the virus, they caution against optimism about having found "the" cause of juvenile diabetes and point out that their findings are no help at all in adult diabetes, which comprises 80 to 90 percent of all cases.[8]

Treatment of diabetes has improved but is still not

satisfactory. Before the discovery of insulin, the life of a
diabetic was bleak. Individuals afflicted with severe cases usually
died after a short illness. A person with a mild case could look
forward to five or possibly ten years of life on a program of rigid
deprivation. The only tool available was diet, and until the
twentieth century doctors relied on their intuition, little being
known about the causes of diabetes or about nutrition. Most pre-
insulin diets were so harsh they became impossible to follow and
some doctors went so far as to lock up their patients to prevent
cheating. Diabetics on rigid diets sometimes even fasted a day every
two weeks. Patients were sometimes forced to eat unpleasant things,
such as rancid meat or melted fat. Nausea was induced to produce
vomiting. One school of thought during this period was that the more
emaciated a patient was, the faster he would recover.[9]

Fortunately, diabetics are no longer subjected to such
torture. The American Diabetes Association now recommends that a
diabetic's diet be kept as flexible as possible, with a wide option
of food choices, taking into consideration the person's personality,
life-style, and physical condition. Diabetics need essentially the
same basic nutrients as non-diabetics, and regularity of meals is
important.[10]

The discovery of insulin in 1921 and subsequent use of animal
insulin have changed the lives of insulin-dependent diabetics.
Insulin was first used for a human on January 11, 1922, by Drs.
Frederick Banting and Charles Best, on a teenager named Leonard
Thompson. "Almost immediately, Thompson improved, and within days
after being on the verge of death, the seventy-five pounder had
dramatically regained his weight and strength."[11] Drs. Banting and
Best later won a Nobel Prize for their work on diabetes.

But though life is easier since then for the diabetic, it is
far from perfect. A diabetic who fails to eat on a regular schedule
risks going into insulin shock, or hypoglycemia, which results from
low blood sugar and can be caused by a missed meal, an unusual amount
of exercise, or a mistake in insulin dosage. Insulin shock comes on
rapidly and is characterized by symptoms such as sweating, intense
hunger, palpitations, inability to concentrate, and unsteadiness.[12]
The victim may appear to be drunk, as in the case of an apparent
drunk my brother, working on the police force, saw being dealt with
by another policeman. My brother, observing the same symptoms of
insulin shock that my diabetic father gets after missing a meal, fed
the man a candy bar. The alleged drunk soon returned to normal with
no memory of his previous experience. After a small dosage of a
concentrated sugar, insulin shock will subside as quickly as it
occurred, but if insulin shock goes untreated, it can lead to a coma
and death.

A diabetic coma results from high blood sugar caused by
overeating or forgetting to take one's dose of insulin. As
distinguished from insulin shock, a coma comes on slowly, taking
days or even weeks to develop, and is characterized by frequent
urination, thirst, hunger, vomiting, tiredness, and a breath odor

sometimes described as smelling like pear drops or new mown hay.[13] Fatal if left untreated, a diabetic coma can be treated with a small dose of insulin buffered with a little sugar to prevent nausea.

Two lines of research are being followed to find a more effective control of adult diabetes. Transplantations of the pancreas have been tried in about ninety cases, but so far the operations have been mostly unsuccessful because of tissue rejection or other complications. One patient, however, lived four and a half years after a transplant and required no further insulin.[14] More hopeful at that moment are experiments being conducted in Toronto, Canada and elsewhere to provide an artificial pancreas which regulates the insulin flow according to the patient's needs. At present the patient wears a pouch around the waist. Drs. Bernard Leibel and Michael Albisser of Toronto's Hospital for Sick Children want someday to develop a "pillbox-sized implant" but warn this is still some years down the road.[15]

Although the future looks brighter for diabetics these days, it should be better. As stated by Dr. Gilman D. Grave of the National Institute of Child Health and Human Development, "Unfortunately. besides intensified surveillance, dietary prudence, nutritional manipulation, exercise, and the avoidance of stress and obesity, modern medicine has little to offer."[16] There is no cure for diabetes, only treatment. In 1974, the year the National Commission on Diabetes was established, 338,000 deaths were caused by diabetes and its complications. In 1975, the number three killer cost the American taxpayer three billion dollars in lost wages, health care, and disability payment.[17] Of the 3,340,000 babies born in 1979, approximately 10,000 will be insulin-dependent diabetics by the year 2000, and we have no way of predicting who they will be.[18] Such statistics call for more research. Although diabetics are grateful for such progress as has been made, for millions like my grandmother and my father, the only real solution is a cure.

FOOTNOTES

[1]Henry Dolger, How to Live with Diabetes (New York: W.W. Norton, 1958, p. 14.

[2]Dolger, pp. 19-20.

[3]Lou Joseph, A Doctor Discusses Diabetes (Chicago: Budlong Press, 1977), pp. 1-2.

[4]U.S. Department of Health, Education and Welfare, Report of the National Commission on Diabetes, Vol. 1 (Washington, D.C.: DHEW Publication No. (NIH) 76-1018, 1975) p. 2.

[5]Ibid., pp. 1-2.

[6]Matt Clark and Marianna Gosnell, "Battling Diabetes," Newsweek, December 10, 1979, pp. 120, 122.

[7]Clark and Gosnell, p. 117.

[8]Peter Gwynne and Emily F. Newhall, "Juvenile Diabetes: A Virus to Blame," Newsweek, June 4, 1979, p. 50.

[9]Dolger, p. 53.

[10]American Diabetes Association, "Special Report: Principles of Nutrition and Dietary Recommendations for Individuals with Diabetes Mellitus: 1979," Diabetes, 28 (November, 1979) 1027-1029.

[11]Joseph I. Goodman, with W. Watts Biggers, Diabetes Without Fear (New York: Arbor House, 1978), p. 18.

[12]W. G. Oakley, D. A. Pyke, and K. W. Taylor, Diabetes and Its Management (Oxford: Blackwell Scientific Publications, 1973), pp. 87-88.

[13]Oakley et al., p. 98.

[14]Clark and Gosnell, p. 122.

[15]Terry Poulton, "Diabetes: There May Be Life Beyond the Needle," Maclean's, March 6, 1978, p. 62

[16]Gilman D. Grave, ed., Early Detection of Potential Diabetes: The Problems and the Promise (New York: Raven Press, 1979), p. xiv.

[17]Joseph, p. 3

[18]Grave, p. xi.

BIBLIOGRAPHY

American Diabetes Association. "Special Report: Principles of Nutrition and Dietary Recommendations for Individuals with Diabetes Mellitus: 1979." Diabetes, 28 (November, 1979), 1027-1030.

Clark, Matt, and Marianna Gosnell. "Battling Diabetes." Newsweek, December 10, 1979, pp. 117, 120, 122, 124.

Dolger, Henry. How to Live with Diabetes. New York: W. W. Norton, 1958.

Goodman, Joseph I., with W. Watts Biggers. Diabetes Without Fear. New York: Arbor House, 1978.

Grave, Gilman D., ed. Early Detection of Potential Diabetes: The Problems and the Promise. New York: Raven Press, 1979.

Gwynne, Peter, and Emily F. Newhall. "Juvenile Diabetes: A Virus to Blame." Newsweek, June 4, 1979, p. 50

Joseph, Lou. A Doctor Discusses Diabetes. Chicago: Budlong Press, 1977.

Oakley, W. G., D. A. Pyke, and K. W. Taylor. Diabetes and Its Management. Oxford: Blackwell Scientific Publications, 1973.

Poulton, Terry. "Diabetes: There May Be Life Beyond the Needle." Maclean's, March 6, 1978, pp. 62-63.

U. S. Department of Health, Education and Welfare. Report of the National Commission on Diabetes. Vol. 1. Washington, D.C.: DHEW Publication No. (NIH) 76-1018, 1975.

CHECKLIST   *Drawing on the World around You*

Preparations.   Check off each item when completed.

Activity 9-1   Finding a Subject . . . .
Activity 9-2   Collecting Resource Material . . . .
Activity 9-3   Organizing Your Material . . . .
Activity 9-4   Introductions and Conclusions . . . .

Goals to Be Achieved.   Write your answers on a separate sheet. Explain fully.

1. Have you expressed a conclusion (central idea, thesis) *of your own* and supported it with interesting and convincing evidence?
2. Does your paper hang together in a logical, unified way, so that a reader can follow easily?
3. Have you carefully checked for all mechanical, grammatical, and typographical errors *in your final draft?*
4. Are you satisfied you have written an interesting, worthwhile paper?

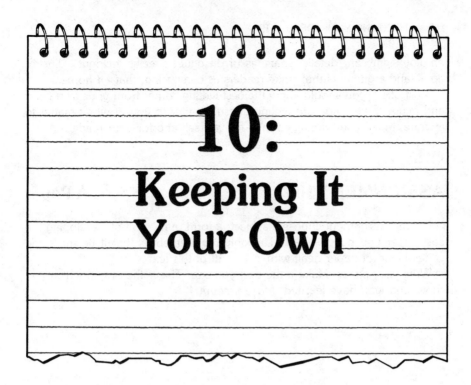

10:
Keeping It Your Own

You have arrived almost at the end of this course. In each chapter so far, one more step has been added toward making your writing effective and interesting. In this chapter there is nothing new. This is your opportunity to put everything together in a way that is meaningful and effective for you.

The crucial thing about this course—or any course, for that matter—is what you know or are able to do *at the end of the term.* The writing problems have become increasingly complex as you have gone along; it is more challenging to write an interesting research paper than to tell the story of your canoe trip down the river. Writing good term papers will also probably be more useful to you in the immediate future as you progress through your college years.

It is well to stop for a moment and see what has been happening. Perhaps now you can see more clearly the "central idea" of this book: *Writing is an expression of your own thoughts, unified by a central idea or purpose and developed in an interesting and complete way through the use of significant details and specific incidents.* By now, you should have a firm grasp on the realization that it is *you* talking, saying things that have meaning for you. This does *not* change as the subject matter becomes less personal. Your thoughts and ideas are as much a part of you and need to be expressed as honestly and effectively as your experiences and feelings.

By now, too, you should be constantly aware of *writing for a reader,* and know that to make your writing alive and interesting to readers you must employ significant details, snatches of dialogue, specific incidents, illustrations, and arguments that strike readers as convincing, that *hit home*.

Most of all, you should know the best writing comes from your own heart and mind. If what you are writing doesn't matter to you, it won't matter to anyone. Make your writing count—for yourself and for your reader.

ASSIGNMENT 10   A Paper

✔   For this assignment choose a subject, a form, a method of developing the best paper you possibly can. The only requirement is that it be the same general kind of paper dealt with in Part III of this text.

Write your paper. Make it the best you can. This is the one in which you show what you have learned. *Make it count.*

Minigrammars

Many students have not been exposed to grammar since the eighth grade and have never learned the "correct" use of language. If they do not learn in college, they probably will never learn. This is a sad—but true—fact.

A STUDENT

GENERAL INSTRUCTIONS

Each of the first five minigrammars begins with a *Diagnostic Section,* consisting of one or more exercises. To determine whether you have good grasp of the grammatical principles discussed in the minigrammar, do the exercises in the diagnostic section. Don't worry if you don't understand or have trouble; the purpose is to *find out* what you know. At the end of the diagnostic section, check the key in the *Key Section* that begins on p. 233. If you have done the exercises correctly, skip the minigrammar. But if you have made even one or two mistakes, read the minigrammar and do the exercises. At the end of each minigrammar, there is a *Check Yourself Section.* If, after doing the exercises in this section and consulting the key, you still feel uncertain, consult your instructor for further assistance.

MINIGRAMMAR

A:
Agreement
between Subjects
and Predicates

DIAGNOSTIC SECTION A

1. On a separate sheet, make a list of all the nouns and pronouns in the following passage.

Example

The boys saw the first one almost immediately.   boys
one

The first thing every morning was a plunge in the lake. Though the water was crisp, it was refreshing. It took my breath away, but the instant it did my breath came back. It was a fantastic, natural feeling, one of the wonders of being alive on those mornings. The early plunge became a ritual. I did not dare to miss it; I felt I would be cheating myself if I did. It was something I had to do. The warmth of the sun felt wonderful. We were cleansed by the clear waters and dried straight from the sun. It was as if the sun were ours, and its rays would touch us before anything else on earth.

2. Make a list of all the verb forms in the following passage. Include verb forms used as nouns and adjectives. Where infinitives occur, copy *to* as in *to go* in the example.

Example

After I tied my shoe, I was ready to go skating.	tied
	was
	to go
	skating

I hazily realized I was awake, and rolled over. But the sounds of birds singing and water splashing tugged at my head until I sat up and looked around. The mountainside was ablaze with sunlight broken into a million diamonds by the dew, while where the three of us lay, the world was still shrouded under the chill haze cast by the opposite peak. Now completely awake, I crept out of my sleeping bag and began to run. The ground passed by in a patchwork of rocks, grass, and mounds of melting snow as I strained toward the oncoming line of sunshine. The air was crisp and thin, and my breathing soon became labored.

3. Make a list of the subjects in the following passage and the predicates that belong to them. Put a single line under each subject and a double line under the predicate. Do not list verb forms that are not predicates.

Example

| A hawk and some other birds sailed in endless circles. | hawk birds sailed |

Whenever the wind blows, they are there, those small free-spirited objects scuttling around in corners. Dead leaves, dirty, black and brown, fragile to the touch, scurry around with the waste paper, looking messy, creating an empty dry sound, and seeming out of place. Man is constantly trying to suppress and destroy these independent objects. We are forever collecting and burning leaves, yet always more are there, rattling around, spiting man. The free spirit of old leaves can really be admired. They seem to be reaching for life after death. They resist captivity, blowing, moving, rambling, rattling. Dead leaves have true independence.

End of Diagnostic Section A. Check the key on p. 233.

In the explanations and exercises that follow, you need not do all the exercises, just the ones that pinpoint the problems you have. When you are fairly sure of yourself, turn to the Check Yourself Section at the end of Minigrammar A (p. 180) and do the subsections there.

IDENTIFYING VERBS

Many grammar problems cannot be dealt with easily unless you can identify subjects of sentences and clauses and the verbs (or predicates) that belong to them. If you have trouble identifying verbs, here are some points that may help you.

1. Most verbs tell what someone does: *sing, run, come, think.*
2. Two common verbs have multiple forms: *to be* and *to have.* (These include *be, is, are, were, being, have, has, had, having.*)
3. Auxiliary or helping verbs form another category: these include *would, should, may, might, can, could,* and *will.* Forms of *to be* and *to have* may also be used as helping verbs.

Example

He *will be coming* soon. The main verb is *coming.* The verb forms *will* and *be* help *coming* to express the idea that the action will take place in the future.

If you can remember these three things, you should be able to locate most verb forms.

Another signal may be the endings *-ing* or *-ed,* though not all words ending in these suffixes are verbs.

Exercise A-1   *Identifying Verb Forms*

List all the verb forms in the following passages. Keep these clues in mind:

1. If you see a verb form like *to be* or *to come,* list the word *to* as well as the verb itself; the two words work together to form the *infinitive* of the verb. Do not list *to* in other instances, e.g., in *to being* in a sentence like "He objected to being told what to do"; the verb forms here are *objected, being, told,* and *to do.*
2. In negatives, the word *not* and the contraction *n't* do not constitute part of the verb, so don't list them.

Both of us were stubborn, self-centered, and unsure of ourselves at thirteen. We met the first day at junior high. I was standing alone by the front entrance. Everywhere I looked there were hundreds of kids. All of them seemed to know where they were going and what they were doing. They only took time to talk to this person or that before continuing on their way. I felt lost and alone, not recognizing anybody or knowing where to go. I didn't know what to do next and was trying to get up courage to ask someone when a girl coming through the door said, "Do you know where we're supposed to go?" Of course I didn't, but I didn't want her to know that.

If consultation with the key shows you can't pick out verbs, swallow your pride or overcome your inertia and seek help from your instructor now. Each exercise builds on the previous one and plowing blindly ahead will only dig you into a hole. Be honest with yourself at every step; it is only yourself you cheat otherwise. *The minute you feel you are out of your depth, ask for help.*

If you recognize verb forms, we can begin to discuss agreement between subjects and predicates. Though not all verb forms are used as predicates, for now we will look only at verb forms that make up predicates. Agreement between subjects and predicates usually involves getting singular subjects with singular predicates, and plural subjects with plural predicates. If you have trouble remembering the meaning of *singular* and *plural*, try associating *singular* with *single*, meaning *one*.

Examples

> *Singular subjects require singular predicates:*
> He (singular) *buys* good clothes. (*Not* He buy good clothes.)
> *Plural subjects require plural predicates:*
> The angry people (plural) *shout* and *scream*. (*Not* The angry people shouts and screams.)

IDENTIFYING NOUNS AND PRONOUNS

Once predicates are located, the next problem is to locate the subject. The traditional way is to ask "Who?" or "What?" in front of the predicate. *Who* buys? *Who* shout and scream? If you can do it that way, fine. Go ahead. But be careful. In a sentence like "One of the girls is sick," the subject is *one*, not *girls.*

Either nouns or pronouns can be the subject of a sentence or clause. Nouns aren't too hard: words like *mother, cat, justice, moon,* and *people* are nouns. They are the names of something. Pronouns are words that can be substituted for nouns or used in the place of them. They include the following:

I, me, my, mine	who, whom, whose
you, your, yours	that
he, his, him	which
she, her, hers	what
it, its	this, these
we, our, ours, us	that, those
they, their, theirs, them	each
everyone	both
any	one
all	every

Exercise A-2   *Identifying Nouns and Pronouns*

List all the nouns and pronouns in the following passage.

I didn't plan to see her last night, but a warmth flowed through my blood when I thought about her. I had visions of her sitting at her desk, bored with her studies, looking foxy as a beauty queen. I thought of all the things we could be doing together. It was just one of those nights when I couldn't get my mind off her. I decided to give her a call, just to see how she was, but I got the "jitters" as I dialed. I felt like a fifteen-year-old again, making my first date with the girl who sat next to me in class. Just as then, I panicked after the first ring, gasped as her roommate answered, and hung up.

IDENTIFYING SUBJECTS OF SENTENCES

Now you should be able to find the subjects and predicates of sentences and clauses. Fortunately there is a predictable pattern in English which helps, though it is not infallible any more than the "who/what" method. But trying it on simple sentences may help you become accustomed to finding the subjects of sentences.

The pattern is that *in a question beginning with a verb form, the first noun(s) or pronoun(s) after the initial verb is (are) the subject(s) of the sentence.* If you can turn the sentence into a question beginning with a verb form, you can find the subject. Look at these examples:

Sentence	Question
He buys good clothes.	Does <u>he</u> buy good clothes? (The first pronoun after the verb form *does* is the subject.)
The angry people shout and scream.	Do the angry <u>people</u> shout and scream? (*People* is the first noun after the verb form *do*.)
One of the girls is sick.	Is <u>one</u> of the girls sick? (*One* is the subject, being the first pronoun after the verb form *is*.)

Note: The above assumes you would not pick *the* or *angry* as a noun or pronoun. If you have trouble with that, see your instructor now.

Exercise A-3   *Identifying Subjects of Sentences*

1. First change each of the following sentences into a question beginning with a verb form. If the sentence has a form of *to be* in it, begin with a form of that verb, as in "Is one of the girls sick?" Otherwise begin your question with *do, does,* or *did.*
2. Underline the subject of each sentence.

1. The beauties of each day never ceased to thrill him.
2. Screaming happily, the children race out to the beach.
3. Blasting into town on their motorbikes came two young men in black jackets.

4. Everybody in town is excited about the President's visit.

5. Both the men and the women voted against allowing nudity on the public beach.

Exercise A-4   *Identifying Multiple Subjects of Sentences*

The following sentences have more than one subject. List all the subjects. Change the sentences into questions if you find it necessary, following the same formula you used in Exercise A-3.

1. Horses, motorcycles, and jeeps are not allowed on this road.

2. Six Boy Scouts, two acid freaks, a retired couple, and a family of four on vacation

   rode the lift to the top of the mountain.

3. Sue, Betty, and I went along.

4. A very large man and a tiny woman entered the restaurant.

A special case: When a sentence starts with the word *there* followed by some form of *to be (There is, There were, There have been),* do not choose *there* as the subject. These phrases are just introductory to get the sentence going. The subject will, however, be the first noun or pronoun in the question you make, just as before.

Example

There were many men on the landing.
Were there many <u>men</u> on the landing? (Eliminating "there" as a possible subject, we come to the true subject: *men.)*

Exercise A-5   *Identifying Subjects in Sentences with* **There** (is, are, were)

List the subject or subjects in the following sentences.

1. There was snow on the ground this morning.

2. There were two apples in the refrigerator.

3. In the barn there were three horses, two cows, and a fat sow with an uncountable

   number of squirming piglets.

(In a sentence like number 3 above, where extra information, such as "in the barn," has been shifted to the beginning of the sentence, put such information *at the end* of the question you form for the purpose of finding the subject. Do the same with information that interrupts the flow of the main sentence, as does "according to bystanders" in sentence 3 of Exercise A-6.)

Exercise A-6   *Identifying Subjects of Sentences*

List the subjects in the following sentences.

1. A balanced social life, as well as steady attention to studies, is an important part of college life.

2. His long record of faithful service and outstanding performance qualifies him for promotion.

3. There were, according to bystanders, many reasons for the fight.

4. The bright red tongue of the wagon stuck out into the road.

5. There is always a chance of coming in first.

6. The effort of lifting the heavy log cost George a great deal in energy and stamina.

7. All the windows and doors were broken and hanging on their hinges.

IDENTIFYING SUBJECTS AND PREDICATES

By now you should be able to find subjects without resorting to questions. Many sentences do not readily convert into questions, so eventually you must move beyond this "crutch." Most of the next sentences are of this kind. Remember that sentences may have more than one subject and/or predicate.

Exercise A-7   *Identifying Subjects and Predicates*

List all the subjects and predicates in the following sentences. Underline the subjects with single lines and the predicates with double lines. (*Note:* if no verb goes with a noun or pronoun, the noun or pronoun is *not* a subject; it is used in another way in the sentence. Similarly, if there is no subject for a verb, the verb is not a predicate. Do not list such nouns, pronouns, and verbs.)

Example

1. The boys and girls ran into the building and climbed over the seats.   1. boys girls ran climbed
2. When I came home, I found two cats on the porch.   2. I came I found

1. George and Jim decided to back Tom for president.

2. When trying to learn a new skill, perseverance and patience will be valuable characteristics.

3. The winning contestant from New York, along with those from New Jersey and Pennsylvania, was being flown to the West Coast.

4. The best and wittiest speaker wasn't Mrs. Grant, but it was she who won the contest.

5. College graduates these days are having a harder time finding jobs, because competition is keen.

6. Marvin was only sixteen years old when he started college.

7. Our college should have won the baseball game yesterday, but it still wouldn't have put them ahead of the pack.

8. There are numerous reasons for choosing to go to college: to prepare oneself to earn a better living, to get away from home, to put off having to assume responsibility for one's own life, to find a husband, or even to dip into the great fund of knowledge and learn as much as possible about oneself and the world one lives in.

9. The Supreme Court decision of 1954 has focused the attention of the nation on the inequities of the separate-but-equal principle of education.

10. Our president, Sam Howard, rigged the election to suit his own purposes.

If you made mistakes in the foregoing exercise, don't despair. These sentences are difficult, purposely made so to see how far you can go in finding subjects and predicates in complicated situations. The important thing is to understand your mistakes. If you do not understand, seek help.

AGREEMENT BETWEEN SUBJECTS AND PREDICATES

Now that you are finding subjects and predicates with reasonable ease, let's go back to making them agree in number. The first problem involves choosing the correct form for present tense verbs (when what is happening in the sentence is going on now; e.g., He *buys* good clothes.). Note that the verb here ends in -s. That is the idea to remember.

In all cases in present tense, except when the subject is a form of you or I, *add -s for singular verbs* (s = singular; say it over a few times until you get it in your mind: in present tense, s equals singular—one—except when the subject is *you* or *I*).

Examples

he buys, she buys, it buys, Tom buys, the woman buys
In all other cases, leave off the s:
I buy, you buy, they buy, the people buy

Exercise A-8

Supplying Present Tense Forms of Verbs

On a separate sheet, list the right forms for the *present tense* of the verbs in parentheses. (Do *not* add any ending other than *s* or *es*).

1. When I am in town, I always _____ a newspaper. (buy)

2. She sometimes _____ a lie if it suits her to do so. (tell)

3. Don't you ever _____ to church? (go)

4. They _____ the office to suit themselves, though we don't always agree with them. (run)

5. Screaming at the top of her voice, Susan _____ across the street. (dash)

6. In a successful class, the teacher and student _____ to develop a productive learning experience. (cooperate)

The second problem in getting agreement between subjects and their verbs is merely a matter of being sure you have identified the subject or subjects properly and then using a singular or plural form of the verb accordingly.

Exercise A-9

Providing Agreement in Number between Subjects and Predicates

List the proper forms for the predicates in the following sentences, choosing from those in parentheses. Be sure you have located the correct subject or subjects. Keep the following points in mind:

1. There may be multiple subjects. (Men, women, and children are coming to the party.) This usually means a plural subject.
2. If multiple subjects are joined by *or* (or *nor*), that means only one *or* the other of the subjects. (Either Tom or Jerry is going.) If all subjects are singular, use a singular verb. If the subjects are plural, use a plural verb. (Either the Smiths or the Joneses are in the lead car.)
3. There may be numerous words or phrases between a true subject and the verb. (Some of the boys have gone.)
4. The words *each, every, nothing,* and *one* signal a singular verb to follow. (Nothing in the cupboard was missing. Every man, woman, and child in the country is coming.)
5. The nouns or pronouns that follow phrases like *together with* and *as well as* are *not* part of the subject. (Bob, together with his mother and father, is on his way.)

1. The house cat and a lion _____ related. (is, are)

2. The captain of the regiment, a dashing figure, _____ received the order to advance. (have, has)

3. Neither you nor your brother _____ twice before you speak. (think, thinks)

4. Each of the children _____ lining up at the front of the hall. (are, is)

5. Which one of those boys _____ fastest? (runs, run)

6. Every bit of garbage and every bottle _____ to be picked up before you leave! (are, is)

7. The socks, shirts, and shorts all _____ in the white wash. (go, goes)

8. Don't any of you _____ near me! (comes, come)

9. Nothing he says ever _____ as if he knows what he is talking about. (sound, sounds)

10. The scenery, together with all the props, _____ sent to the wrong town. (were, was)

If you feel fairly confident about your ability to pick out subjects and predicates and to make them agree in number, try the Check Yourself Section that follows. If you make more than one mistake, see your instructor before you go on to the next minigrammar, which will assume you now have no difficulty in picking out subjects and their predicates.

CHECK YOURSELF SECTION A

Do both of the following subsections before you look at the key.

1. List all the subjects and their predicates in the following section. Do *not* list any noun, pronoun, or verb form that is used in other ways in the sentence. Do not consider infinitives (*to be, to come,* etc.) as part of any main verb. Underline with single lines for subjects, double lines for predicates.

With the problem of energy becoming more publicized every day, it is time we took a look at how much potential trouble actually exists. For many years this country has produced its energy from sources that are exhaustible. Coal and wood were first; next came natural gas and oil with their derivatives gasoline, kerosene, and other energy fuels. This country has been industrialized for less than one hundred years, and already we have used almost all our known energy deposits. We import fuels, and although the big companies assure us there are numerous areas that may yield tons of fuel, they haven't been discovered yet. What are we going to do when we "run out of gas" and cannot import enough to satisfy our needs?

2. Choose the appropriate verb forms in the following passage and list them on a separate paper.

When I _____ (looks, look) at the front of the room, I _____ (feels, feel) like a prisoner in a computerized, sterile, stainless steel environment. The beige paint on the walls _____ (appears, appear) drab and bland, as if attempting to stifle man's quest for color and life. The gleaming aluminum chalk tray, electric plug, and light switch _____ (is, are) symbols of man's technology ruling man. A hospital would look like this if they taught classes in it. Everything _____ (has, have) a precise location. It _____ (doesn't, don't) seem natural. The chairs _____ (isn't, aren't) built for comfort; they _____ (looks, look) all alike. Rows of green desks _____ (makes, make) a mechanical pattern. The only signs that man _____ (was, were) ever here _____ (is, are) the chalk dust on the board, the scuff marks on the floor, and two bulletins on the bulletin board. The hum of the air conditioner and the thermostat on the wall _____ (is, are) a constant reminder of technology's effort to push back nature.

End of Check Yourself Section A. Check the key now.

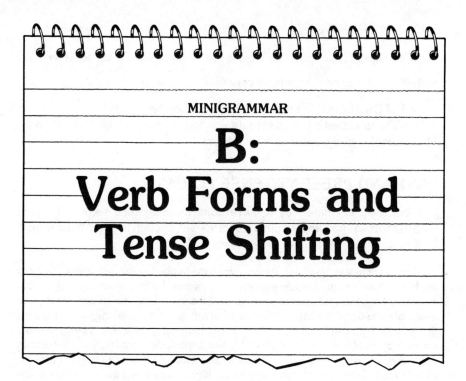

B:
Verb Forms and Tense Shifting

DIAGNOSTIC SECTION B

1. Copy the following passage and underline all verb forms.
2. Verb forms that have subjects are called predicates. Underline all the predicates with a double line. Be sure to include auxiliary (helping) verbs.
3. Some of the predicates are not in Standard English. Cross those out and write the Standard English forms above them.

Example

                                                    pulled

    Mom and Dad found it: a tarnished silver trumpet with valves that just pull themselves up after they were pushed down.

I didn't want to start band, but they convince me to play. At the first lesson, I takes out my horn, showed it to my teacher and was curtly inform it ain't worth five dollars. But somehow, with lessons, practice sessions, and tears, I managed to get through the first lesson book and into the band. I learn fast that sitting at the end of the trumpet section in the junior high band wasn't enjoyable. Finally, thoroughly frustrated, I begun to show up at study hall instead of band class. My band instructor, very angry when he finds out, yank me out of study hall. I went back to band and hate it, but I kepted at it.

183

From last chair in junior high I progress to first in senior high. That's how I learn the truth of the old saying, "Anything is possible."

End of Diagnostic Section B. Check the key on p. 236.
Don't be too upset if you made mistakes in this section. It isn't an easy one. Many people have trouble with verb forms.

PAST AND PRESENT TENSE FORMS

There is an alternate way to have done the diagnostic section. If yours reads as follows, you know your verb forms well enough to skip Minigrammar B, if you wish.

I don't want to start band, but they convince me to play. At the first lesson I take out my horn, show it to my teacher and am curtly informed it isn't worth five dollars. Bu. somehow, with lessons, practice sessions, and tears, I manage to get through the first lesson book and into the band. I learn fast that sitting at the end of the trumpet section in the junior high band isn't enjoyable. Finally, thoroughly frustrated, I begin to show up at study hall instead of band class. My band instructor, very angry when he finds out, yanks me out of study hall. I go back to band and hate it, but I keep at it. From last chair in junior high I progress to first in senior high. That's how I learn the truth of the old saying, "Anything is possible."

The difference between the paragraph in the key and this one is a difference in *time*. The one above is in *present tense*, meaning things happen in the present, *now*. The paragraph in the key is in *past tense*, meaning that things have already happened, that they are in the *past*. Sometimes you will want to use one tense; sometimes, the other. There are other tenses, but for now learn to recognize these two and be able to name them, so that we can use the terms in the future.

Exercise B-1   *Identifying Past and Present Tense Verb Forms*

Identify each of the following sentences as either *present* or *past*, depending on the time indicated by the form of the predicate.

1. It was a discouraging start.
2. In eighth grade, I persuade my parents to let me have a better horn.
3. Just when I got the hang of playing, we began to march outside.
4. I can't keep in line, let alone play and stay in step.
5. I still needed a better horn, so I started delivering papers to save up for the trumpet I had my eye on.

6. I have been looking forward to high school, but right away I find out that band is tougher than I expected.

7. People who sit at the top of each section usually have three years under their belts.

8. Heading down to a music camp the next summer is great.

9. Only a lone senior sat ahead of me my sophomore year; his sound was silky smooth.

10. My trumpet screams out high notes and finishes with a flurry that leaves the air shimmering; the crowd loves it!

Exercise B-2   *Using Present Tense*

Write the above ten sentences as a paragraph, keeping it all in present tense.

Exercise B-3   *Using Past Tense*

Write the same ten sentences as a paragraph, keeping it all in past tense.

CONSISTENT VERB FORMS

By now you should have the concepts of present and past tense firmly in mind. In your writing, it is generally best to be consistent, keeping to one tense in any given piece of writing and not shifting back and forth. The student who wrote about his trials and tribulations with the trumpet did not shift as indicated in Exercise B-1; the tenses were jumbled to give you practice in recognizing them. At times, of course, you want to shift for a good reason; the trumpet player put everything in past tense until he came to his final night of glory, when his instrument screamed and shimmered. Then he shifted to present tense, to convey the impression that his performance was occurring *as the reader watched.* This sort of shifting is often effective, but until you are sure of yourself, you had better not try it.

We have already talked about present tense forms in Minigrammar A; if you are not sure yet when to add the problematical s, review that section now.

The next problem is the selection of correct past tense forms. In both present and past tense, many confusions arise because speech patterns are different from written patterns. Lots of people neither hear nor pronounce the s at the end of present tense verbs. Similarly, the *-ed* at the end of past tense verbs creates difficulty. Some speak a dialect that does not use the *-ed* form. Sometimes the word is spelled differently from the way it is pronounced, as in the verbs *stopped* (pronounced *stopt*) or *pronounced* (pronounced *pronounst*). Sometimes the *-ed* at the end of the verb merges into the opening sound of the next word, as in *used to* and *supposed to*. In written work, the accepted Standard English is "I us*ed* to go to the park," *not* "I use to go to the park," and "He is suppos*ed* to come tonight," *not* "He is suppose to come tonight." Regardless of how the verb *sounds* to you, when you write you are expected to use the Standard English form.

There is a whole category of verbs, called irregular verbs, that don't use an *-ed* to denote the past tense. The only way to be sure of these verbs is to memorize them. Most of you were at one time asked to memorize the *principal parts* of verbs, and by now most of you use these principal parts without a second thought. But some verbs may give you trouble.

The first principal part is the present tense form when the subject is *I, you,* or *they* (or a plural noun). It is also the form that combines with *to* to form the *infinitive (to be, to come)*. The infinitive is important both because it is used a great deal, and because it is, so to speak, the *name* we give the verb: when we talk about a verb we usually give its infinitive form, e.g., "The verb *to be* is often overused."

The second principal part is the past tense form for the verb.

The third principal part is called the *past participle* and is used when there are helping verbs in the past tense. Past participles are used in verb phrases like "has been called," "were bitten," "have gone," "would have fallen."

Note: The word *of* is not a helping verb. Many people hear — and therefore write — "would *of* fallen" for "would *have* fallen" or "could *of* gone" for "could *have* gone." If you are one, watch out particularly for this problem in your writing.

(There is another "part" to the verb, called the *present participle*. This is formed by adding *-ing* to the present infinitive [*go* + *ing* = *going*] and is often used with present tense helping verbs, e.g., "He is going.")

Exercise B-4   *Learning Irregular Verb Forms*

Following is a list of irregular verbs, with their principal parts. Cover the second two columns with a piece of paper, and write down the past and past participle forms for each infinitive or present tense verb. List those you missed. Wait until another day and then repeat the process with your new list. Keep doing this until you make no mistakes. Then go back and do the whole list again. *Make a mental note of the verbs you have trouble with,* so that when you use them later, red flags of caution will go up and you will be particularly careful.

Infinitive (present)	Past tense	Past participle
arise	arose	arisen
be	was	been
begin	began	begun
bite	bit	bitten
blow	blew	blown
break	broke	broken
bring	brought	brought
burst	burst	burst
cast	cast	cast
catch	caught	caught
choose	chose	chosen
come	came	come
dig	dug	dug
dive	dived, dove	dived
do	did	done
draw	drew	drawn
drink	drank	drunk
drive	drove	driven
eat	ate	eaten
fall	fell	fallen
fight	fought	fought
flee	fled	fled
fly	flew	flown
forget	forgot	forgotten
freeze	froze	frozen
get	got	got, gotten
give	gave	given
go	went	gone
grow	grew	grown
hide	hid	hidden
know	knew	known
lay	laid	laid
lead	led	led
lend	lent	lent
lie (recline)	lay	lain
pay	paid	paid
ride	rode	ridden
ring	rang	rung
rise	rose	risen
run	ran	run
see	saw	seen
set	set	set
shake	shook	shaken
shine (as the sun)	shone	shone
shrink	shrank	shrunk
sing	sang	sung
sink	sank	sunk
sit	sat	sat
speak	spoke	spoken
spring	sprang	sprung
steal	stole	stolen

Infinitive (present)	Past tense	Past participle
strive	strove	striven
swear	swore	sworn
swim	swam	swum
swing	swung	swung
take	took	taken
tear	tore	torn
throw	threw	thrown
wake	woke, waked	waked
wear	wore	worn
weave	wove	woven
wring	wrung	wrung
write	wrote	written

Most verbs, however, form both their past tense and their past participle by adding -ed (kick, kicked, kicked). If there is already an e at the end of the verb, only a d is added (shuffle, shuffled, shuffled). Sometimes the final consonant is doubled, usually to indicate pronunciation (planed, as in "He planed the board" and planned, as in "He planned a trip"). If there is a y at the end of the verb, preceded by a consonant, the y is changed to i before the -ed is added (carry, carried, carried). If the y at the end is preceded by a vowel, simply add the -ed (play, played, played). These few hints won't guarantee you one hundred percent against error, but they will go a long way.

Examples

Infinitive (present)	Past tense	Past participle
stop	stopped	stopped
pile	piled	piled
fry	fried	fried
pull	pulled	pulled
sway	swayed	swayed

Exercise B-5   *Practicing Principal Parts of Verbs*

Copy the following present tense verbs and add the past tense and past participle.

try	satisfy	mount
hunt	troll	run
judge	hide	plead
urge	sprout	flop
cast	wash	conceive

pay	plow	catch
set	choose	bring
sit		

Exercise B-6   *Using Past Tense*

Change the following passage from present tense to past tense.

Traveling with the carnival, we come to a small town with a population of about a thousand. This is the last county fair we are supposed to play in this year's circuit of the north. When we arrive, it is cold and damp. Soon it begins to rain. What a drag: another hick town! But that's where the money is.

The fellows start setting up the rides and concession stands. There comes the clang, clang sound of iron against iron. Someone yells, "You s.o.b., watch it!" Up come the steel skeletons of the rides above the building, outlined against the sky and trees. Everyone is hurrying, for the opening is only a few hours away.

Exercise B-7   *Using Present Tense*

Change the following passage from past tense to present tense.

At last, opening! The night was bright with colorful lights from the rides and they seemed to say, "Come take a ride on me, and I'll give you the thrill of your life!" From the carousel came the sound of the calliope playing a catching tune, and before I knew it, I was humming: de-de-dum, de-de-dum, da-da-dum.

Across the way, a girl yelled, "Snow cones, snow cones, get your snow cones!" Ah, what was that smell? It was onions frying. I envisioned the hamburgers and French fries. The aroma floated through the air and made me hungry. Growl, there went my stomach!

VERB FORMS USED AS NOUNS AND ADJECTIVES

By this time, you should be reasonably secure about subjects and predicates, and about how to make them agree in both number and tense. Not all verb forms are employed as predicates, however. Now that you know subjects and predicates, you should be able to recognize verb forms that are not a part of a predicate.

Verb forms may be used as nouns. *To run* is an action, of course, as in "I try *to run* five miles a day," but *to run* may also *name* the action and function in the sentence as, for example, the subject of the sentence: "*To run* five miles in the open air strengthens my heart, lungs, and legs." The predicate of this sentence is *strengthens*. The answer to the question "*What* or *Who* strengthens?" is "To run five miles in the open air." This phrase is the complete subject of the sentence; the simple subject is *to run*. In the following examples, verb forms used as nouns are underlined with a single line. The predicates of the sentences are underlined with a double line.

Examples

Singing is one of my favorite hobbies.
Having prepared for the test resulted in my acing it.
My goal was to sleep about twenty-four hours.

Exercise B-8   *Recognizing Verb Forms Used as Nouns*

In the following passage, list the verb forms that are used as nouns. Make a second list of verb forms used as predicates. (Be sure to include helping verbs.)

Observing my watch can be fascinating. The movement of the second hand is predictable and controlled, round and round, seemingly forever, always at the same rate. The watch is a machine; it can do only what is intended for it. To perform any other function is unthinkable; to talk to you or to smile at you would be totally impossible. The only function of my watch is to tell you the time of day. Watching the hand go around and around is almost like being hypnotized, and suddenly I feel that I too am becoming a machine.

Verb forms may also be used as adjectives. Almost invariably these are participles, either present (the "-ing" form) or past participles. Thus *running* may be part of a predicate (I was running down the hill), the name of something and therefore a noun (Running is good for the health), or it may help describe a noun and thus serve as an adjective (The *running* brook sang to me all night). In the following examples, all the italicized verb forms are adjectives, because they help describe a noun.

Examples

There are twenty people in my *writing* class.
The children, *laughing* and *singing*, raced away from the school.
The sky was a mass of *glowing* color.

Exercise B-9   *Recognizing Verb Forms*
                                    Used as Adjectives

List the verb forms in the following passage that are used as adjectives. Then list the verb forms used as predicates.

My watch reminds me of the time of black slaves in America. Like the watch, slaves were looked upon as performing machines, their actions as controlled as the ticks of a clock. If they didn't work, they were considered as malfunctioning, with no value. Sometimes we think of black slaves as a dancing, singing, happy people, but when I look at my watch I know there is another side to the picture—a dark, forbidding side that no amount of laughter and song can hide.

CHECK YOURSELF SECTION B

1. Copy the following passage and underline all the verb forms with a single line.
2. Underline all predicates with a double line.
3. Where forms are not in Standard English, cross them out and write the Standard English form above. Keep the passage in past tense.

I conned the fellows into spending their money. "Come on in. Take a chance. Win a giant teddy bear!" I can't help but watch the confidence on their faces and then the disappointment. I thinks, "Sucker!"

Here come my relief. I could take a break and see how the others were doing. I starts walking amidst the spectators and came upon the rides. The sound of tapes blasting out hard rock songs is enough to make me deaf. The ride boys flirt and try to make the locals. I use to fall for them myself, but not any more. I reached my destination, the cook shack, and some of the fellows are already there for their break. Sam asks, "How about some carney steak?" Would you believe it's fried bologna? It sure tasted good with lettuce and mayonnaise.

End of Check Yourself Section B. Check the key now.

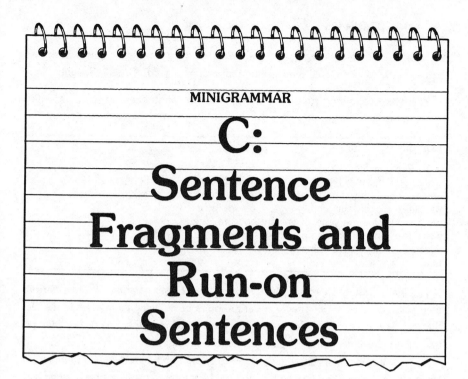

MINIGRAMMAR

C: Sentence Fragments and Run-on Sentences

DIAGNOSTIC SECTION C

1. Each group of words in the following passage is numbered. Identify each group as either a complete sentence (S) or a sentence fragment (SF).

Example

1. The sky was dark and foreboding in the west, but the morning sun was bright.   **2.** Slowly changing the darkness to a reddish-gold.   **3.** I felt close to God.   **4.** Because He created that scene.

1. S
2. SF
3. S
4. SF

---

1. "Come on, everybody up.   **2.** We've only got half an hour," Dad yelled in the doorway.   **3.** Those words heralded the beginning of Sunday mornings. **4.** And I dreaded the sound of them.   **5.** I went through the ritual of dressing, eating breakfast, and piling myself into the car with the rest of the family.   **6.** Then the silent ride to the white building, the walk up the steps, and the limp shake of the pastor's hand.   **7.** Yech.   **8.** We all filed into our usual pew, and I sat by the usual person, Mrs. Grant.   **9.** "Isn't it a beautiful day?" she asked no one in particular.   **10.** I nodded.   **11.** Because I always felt those unexciting questions were directed at me.   **12.** Silence.

13. "Today is the quarter of the year," the pastor announced.   **14.** The celebration of our Lord's Supper."   **15.** "Oh, goody," I thought.   **16.** A longer sermon.   **17.** More singing.   **18.** Well, at least the grape juice wasn't so bad.   **19.** Which would redeem the hour a little.   **20.** Or so I thought.

2. In the following passage, identify run-on sentneces by ROS. Identify sentence fragments by SF. Identify complete sentences by S.

Example

    1. Being a little kid is hard.   **2.** Especially when you believe everything that grownups tell you.   **3.** I did, I just naturally thought older people were always right.   **4.** For instance, my parents told me vegetables were good for me but I was one of those normal kids who hated vegetables, especially spinach, which made me totally sick.

    1. S
    2. SF
    3. ROS
    4. S

---

    1. Finally I refused even to touch spinach.   **2.** My parents pleaded with me, they yelled at me.   **3.** They were at the point of resigning themselves to the fact that their son just never would be a spinach eater when my father, in one last attempt, told me to eat spinach and it would put hair on my chest.

    4. Now this idea impressed me.   **5.** Because I had a brother who had hair on his chest and once when I asked him about it he informed me it was because he was already a man and I wasn't.   **6.** Well, deciding I was ready to be a man, I took a sudden liking to spinach.   **7.** I ate two or three helpings each time it was served, I used to beg for it at every meal.   **8.** My parents couldn't figure out what had happened they were shaking their amazed heads over me.

End of Diagnostic Section C. Check the key on p. 240.

SENTENCE FRAGMENTS

    Sentence fragments and run-on sentences are two of the principal stumbling blocks for inexperienced writers. It would be wrong to call either of these problems *errors*, because experienced writers often use them effectively. For instance, a random opening of Thoreau's *Walden* yields the following passage:

For numbers and for carnage it was an Austerlitz or Dresden. Concord Fight! Two killed on the patriots' side, and Luther Blanchard wounded!

Whatever "Concord Fight!" is (probably an exhortation to the people to rise to arms), "Two killed on the patriots' side, and Luther Blanchard wounded!" is clearly a sentence fragment. Possibly if Thoreau had written this passage as a part of a freshman English essay, some mid-nineteenth-century teacher would have red-penciled it, because this kind of inflexible attitude toward grammar was prevalent in those days—and is adhered to in many English classes today.

But just because sentence fragments and run-on sentences can be used effectively does not mean "anything goes." If you are to use them, you must know what you are doing and why. To know that, you must be clear about what a sentence is. You must know how a sentence differs from a sentence fragment and from a run-on sentence.

We will take up sentence fragments first. What is a sentence fragment? It is usually defined as an incomplete thought, while a sentence is defined as a complete thought. This isn't a very helpful definition. "And so Uncle Wiggly put a fence around his carrot patch" is a sentence which doesn't sound like a complete thought because we don't know what "and so" refers to. On the other hand, in the sequence "Why do I write this book? Because I think I have something to say," the words "Because I think I have something to say" sound like a complete thought, but these words constitute a sentence fragment.

Get out of your head, if you have it there, the idea that you can tell a sentence because it expresses a complete thought.

Another misconception is that a sentence has a subject and predicate, but a sentence fragment does not. "Because I think I have something to say" has *two* subjects and predicates and is still a sentence fragment.

The best way, I think, to identify sentence fragments is to look for danger signals. The following discussion and related exercises will help you learn to watch for three of them. They don't cover every sentence fragment, but if you learn to recognize the three given here, you should have little trouble.

Danger signal 1: *"-ing" and "-ed" verb forms (participles) at the beginning of a group of words.*

Example

He decided to go to the movies. *Having nothing better to do.*

Having is a participle; the italicized words are a sentence fragment. All you need to do is combine the two word groupings: "He decided to go to the movies, having nothing better to do." Or: "Having nothing better to do, he decided to go to the movies." Quite often, all you need to do to eliminate your accidental or ineffective sentence fragments is to hook them to the sentence in front of or behind them.

An "-ing" or "-ed" verb form at the beginning of the sentence does not automatically mean you have a sentence fragment, as verb forms are sometimes used in the place of other parts of speech. An example is their use as nouns in *"Seeing is believing."*

Don't assume because something "sounds all right" to you that it is all right. When you are speaking or writing for your peers, those who speak and think as you do, then what sounds all right is all right. Few of you, however, will spend the rest of your lives speaking to or writing for only your peers; the mark of education may be your ability to meet the expectations of those who have concepts different from yours of what constitutes acceptable writing.

Exercise C-1 — *Identifying Participial Verb Forms and Their Use*

List all the "-ing" and "-ed" verb forms in the following passage. Not all are used as verbs; some are used as nouns or adjectives. Label the verb forms N if they are used as nouns, A if used as adjectives, and V if used as verbs.

Example

When I am swinging high, I feel a confused excitement; a rushing of mixed joy and fear surges through me.	swinging V
	confused A
	rushing N
	mixed A

Sensations!

Shutting my eyes against the many prejudices of color, size, shape, religion, and sex in the world. Shutting each one out separately but firmly behind the locked doors of my vision. Relaxing. Forgetting everything except myself. One space of my mind follows the cool, crooning voice at the center of the room which tells me what to do. What am I? Completely relaxed. No feeling. But wait! I am breathing. I feel like a butterfly. I'm soaring. Nothing but this exquisite air.

One thing to keep in mind is that in a *complete sentence,* an "-ing" or "-ed" form used as a verb will always be associated with a helping verb:

Complete sentence	**Sentence fragment**
Her credentials were being checked.	Being she was invited

In the first instance, the helper "were" is associated with "being"; in the second, there is no helper associated with "being."

Exercise C-2 — *Locating Sentence Fragments (Participial Phrases)*

On a separate sheet, identify the following word groups S if they are complete sentences and SF is they are sentence fragments.

1. We were having a good day
2. Doing just what we wanted to do
3. The wind was blowing up a storm
4. But we were having too much fun to pay any attention

5. Soon, however, noticing the quickening gale, the stirring of the leaves in the trees, the rain beginning to patter down on the sand

6. We ran for shelter

7. But we had waited too long and were soaked before we reached the old barn on the hill

8. We had learned our lesson, and the next time the weather began to threaten, we gathered up our things quickly and escaped the downpour

9. Proving you can teach young dogs new tricks

Exercise C-3   *Eliminating Sentence Fragments*

Write the Exercise C-2 groups into a paragraph, changing no words or their order but inserting punctuation and combining sentences so that there will be *only complete sentences*. Do *not* combine with one another units *that are already sentences*.

Danger signal 2: *certain pronouns at the beginning of a statement.*
Some pronouns, when they begin a unit of words, can get you into trouble. The principal ones to look out for are:

who	what	those	one
which	that	this	

In the following examples, the italicized words are sentence fragments introduced by the listed pronouns.

I went to see my favorite uncle. *Who told me he was moving to Alaska.*
He took the afternoon off to go to a ball game. *Which made his boss very angry.*
He told me something extremely important. *What I should have known without being told.*
The world gasped at his news. *That under no circumstances would he run again for the Presidency.*
Charitable organizations always need new recruits. *Those who are willing to work hard and selflessly.*
I made a New Year's resolution. *This being that I would give up smoking.*
Psychologists tell us that to each man his name is very important. *One of his dearest possessions, in fact.*

One caution: we are talking about statements, not questions. Most of these prounouns can be used to introduce questions that are complete.

Complete	Fragment
Who went to the store?	Who went to the store.

Often a sentence fragment of this sort can be combined with a complete sentence in its immediate vicinity. This is true of most of the examples. Care must be exercised, however. Sometimes it is necessary to recast the resulting sentence to cut needless wordiness. "I made a New Year's resolution, this being that I would give up smoking" would be more efficient and effective if reworded: "I made a New Year's resolution to give up smoking."

Parallelism often works well in combining sentence fragments with a complete sentence. "He told me something extremely important, what I should have known without being told," is awkward, but "He told me *something* extremely important, *something* I should have known without being told," works well, with the parallelism signalled by the repetition of the word "something." A whole series of fragments, all beginning with the same word, can be attached to a main clause with nice effect. For instance: "Psychologists tell us that to each man his name is important, *one* of his dearest possessions, *one* he will give up only with a great struggle."

Exercise C-4   *Locating Sentence Fragments (Pronoun Clauses and Phrases)*

On a separate sheet, identify the following word groups by S if they are complete sentences and by SF if they are sentence fragments.

1. All of us think and act the way we do for various reasons

2. Which to a large extent depend on the way we grew up

3. We have been greatly influenced by our families and friends

4. I would like to tell you about one of the greatest influences on me

5. One which most people never have

6. One which I have rarely talked about and have never written about

7. She was one of those unfortunate people born mentally retarded

8. Those with no real muscle control

9. Who can never walk, talk, or even sit up

10. Yet she was a constant source of joy for us and was easily entertained

11. Which we would spend hours doing, entertaining ourselves at the same time

12. She loved to be held or petted or talked to, and I learned much about patience and love by caring for her

13. Things that I might otherwise never have understood

14. There is one thing I know

15. That my little sister, who died suddenly on a cold night last winter, made me more appreciative of life and of how lucky I am

Exercise C-5   *Eliminating Sentence Fragments*

Without changing any of the words or the word order, combine the Exercise C-4 groups into complete sentence units.

Danger signal 3: *groups of words that tell when, where, why, how, or that otherwise qualify some statement.*

This is a cumbersome way to describe adverbial clauses. Many students, however, have particular trouble recognizing adverbs. This kind of sentence fragment also begins with words that, when you see them, should raise a flag of caution in your mind. Sometimes these words do not signal fragments, but when you use them, stop and consider, until your recognition of sentence fragments becomes automatic. There follows a partial list of the particular words; these are the most common ones and if you are accustomed to them, you will find it easier to recognize others that fall in the same category.

when	although	unless	after
where	while	until	why
as	because	in order to	whenever
for	if	before	wherever

Two that seem to give particular trouble are because *and* for. Raise an especially big caution flag in your mind for these.

Examples

We need to understand what a great athlete is. *For we live in a time when athletics is important to nearly all young men and women.* (Adverbial clause telling "why" about main statement)

Athletes who get involved with gamblers are looked down on by many youngsters. *Because they picture them as crooks and no longer the type of athletes they want to pattern themselves after.* (Adverbial clause telling "why" about the main statement)

Self-discipline is important to any human being. *Although to an athlete it means more than simply obeying the rules.* (Adverbial clause qualifying the main statement)

Athletes, like everyone else, need a place to be by themselves sometimes. *Where they can think over problems and gain inner strength.* (Adverbial clause telling "where" about the main statement)

An athlete needs dedication, self-discipline, a strong mental attitude, and the ability to endure criticism. *As without these, he is only a "could be."* (Adverbial clause telling "why")

In each case, the two statements can be combined to eliminate the sentence fragment, e.g., "We need to understand what a great athlete is, for we live in a time when athletics is important to nearly all young men and women."

Exercise C-6   *Locating Sentence Fragments*
                                          (Adverbial Clauses and Phrases)

On a separate sheet, identify the following word groups by S if they are complete sentences and by SF if they are sentence fragments.

1. Should certain classes be required of every person who graduates from college

2. I don't think so

3. Because in some of the specific courses which are required we students "don't learn a thing"

4. Sometimes we put forth very little effort

5. Especially when we didn't elect the course in the first place

6. Some required courses are rinky-dink, general in perspective, and too simple for many students from good high schools

7. Instead of particular courses, we should be required to choose a certain number of hours in each subject group from a published list of courses

8. Where the courses would be described in enough detail so we would know what to expect

9. With this information we could choose classes which would expand our minds and prove a challenge

10. Although I suppose some students would still be looking for the easiest way out of any requirement

Exercise C-7   *Eliminating Sentence Fragments*

Rewrite the material in Exercise C-6 into complete sentences.

RUN-ON SENTENCES (COMMA SPLICES, FUSED SENTENCES)

Fragments are groups of words that don't form a complete sentence, and as you become more aware of them, you should be developing a better sense of what is and is not a sentence. Run-on sentences require the same understanding of sentence structure. They are the other side of the coin from fragments. Instead of being incomplete, they are more than complete: two or more sentences are strung together either with no punctuation (a fused sentence) or with only a comma between them (a comma splice).

Example

John came to see me this weekend, we had a great time. (Comma splice)
John came to see me this weekend. (Complete sentence)
We had a great time. (Complete sentence)

There are basically three ways to eliminate run-on sentences. You can divide them into two separate sentences as shown above, each with its own capital letter at the beginning and period at the end. A second way to avoid a run-on sentence is to join the two sentences with a semicolon (;), or sometimes a colon (:). This is done when the thoughts in the two sentences are so closely related you don't want them separated by a period.

John came to see me this weekend; we had a great time.

Finally you can use a connecting word that helps show the relationship between the units.

When John came to see me this weekend, we had a great time.

One of the things this last solution does is to help emphasize the most important idea: that we had a great time. You do this by putting the main idea in the main or independent clause. If you wanted to make the two ideas of equal importance, you might have said "John came to see me this weekend, and we had a great time."

Caution: Do not confuse a run-on sentence with a sentence that is loosely constructed and seems to run on and on, becoming long and difficult to follow. A run-on sentence has only one, very special, meaning: two or more sentences have been fused into one without proper punctuation.

Examples

I felt bigger and stronger my voice sounded deep and booming in my ears. (Run-on sentence: a fused sentence)

Every night I ran to the mirror over the bathroom basin and checked to see if any hair had grown on my chest but I always came away disappointed, thinking that perhaps I hadn't eaten enough spinach that night and vowed to eat more helpings next time. (Grammatically one sentence but too long to follow easily)

Long sentences are not necessarily bad sentences. If you have difficulty following a long sentence, you may need to sharpen your reading ability. One way is to learn to write more complicated sentences yourself; when you can do it, you can see more easily what others are doing.

Exercise C-8   *Recognizing Run-on Sentences*

On a separate sheet, identify the following word groups, labeling them ROS if they are run-on sentences and S if they are not run-on sentences.

1. Finally I began to get discouraged, when my parents told my little sister that eating peas would make her hair curly, I took her aside after dinner and told her not to believe a word of it

2. I learned again the hard way during one of my most gullible summers, during which my father built my brother and me a sandbox in the backyard with wooden sides and the ground for a bottom and he filled it with sand from a nearby beach

3. My uncle came over one day when I was playing in it alone just before he left he asked me if I knew that if I kept digging straight down I would dig all the way to China

4. No I didn't know it but the idea enthralled me

5. I dug through the sand and came to the brown soil below I was really excited

6. I couldn't wait to get to the bottom and look through and see little Chinese people walking around and riding in those buggies that weren't pulled by horses but by people, like I'd seen in pictures

7. I dug all the way to the black below the soil and I was beginning to get tired and frustrated

8. When my father saw the hole he was angry and made me fill it back up I wasn't allowed to play in the sandbox for a week

Exercise C-9 *Correcting Run-on Sentences*

Revise the following sentences so that there will be no run-ons.

1. I was furious with my uncle when I started thinking I was sure I could have dug in that stupid hole all night and never reached China.

2. I came to the conclusion grown-ups weren't really so smart they had a lot of dumb ideas and didn't know much about anything.

3. Ever since, I've only half believed ideas that sounded a little fishy I usually check out advice before I follow it.

A special case: There is a class of words that gives people a particular kind of trouble, words such as *however, therefore,* and *then.* People often use them to connect two complete sentences, but this is *not* one of their functions.

Example

I wanted Harry to come with me, however he had agreed to play tennis with Nan, so he couldn't make it.
I wanted Harry to come with me. (Complete sentence)
However he had agreed to play tennis with Nan, so he couldn't make it. (Complete sentence)
I wanted Harry to come with me; however, he had agreed to play tennis with Nan, so he couldn't make it. (Proper punctuation, separating the sentences with a semicolon)

Exercise C-10   *Correcting Run-on Sentences Using* **However, Therefore,** *and* **Then**

Rewrite the following sentences to eliminate run-ons.

1. Everyone would like to become famous, however, only a few actually do.

2. It was a dark, cloudy day, therefore we stayed in and played cards.

3. Mary did everything she could to block Tom's appointment, nevertheless, he was given the position.

4. The children dashed across the bridge, then they saw the danger they were in.

5. I couldn't see his point, however, I still had the same opinion as when I began talking to him.

CHECK YOURSELF SECTION C

Do both the following subsections before looking at the key.

1. On a separate sheet, identify complete sentences by S and sentence fragments by SF. Then rewrite the passage, using essentially the same words and word order, to eliminate all sentence fragments.

1. The world is a strange and often difficult place in which to live. **2.** A world in which we see many diversities. **3.** Seeing men landing on the moon one second and men starving in our own country the next. **4.** We are supposed to live in the richest country in the world. **5.** But we still have hungry kids who don't have enough energy to go to school. **6.** The unfortunate fact is that rich, affluent people don't open their eyes to what is going on around them. **7.** Although we are not exactly opening our eyes to the facts either. **8.** Until we do, the world will remain its old, poor, and starving self. **9.** Where children die at a rate that would astound us if we knew. **10.** And we sit here doing nothing about it. **11.** While you have been reading this, nine children have died in the United States.   **12.** And somewhere in the world, thirty children.   **13.** This being of starvation alone.   **14.** Isn't it time to be doing something?   **15.** Like writing your congressman or helping through CARE or UNESCO?

   2. On a separate sheet, identify each group of words by S or ROS. Then rewrite the passage to eliminate all run-on sentences, without substantially changing the word order. You may, however, revise long sentences to eliminate confusion or wordiness if you choose.

   1. I will never know how someone can just flatly state "Boy! I just hate to write," or "Teacher, teacher! I just L-O-V-E to write."   **2.** Writing is a broad and diverse activity, it's impossible to give a 100 percent truthful opinion in a few words.   **3.** For a month and a half this summer I kept a journal while I was out west traveling and it was no chore for me to pick up a pen and write three pages of events, experiences, and emotions in that journal I don't think I enjoyed anything as much on the trip as lying down by the campfire and writing about all the wonderful and miserable things that had happened that day.   **4.** The best part of keeping that journal is now that I'm home I have a set of memories inside that beat-up blue notebook worth more than a thousand color slides.   **5.** But my feelings can jump to the other spectrum too, if you have ever filled out an application that wanted you to state in three hundred words what your future occupational plans were you know what I mean.   **6.** Or maybe you have had an experience as I have with the epitome of all miserable writing assignments by an old, senile teacher who wanted a five-page combination report and reaction to present-day draft dodgers.   **7.** After four nights in the library and a whole lot of B.S. I had a paper that got me an A, more important, I had developed a lasting dislike for composition classes.

   End of Check Yourself Section C. Check the key now.

D:
Pronoun Usage

DIAGNOSTIC SECTION D

In the following passage, there are numerous instances of unclear or incorrect pronoun usage:

1. On a separate sheet, list all pronouns except "I." Write the referent for each pronoun (its antecedent, if that's the term you understand). If there is no referent, write "None."
2. Identify each pronoun used in a faulty way and state briefly what the problem is.

Example

1. I always knew what a good theme was (or so I thought) until my freshman year in college. **2.** In junior high and high school, which I attended in a small town, good writing was using big "million dollar" words that I didn't know the meaning of. **3.** It was stretching my thoughts into three pages when a page would easily tell it all.

1. *my:* the referent is "I."
2. *which:* the referent is "junior high and high school." *that:* the referent is "words." In this sentence, there is a problem with the referent of *which,* because it is not clear whether *which* refers just to high school or to both junior high and senior high schools.
3. *It:* the referent is "good writing." *my:* the referent is "I." *it* and *all:* the referent for both is "my thoughts." In this sentence, the second *it* raises problems because it refers to something different from the first *it* in the sentence. In addition, the referent (or antecedent) for the

second *it* is "my thoughts" which is plural. The sentence would be better if it read "It was stretching my thoughts into three pages when a page would easily tell *them* all."

---

1. Good writing was using the style my teacher liked best, so if they liked big fancy words and I used them, I was sure to get an "A —Very good."   **2.** Now, in my freshman year in college, I'm told that is all wrong.   **3.** Today, good writing is "free writing."   **4.** It's letting yourself go.   **5.** Thoughts and ideas should flow from my brain.   **6.** No "million dollar" words.   **7.** No exaggerations.   **8.** No stretching it out with unnecessary repeated lines.   **9.** Watch for sentence fragments.   **10.** Be sure it flows freely from idea to idea.

End of Diagnostic Section D. Check the key on p. 244.

VAGUE PRONOUN REFERENCES

As you should know by now, a pronoun stands for a noun or is used in place of a noun. Concentrate on that for a moment: a pronoun is used in place of *one, specific, identifiable noun.* There are some exceptions, but you should make it a practice to be sure your pronouns refer to a *particular* noun. This will solve a great many of your own pronoun problems.

(There is a partial list of pronouns in Minigrammar A, p. 174. If you have trouble identifying pronouns, check that list. Then take any passage of written material and practice finding pronouns.)

The following examples demonstrate some common types of the ambiguous (or unclear) use of pronouns. All contain vague pronoun referents, a problem for which even the best writers have to keep a constant vigil.

Examples	Possible revisions
The teacher told Tom the principal held him responsible. (Who is being held responsible—the teacher or Tom?)	According to the teacher, the principal held Tom responsible. "The principal holds me responsible," the teacher told Tom.
I had to sit in the bleachers, which annoyed me greatly. (The bleachers annoyed you? Obviously not, but there is no other particular referent.)	It annoyed me greatly to have to sit in the bleachers. Having to sit in the bleachers annoyed me greatly.
There was this girl coming down the street. (What girl? What does "this" refer to?)	There was a girl coming down the street.

Exercise D-1 *Locating Vague Pronoun References*

For each sentence in the following passage, determine whether there is a vague pronoun reference. If there is a vague reference, rewrite the sentence to clarify the meaning; if not, write "No vague pronoun."

1. I wake up in the morning and stretch the cramped areas of my body, and the eight—sometimes nine—hours of slumber slowly ebb away as they begin to come alive. **2.** My senses begin to compute the environment around me and convey it into thoughts of doubt and anxiety. **3.** A new day is beginning as the brisk, blue February sky spawns spent white pillows of God, seeming to rejoice in its unveiling as golden strands of sunlight shower warmth and beauty upon the earth. **4.** As I draw the curtains to shut it out, the solemn intangibility of semidarkness engulfs me, and I think how the world is pulling closed its curtains by persistent violence and neglect. **5.** But then I think again. **6.** I think of how it was only in the dawn of time that the purest harmony was bestowed upon us. **7.** I think: if only everyone could live prosperously and harmoniously with one another, with none of the insolent "minorities" or the "clean whities" ruining their chances of survival. **8.** Then I find myself at my desk writing it all out to ease the angry thoughts swelling in my head. **9.** The graphite-tipped pencil seems to write on its own. **10.** It isn't laid down according to strict rules and regulations, but spews forth thoughts as they come—carelessly, sincerely, thoughts of anger!

AGREEMENT BETWEEN PRONOUNS AND THEIR ANTECEDENTS

Agreement, especially in number, between pronouns and their referents is another common problem. Sometimes a writer simply forgets how the sentence started. Or sometimes the writer's mental image doesn't correspond to the one written on the page. In a sentence like "A student often gets behind because they don't realize how fast the end of the term creeps up," perhaps the writer was thinking about all students but wrote "a student."

There are several ways to remedy failure to provide agreement between pronuns and their referents. Both parts of the sentence above could be made singular; i.e., "A student often gets behind because he doesn't realize . . ." is a possibility. Once it was quite acceptable, but lately people object to what is called the generic use of *he* to refer to both males and females (see "The His/Her Problem," p. 208). You could say ". . . because he or she doesn't realize . . .," but that is awkward. It is probably better either to change the whole sentence to plural, i.e., "Students often get behind because they don't realize . . ." or reword the sentence entirely, i.e., "A student, not realizing how fast the end of a term creeps up, often gets behind." Be sure, however, that if you reword the sentence you still say exactly what you want to say; the revision above slightly changes the original meaning.

Watch out for *each* and *everyone!* These mean *each one* and *every one;* they are singular. *None* also presents problems; it is technically singular, meaning *no one.* In everyday speech, we use *everyone* and *none* as if they were plural, as in *"Everyone* brought *their* swimsuits" or *"None* of the girls *are* going swimming." Although this common usage is gaining acceptance, for the time being, try to remember, when you are writing Standard English, to make them singular, i.e., *"Everyone* brought *his* swimsuit," and *"None* of the girls *is* going swimming."

Usage, by the way, does control grammar in significant ways. Many expressions once considered totally wrong are now accepted rather generally, like the plural usage of *everyone.* The same professor who insists you write *"Everyone* brought *his* swimsuit," may say *"Everyone* should bring *their* texts to class tomorrow," and neither he nor you will think twice about the grammatical correctness of what he has said. Opinion on such matters is so divided that the compilers of *The American Heritage Dictionary of the English Language* submitted questions of usage to a panel of about one hundred experts—novelists, essayists, journalists, and professors—and then recorded the responses, showing the percentages for and against. For instance, here is a part of the usage section for the verb *compare:*

> Usage: In formal usage, *compare to* is the only acceptable form when *compare* means representing as similar or likening, according to 71 percent of the Usage Panel: *compare a voice to thunder.*

Some English manuals are very strict about usage, others quite permissive. Much depends on the manual of usage you—and/or your instructor—happen to be relying on. In cases of doubt, it is better to be safe and follow majority rule.

In pronoun referents also watch out for *either . . . or,* meaning one *or* the other. "Either the boy or the girl" demands a singular pronoun in the following part of the sentence, an almost impossible requirement. Rewording the sentence would be in order. On the other hand, "Either the men or the women," since it refers to plural subjects, demands a plural pronoun; this can be handled neatly with "their."

Both . . . and means at least two things are involved and always requires plural pronouns in the balance of the sentence.

Don't try to memorize which expressions require singular pronouns; use your common sense. If you think what the words *mean,* you can't go far wrong.

The "His/Her" Problem

In recent years, the practice of using the masculine pronoun (*he, his, him*) to refer to both sexes in a general reference has become obsolete. We can no longer say "Each member of the legislature took *his* seat" unless there are only male members. So far, no acceptable substitute has been developed;

although you occasionally see "his/her," it is considered awkward. Sometimes a writer will use feminine pronouns in one section to offset the use of masculine pronouns elsewhere; this also sounds awkward and affected. An attempt to coin new forms, such as "s/he," seems equally artificial.

Avoiding the problem requires considerable flexibility in the use of language. Let's see what options we have. The first possibility is to say "Each member of the legislature took *his or her* seat." The somewhat cumbersome "his or her" should be resorted to infrequently, but if used with good judgment, it is quite acceptable. The second option—often the easiest—is to shift the entire passage into plural: "*All members* of the legislature took *their* seats." A third remedy might be to use the passive voice, though this can weaken your statement and should also be used with discretion: "Each seat *was taken by* a member of the legislature." Sometimes you can simply avoid using *any* pronoun, e.g., "Each member of the legislature took *a* seat."

Experiment until you find the solution that works best in the context of your passage.

PRONOUN SHIFTING

One other thing to watch about pronouns: As a general rule, don't shift from one *person* to another. If you start in the first person, using *I, me,* and *my*, stick to first person *unless you have a good reason to shift*.

Example	Better
I walked down to the stream by myself and thought about the events of the past. You could hear the murmuring of the stream and the stirring of the wind in the branches, and it seemed very peaceful there.	I walked down to the stream by myself and thought about the events of the past. I could hear the murmuring of the stream and the stirring of the wind in the branches, and it seemed very peaceful there.

Exercise D-2   *Correcting Faulty Pronoun Agreement*

In the following passage, rewrite the sentences in which the pronouns do not agree with the noun or pronoun to which they refer. Be a "purist," regardless of what the usage dictionaries tell you.

1. What is writing?   **2.** No, I don't mean the *Webster's Dictionary* definition.   **3.** I'll bet way back in elementary and junior high school, almost everyone was like me and thought writing was a pain, probably because they didn't understand its significance.   **4.** Sometimes a person can have fun and learn to appreciate writing more if they play around with words a little.   **5.** You may have written a silly poem once in your life, but if you haven't, try one.   **6.** I used to (and sometimes still do) write this kind of nonsense.   **7.** Here's a poem from a couple of years back:

Sooner or later
Sinner be free,
Chomp that eraser,
Fun rips my knee.
Now you fools,
Carve the sphinx.
"What's that you say?"
Better savor your winks.

8. Of course, each person may have their own way of getting past their first reluc-tance to start using language as an effective tool.   **9.** What my poem means is somewhat beyond me.   **10.** Writers run into trouble if neither he nor his readers can understand what they are talking about.   **11.** If ideas come out scattered as in the poem above, how then can anyone even know what they're trying to say?

12. I'll tell you my principle for writing, which is simply to write as honestly as I can and let my mind and body be relaxed.   **13.** (Don't get so comfortable you fall asleep.)   **14.** If one has to, they can prop their feet up on a chair, but they shouldn't let other ideas and thoughts hinder what they wish to express on paper.   **15.** Maintain your train of thought and let what you write speak for you.

CHECK YOURSELF SECTION D

Rewrite the following passage, improving the pronoun usage.

Teachers Unite

It's no wonder a student is mixed up about writing by the time they get to college. Here's how their earlier schooling probably has gone. In kindergarten they are taught writing consists of printing the alphabet in large capital letters, which seems pretty reasonable at the time. But then in first grade they find out there is such a thing as a lowercase letter, and when and where to use them. By the end of the first year, everybody knows how to hold their pencil correctly and to print perfectly, which they are proud of.

Alas, to their surprise upon entering second grade, the boy or girl is *punished* for printing. Then in third grade all you hear is "Don't write backhand," "Sit up straight," "Don't hold your fingers too close to the lead."

In the next three grades, they learn mostly about putting writing skills into practice.

One of the things they learn to write are reports about something or somebody that really means nothing to him. It doesn't matter how good the report is, only if they are long enough.

In junior high, you find out it is against the law to copy what someone else has written without giving them credit for it. Also English isn't English anymore; it's Grammar. About this time, they begin to think writing is pretty heavy, which makes a guy wonder if they want to write any more. In high school, the student gets more things thrown at him; they have to write big papers with an introduction, five to ten footnotes, a bibliography with at least five sources used, an outline, and a summary.

Now in college there is this emphasis on writing out of my own mind. In each of my experiences, they expect something different. I wish someday every teacher in schools and colleges would get together and decide what they expect of students.

End of Check Yourself Section D. Check the key now.

MINIGRAMMAR

E:
Faulty
Sentence Logic

DIAGNOSTIC SECTION E

Each of the following sentences is in some way unclear and needs rewording to fit logically into the paragraph. Rewrite the entire passage so that it flows smoothly and logically.

1. In eighth grade, Saturday afternoon excitement consisted of going to a local shopping mall for a day. **2.** Watching people and hanging around was fun, but shoplifting was really exciting. **3.** It was a big deal to see who could steal most in one day. **4.** Ranging from candy to perfume, we stole all sorts of things. **5.** Big things, clothes, typewriters and things like that, we didn't bother with and besides were too dangerous to try to steal. **6.** Candy, cosmetics, and jewelry were something else.

7. This particular Saturday morning browsing around Montgomery Ward's makeup counter, a new type of mascara caught our eyes. **8.** It was on a rack hanging right in front of us. **9.** Staring us in the face, we knew what each other were thinking with no sales lady behind the counter. **10.** We drew straws between Linda, Peggy, Martha, and I was elected.

End of Diagnostic Section E. Check the key on p. 246.

THE MAIN IDEA IN THE MAIN CLAUSE

Many times what you write or read just doesn't "sound right." Sometimes you can understand it all right; other times you have to read it two or three times before its meaning is clear. Numerous reasons exist for this confusion, some of which have already been touched on. For instance, the pronoun references may be ambiguous or you may not have punctuated or arranged the sentence in the clearest possible way. Often you will have difficulty seeing your own problems even when you see the logical faults in someone else's writing, because you know what you mean. Therefore, you need to be especially careful to become aware of the kinds of things that may cause faulty sentence logic. Not all are included in this minigrammer; the most important thing is for you to develop a habit of *watching every sentence* to be sure you have said exactly what you mean to say and that each sentence fits logically and smoothly with those around it.

Sometimes confusion results when you fail to put your main idea in the main clause, thus creating a problem of emphasis. In the following examples, the main clauses are italicized:

Linda opened her bag, while I grabbed the charcoal brown mascara off the rack and dropped it in.

While Linda opened her bag, *I grabbed the charcoal brown mascara off the rack and dropped it in.*

Probably, in view of the situation set up in Diagnostic Section E, the most important idea here is that the storyteller grabbed the mascara, not that Linda opened her bag. The second version of the sentence would therefore fit more clearly into the passage as a whole.

Exercise E-1   *Putting the Main Idea in the Main Clause*

In the following passage, rewrite each sentence, reversing the clauses so that the original main clause becomes a dependent clause. Underline the new main clause. Then decide which version of each sentence fits best into the whole shoplifting story that is developing. Do any further revising that seems advisable, remembering what you have already learned about achieving coherent sentences.

1. Next, after Linda grabbed two more tubes and dropped them in her purse, we nonchalantly looked around a few minutes and walked away.   **2.** We left, after staying in the store for a while and feeling successful about our rip-off.   **3.** When we were outside the store, we heard a man talking to us.   **4.** He pointed to a corner, while he said in an accusing voice, "Girls, come with me."   **5.** He followed us as we walked the way he directed.   **6.** When we were in the corner, he asked, "What do you have in those bags that doesn't belong to you?"

MISPLACED MODIFIERS

Sometimes sentences become distorted because of misplaced modifiers—words, phrases, or clauses that seem to modify a part of the sentence other than what was intended, as in the case of "clearly suspicious" in the following sentence.

The man stared at Linda and me in particular, though Peggy and Martha crouched behind us, *clearly suspicious*.

In our little shoplifting story, the "clearly suspicious" person is the man, not Peggy and Martha. A clearer, more logical wording would be as follows:

The man, *clearly suspicious*, stared at Linda and me in particular, though Peggy and Martha crouched behind us.

Always place modifiers as close as possible to the word modified. Watch out in particular for the word *only*, which often gets misplaced. (Words like *almost, just, hardly,* and *merely* create similar but less frequent problems.) The logic in the following sentence is distorted.

We only kept silent because we didn't know what else to do.

The girls didn't "only keep silent"; what the writer is trying to say is that they kept silent "*only because they didn't know what else to do*."

Exercise E-2   *Correcting Misplaced Modifiers*

Rewrite the following passage to correct the misplaced modifiers. Rearrange the material as you see fit to make the sentences flow more logically.

1. We continued to cower there in the corner, feeling stupid and scared.
2. People were staring at us as they walked by curiously.   **3.** I forced my eyes away from Linda's purse which kept wandering in that direction.   **4.** The man motioned for us to go inside finally and walk through the store, which made me feel like a criminal.   **5.** I thought we would never reach the elevator as he stayed close behind us.   **6.** All the way up, I tried to keep myself from crying

DANGLING PARTICIPLES

A special and very common type of misplaced modifier is called a *dangling participle.* Be careful that any participle (the "-ing" or "-ed" forms of the verb) used as an adjective clearly modifies a noun or pronoun *in your sentence* and is placed as close as possible to the word it modifies. Participial phrases at the beginning of sentences are particularly troublesome, because, with few exceptions, the reader expects the participle to modify *the subject of the main clause.*

Trembling as the elevator arose, *we* felt the success we had experienced a few minutes earlier drain away.

Here it is clear who was trembling: "we"—the shoplifters. But often a writer becomes careless and produces a less clear statement.

Trembling as the elevator arose, the feeling of success we had experienced a few minutes earlier drained away.

What or who is doing the trembling here? The feeling of success?

Exercise E-3   *Correcting Dangling Participles*

Rewrite the following passage to correct the dangling participles or any other misplaced modifiers. Rearrange or revise as you see fit for a clearly logical flow.

1. Seeming like ages, the elevator stopped at the third floor, where the offices were. **2.** The man kept right behind us, walking down the hall miserably. **3.** Entering the office, a heavyset man was sitting at a cluttered desk, looking as if he expected us. **4.** His face wore a mean look, frightening us all the more. **5.** He motioned us to sit down in chairs, leaning forward and studying our faces intently.

FAULTY PARALLELISM AND FAULTY PREDICATION

Faulty parallelism and *faulty predication* are two other ways in which sentence logic becomes distorted. As you know, parallelism results when two parts of a sentence are structurally similar. Often a sentence is hard to follow if the structural similarity is not maintained.

Example

Handing us a card to fill out and they wanted our name, address, phone number, age, parents' names, and merchandise stolen, the manager continued to watch us.

The manager performs (in addition to watching) two actions: he hands the girls a card and he asks for certain information. The sentence would read more smoothly and clearly if the references to both of these actions were contained in grammatically similar phrases, e.g., "*Handing* us a card and *asking* each of us to fill in her name, address, age, parents' names, and merchandise stolen, the manager continued to watch us." Both actions are now introduced by participles (*handing, asking*) and both are clearly actions of the manager. Another possible wording, but one still preserving the parallelism, might be: "As he *handed* us a card and *asked* each of *us* to fill in her name . . ., the manager continued to watch us."

Faulty parallelism often occurs in connection with paired groups of words like *both . . . and* and *either . . . or*. To preserve a smooth and logical flow, be sure the material following each half of such pairs is in parallel form.

> We *either* had a choice of trying to lie our way out *or* answering truthfully and admitting we were shoplifting.

The logic is distorted in the above sentence because the word groups following "either" and "or" are not parallel.

> *either* "had a choice of trying to lie our way out"
> *or* "answering truthfully and admitting we were shoplifting"

To achieve a logical, balanced statement, the sentence might be rewritten:

> We had a choice of *either* trying to lie our way out *or* answering truthfully and admitting we were shoplifting.

Faulty predication means that a sentence starts one way and finishes another; that is, the first half doesn't fit logically with the second half.

> What he did after that was the worst thing when he called our parents to come and and pick us up.

The main clause, "What he did after that was the worst thing," should logically be followed by an explanation of what he did, and although the writer does tell us, she distorts the logic by starting the clause with "when." The sentence might be rewritten thus:

> What he did after that was the worst thing: he called our parents to come and pick us up.

Exercise E-4   *Correcting Faulty Parallelism and/or Predication*

Rewrite the following passage to correct faulty parallelism and predication. Revise the sentences as necessary to improve logic and clarity.

1. As we sat there imagining what our parent's reaction would be, I wondered if I would be grounded and would my dad hit me.   **2.** When I heard his voice coming over the phone in reply to the manager did not make me feel any better.   **3.** His voice both sounded shaky and he was angry.   **4.** I couldn't hear what was said but the reply of the manager was what I did hear. "No. No mistake. It's your daughter. We caught her shoplifting."   **5.** I strained to hear and another pause occurred in the manager's conversation before he said, "Please come down to pick her up. It's routine."

FAULTY USE OF *TO BE*

The verb *to be* (*is, are, was, were, am,* etc.) is often at the root of faulty predication and deserves special attention. When used in a sentence as the main verb, in which case it is called a *linking verb*, it is like an equals sign (=) in that what goes before it should be logically "equal to" what follows. Even though a reader may be able to grasp the meaning, a distortion of logic through faulty use of *to be* is often disturbing.

The turning point of my life was what was going through my head just then.

A turning point is not something that "goes through one's head." We understand the writer; she knows she is at a turning point in her life. She should have said it that way. Often the best way to eliminate the problem is to *rewrite the sentence using a different verb:*

I knew I was at a turning point in my life.

Many examples of faulty predication resulting from the use of *to be* involve completers beginning with *where* and *when*.

The realization was when I thought how shocked my parents would be.

When signals a time reference; *where* is a location word. Yet they are commonly used illogically, as above. The word *realization* is not somehow *equal* to a time (implied by "when"). Again the best solution is to rewrite, choosing a different verb and perhaps expressing the whole idea more precisely.

The realization I was growing up came to me as I thought how shocked my parents would be.

A special problem occurs when a participle is used after a form of *to be.* In the following sentence, is "seeing" (a participle) part of the predicate?

I thought to myself, "Maybe growing up is seeing the consequences of what one does."

"Growing up" is the subject of the sentence in quotes. If "is seeing" is the predicate of the sentence, that means "growing up" is doing the seeing—not very sensible. One possible remedy in such a case is to substitute infinitives for the participles:

Maybe *to grow up* is *to see* the consequences of what one does.

Or, as suggested before, rewrite the sentence to avoid the verb *to be*.

Maybe one begins to become an adult when one sees the consequences of one's actions.

The verb *to be* is much overused; avoiding it when possible is, in general, a good practice.

Exercise E-5   *Correcting Faulty Predication*

Rewrite the following passage to correct faulty uses of *to be* and to make the paragraph flow more smoothly and logically. Eliminate forms of the verb *to be* where practical.

1. A terrible feeling is wishing the ground would open up and swallow you. **2.** My father's arrival was when I wanted to disappear into thin air.   **3.** The importance of having my parents' respect was where it hit me the hardest.   **4.** All the way home to say I was overcome with guilt was putting it mildly.   **5.** Since that Saturday, I have never stolen another thing.

CHECK YOURSELF SECTION E

Rewrite the following passage to make it read more smoothly and logically.

Death is one of the hardest things to understand. Accepting it is one thing, but it is another thing to understand it. Having been hit with death in many different ways, each time it hurt me and left me with an empty feeling. As time went on and the pain lessened, however there were always certain things that reminded me of it. I always thought of death happening only to the old and sometimes of course it happened to the sick too, but mostly murders and accidents in the newspapers were the things that reminded me of death. They never hit young and healthy people was what I wanted to believe. My belief which I cherished was that it only happened in James Bond movies and some far-off place was where it took place. Our small town was quiet and safe. A seventeen-year-old friend of mine one Sunday was hit by a car riding his motorcycle dying instantly. Because he was thrown completely off his bike about twenty feet never gave him a chance. All I could think why it should have taken place was why God had taken him when he had only begun his life.

End of Check Yourself Section E. Check the key now.

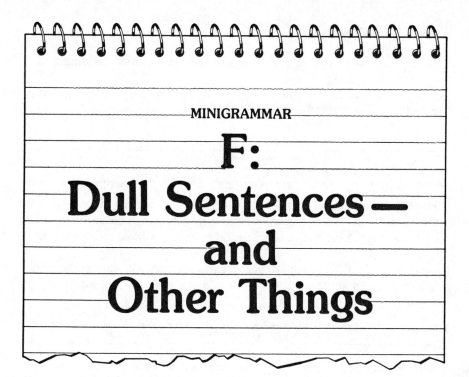

F:
Dull Sentences—
and
Other Things

There is no diagnostic section with this minigrammar, because it is a bit different from the others, and you should work through it, whatever your level of writing achievement may be.

By now, you should understand the basic problems of "writing correctly." You may not have assimilated them fully; perhaps you still need to think twice about whether your subjects and predicates agree, whether you have written a run-on sentence, whether your pronouns are clear and unambiguous. If you have special problems, you should by now have brought them to your instructor for special help.

Probably many times you have felt like a slave to language, letting it dictate to you. Gradually, however, you should be experiencing a greater sense of control and an ability to become to some extent the master of the words you use, not their slave.

You should be becoming aware there are alternative ways of doing things, many ways of handling language, all of which are correct, but some of which are more effective than others.

VARIETY IN SENTENCE STRUCTURES

A time-honored dichotomy is the relationship between uniformity and variety. In language, uniformity is embodied in the rules we all follow. Variety comes out of the flexibility—the various ways of using language—and our ability to rearrange words according to our desires, to "play around" with them. Variety is the key to keeping sentences from becoming dull, monotonous, boring.

Usually sentences become boring when (1) they are all about the same length, (2) they have the same structure, or (3) they begin with the same word. Look at these two sentences.

I hate to get up in the morning.
I'd rather stay in bed until noon.

These sentences suffer from all three problems mentioned. They are about the same length: the first sentence has eight words; the second has seven. Both sentences have the same structure: subject, predicate, completer. Both begin with "I."

There are numerous ways to vary these sentences. The simplest would be to join them in some way, without of course turning them into a run-on sentence:

I hate to get up in the morning; I'd rather stay in bed until noon.

Another way might be to change the structure of one sentence.

I hate to get up in the morning. Why can't I stay in bed until noon?
I hate to get up in the morning. Staying in bed until noon is what really turns me on.

Both length and structure may be changed to provide greater variety:

Get up in the morning? Not I. If I have my choice, I'll stay in bed until noon.

Exercise F-1   *Eliminating Dullness Resulting from Similar Length and Structure*

Rewrite the following passage to eliminate dullness in the sentences. Try several different combinations. Play around with the sentences until you have a revision that pleases you. *Do not begin any two consecutive sentences with the same word.*

I love to go camping. I go every summer at least once. Usually we camp in the mountains. Sometimes we camp at the ocean. My favorite place is by a swift mountain stream. There are tall evergreens. A snow-capped mountain appears in a gap in the trees. It is a beautiful scene. I like to hear the rushing water at night. I can look from the open tent flap. I see stars twinkling in the dark sky. The outline of the mountain is barely visible in the moonlight.

SENTENCE COMBINING

There are a few rather mechanical ways that may help you to vary sentence structures:

1. Combine two sentences with the same subject or predicate into one sentence with a compound subject or predicate.

Two sentences	Combined
Sally went to town. I went too.	Sally and I went to town.
I crept up to the house. I looked into the window	I crept up to the house and looked into the window.

2. Sentences may be joined by a semicolon (;) or by a coordinate conjunction (usually *and, but, or*) if the ideas in each are equally important.

Two sentences	Combined
The two men rode their motorcycles to the fair. The boys followed on bicycles.	The two men rode their motorcycles to to the fair, and the boys followed on bicycles. The two men rode their motorcycles to the fair; the boys followed on bicycles.

3. When two sentences work together but one has a more important idea, make a main clause of the important idea and turn the other into a subordinate clause showing relationship, using words such as *which, who, that* or *because, since, although* to introduce the subordinate clause.

Two sentences	Combined
The train ran right through the middle of town. It always rattled and clanged, its couplings banging against one another with a deafening clatter.	The *train*, which ran right through town, *always rattled and clanged, its couplings banging against one another with a deafening clatter.* The *train*, which always rattled and clanged, its couplings banging against one another with a deafening clatter, *ran right through the middle of town.* (Main clauses italicized.)
I finished all my homework. I went to a movie.	After I finished all my homework, *I went went to a movie.* *I went to a movie* after I finished all my homework. Before I went to a movie, *I finished all my homework.*

4. Forms of verbs marked by *-ing* and *-ed* (called *verbals*) can be used to achieve sentence variety.

Two sentences	Combined
The old man went home to die He had completed his mission in life.	Having completed his mission in life, the old man went home to die.

Exercise F-2   *Using Techniques for Varied Sentence Structures*

Combine the following sentences, using the methods indicated by the numbers in the parentheses and referring to the explanations above. If you are unsure about the grammar of your version, consult your instructor.

1. The moon shone brightly on the lake. It lighted up the whole scene almost as if it were day. (1)

2. Dark clouds began to rise off on the horizon. Soon they began to creep upward. (2)

3. The moon continued to shed its brilliance over the lake. It rode serenely in the night sky. (3)

4. The clouds rose ever higher. Soon they covered the moon completely. (4)

5. The wind began to blow. Waves appeared on the lake. (2)

6. The houses on the shore disappeared from view in the blinding rain. The little boats bobbing at the dock disappeared too. (1)

7. The wind grew stronger. It came out of the west. (3) or (4)

8. Soon we realized we were in a real storm. Our little boat was in terrible danger of being swamped. (2)

9. At last we heard the sound of a powerful motor coming out of the rain. It seemed like an age. (3)

10. We headed homeward in the motor boat. We towed our little rowboat behind. (4)

Exercise F-3   *Varying Sentence Structures in a Paragraph*

Write the sentences from Exercise F-2 into a paragraph, making sure (1) that each sentence flows logically and coherently into the next one and (2) that there is sufficient variety of sentence length and structure to keep the paragraph from becoming monotonous. You may change the sentences in any way you wish, but retain the essential meaning and the significant details.

OTHER THINGS

Numerous relatively minor but recurring problems keep popping up in student papers. You need to be aware of them and check your writing for them.

Intensives

At least five words people use to give added intensity to their writing often can—and should—be omitted. Usually they add little and sometimes actually weaken the impact.

These words are *very, really, much, so,* and *just.* Watch out for them!

The following examples were taken from student papers. In no case does the intensive justify its use. Remember: *Every unnecessary word slows down the forward movement of your writing.* Intensives have legitimate uses, but all can be misused.

---

1. The test papers were distributed and the test began. Everyone was ~~very~~ quiet. Everyone but me.
2. Last month I almost got killed. It's ~~really~~ funny to me now, but it sure wasn't then.
3. It's ~~really~~ sad how teachers can sometimes, instead of arousing your interest in something, make you lose it completely. This is ~~so~~ true in writing, because it is something you will be doing for the rest of your life.
4. In learning to endure physical work beyond the discomfort of pain, a runner gains a psychological advantage. He is ~~much~~ better able to handle difficult tasks in all aspects of life.
5. Imagine, if you will, that we have ~~just~~ turned back the hands of time and are about to witness the first human being ever to write. Here he comes.

The Verbs *to Be* and *to Get*

Two of the most overused words in the English language are the verbs *to be* and *to get.* Watch for them in your writing. It isn't wrong to use them, but try to cut down the frequency with which you do. In particular, see if you can find other verbs to substitute for *to get,* as usually there is a better and more interesting word.

Overuse of *to be*	Passage rewritten
I *was* in Miss Riley's fourth grade class She *was* a tall, dark-haired lady with brown eyes. She used bright red lipstick and wore pleated, plaid skirts with button sweaters and low-heeled shoes. Her	My fourth grade teacher *was* Miss Riley, a tall, dark-haired lady with brown eyes. She used bright red lipstick and wore pleated, plaid skirts with button sweaters and low-heeled shoes. Her

nylons caused the dark, heavy hair to lie flat against her legs.

Miss Riley *was* a Catholic. Her unconcealed pet *was* Tim, who *was* also a Catholic. Monday morning she would discuss church with him in class, while the rest of us sat and waited for them to get done talking. She *was* hard on my ego. Three or four of us *were* gathered around her desk one day talking about how strong we *were*, and we shoved up our sleeves to show her how hard our biceps *were*. She felt Tim's arm and the arms of a couple of other boys and *was* duly impressed. I *was* left standing with my sleeve shoved up.

[11 forms of *to be*]

nylons caused the dark, heavy hair to lie flat against her legs.

Miss Riley, a Catholic, had an unconcealed pet, Tim, also a Catholic. Monday morning she would discuss church with him in class, while the rest of us sat and waited for them to get done talking. She *was* hard on my ego. One day as three or four boys and I gathered around her desk boasting about our strength, we shoved up our sleeves to display our hard biceps. Duly impressed, she felt Tim's arm and the arms of a couple of other guys. I *was* left standing with my sleeves pushed up.

[3 forms of *to be*]

Overuse of *to get*

We *got* up about eight in the morning, and the sun was *getting* bright, so we decided to go sightseeing around Hong Kong, where we were on shore leave, and *get* a few pictures. Grabbing our cameras, away we went. We finally *got* a taxi, but it didn't look like one. It was a black Mercedes Benz, and it looked like the guy had spent all morning polishing it and had *gotten* the red interior as pretty and clean as the outside. I *got* a shock to see the driver wearing a sports jacket and tie. I couldn't remember ever seeing a taxicab driver in the U.S. dressed up like this guy.

[6 forms of *to get*]

Passage rewritten

We *got* up about eight in the morning, and the sun was shining, so we decided to go sightseeing around Hong Kong, where we were on shore leave, and take a few pictures. Grabbing our cameras, away we went. We finally flagged a taxi, but it didn't look like one. It was a black Mercedes Benz, and it looked like the guy had spent all morning polishing it. The red interior was as pretty and clean as the outside. It shocked me to see the driver wearing a sports jacket and tie. I couldn't remember ever seeing a taxicab driver in the U.S. dressed up like this guy.

[1 form of *to get*]

A final word: You will not be completing this course in a couple weeks; you will be completing it in a couple *of* weeks. Get that *of* in there!

Exercise F-4   *Reducing Forms of* to Be *and* to Get

In the following passage, reduce the forms of *to be* by at least half. Eliminate all forms of *to get* and all intensives. Watch out for other problems, too.

The walls were very simple—concrete of a dull, off-white color. On the pale brown lockers, all in rows, were pieces of tape, someone's phone number, and other scribblings. Alongside the lockers were a couple thin, narrow wooden benches. On the blackboard in front, one got a glimpse of different offensive and defensive plays that looked just like a four-year-old was playing with some chalk.

There were sinks and mirrors lining the wall in front of the showers. In the soap dishes the soap was getting soft, like mounds of semimelted snow. Papers, used strips of tape, and pieces of dried mud from yesterday's practice were scattered on the floor, and the benches really were pretty much like canoes floating in a polluted stream.

As the players were drifting in, comments, usually foul and sarcastic, got exchanged. The sound of clicking, cleated footsteps on the cement floor and the slamming shudder of the outside door meant, "Hurry. We've got to get to practice."

CHECK YOURSELF SECTION F

In the following story, do whatever you can to improve the mechanics, spelling, and grammar.

In Search of the First Writer

Imagine if you will, that we have just turned back the hands of time and are about to witness the first being ever to write. Here he comes. The instrument he carries was probably designed especially for the purpose of writing. Notice how the caveman firmly grasps onto the stick and moves it along the stone wall. Here comes another man. Lets listen in on the two.

"Hey red, what ya got goin?"

"I just invented a new way to sharpen our spears."

Oh well, I guess we went back a little to far. Lets try it again. Moving up twenty years we run across the same men and the same wall.

"You know something Fred?"

"What Barney?"

"We've sharpened all our spears on this wall. Without knowing it we have filled this wall with marks, grooves and lines. Are you thinking what I'm thinking?"

"Ya, lets move to a new wall."

"Sounds good! Lets go."

Forget it, these two idiots probably haven't yet discovered there feet let alone writting.

We now move to a new place and time farther up in human development. Here comes a dud in a dugout canoe let's see if he can tell us who the first writer was.

"Sir, Sir, could you pull your boat over to the bank and talk with us a while. Thankyou. Are there any people around here that do any carving or painting on walls?"

"No, if its important we usually write it on paper."

"You mean all of your kind write?"

"Sure, doesn't everyone!"

"Could you tell us who started it?"

"Horse, the biggest guy around. He owns the papyrus plantation."

"And how might we find him?"

Go up the river and hang a right two pyramids past the waterfall. It's the first oasis on the left. You can't miss it."

As we approach his home we can't help but notice how wealthy he must be. His house is very large and his plantation streaches for miles. A slave leads us to the owner.

"Mr. Horse we are from the future and have been told that you are the first person to write. Is it true and if so could you tell us how it all came about?

"Yes, it is true and it all started one day when we weren't so well off. Sam our neighbor, Betty Lou my wife and I were all sitting around the house one day sipping coke and trying to figure out what to do with all the papyrus weeds on our lawn. (We later learned he invented coke.) This guy from India comes by and trys to sell us this black liquid. He tells us you can polish your shoes with it. Fine and dandy, but we haven't got any shoes. Being a high pressure salesman he said its uses are in the thousands. It makes an excellent rock I said as I through the bottle across the yard. When the jar hit the ground it opened and splattered on the plants. Upon closer observation of the plants we found some far out designs. I grabbed Sam's touthpick and tried putting the liquid on the plants myself. And the rest is history."

There you have it folks, straight from the Horses mouth. You have witnessed for yourself that writting from the beginning of time was a farce. Therefore I submitt that this writting is also a farce. But fear not, out of every evil comes some good, and in this case an immoral moral.

Moral: Money is everything and don't let anyone tell you different.

Appendix

Keys

KEY TO MINIGRAMMAR A

Diagnostic Section A

1.
thing	one	warmth
morning	wonders	sun
plunge	those	We
lake	mornings	waters
water	plunge	sun
it	ritual	It
It	I	sun
my	it	ours
breath	I	its
instant	I	rays
it	myself	us
my	I	anything
breath	It	else
It	something	earth
feeling	I	

2.
realized	tugged	lay
was	sat	was
rolled	looked	shrouded
singing	was	cast
splashing	broken	crept

sleeping	melting	breathing
began	strained	became
to run	oncoming	labored
passed	was	

3. wind blows
   they are
   leaves scurry
   Man is trying
   We are collecting burning
   more are
   spirit can be admired
   They seem to be reaching
   They resist
   leaves have

Exercise A-1

were	took	to ask
centered	to talk	coming
met	continuing	said
was	felt	Do
standing	recognizing	know
looked	knowing	are ('re)
were	to go	supposed
seemed	did	to go
to know	know	did
were	to do	did
going	was	want
were	trying	to know
doing	to get	

Exercise A-2

I	queen	she
her	I	I
night	all	"jitters"
warmth	things	I
my	we	I
blood	It	fifteen-year-old
I	one	my
her	those	date
I	nights	girl
visions	I	who
her	my	me
her	mind	class
desk	her	I
her	I	ring
studies	her	her
beauty	call	roommate

Exercise A-3

1. Did the <u>beauties</u> of each day ever cease to thrill him?
2. Do the <u>children</u> race out to the beach, screaming happily?
3. Did two young <u>men</u> in black jackets come blasting into town on their motorbikes?
4. Is <u>everybody</u> in town excited about the President's visit?
5. Did both the <u>men</u> and the <u>women</u> vote against allowing nudity on the public beach? (If you underlined <u>both</u>, that is all right.)

Exercise A-4

1. horses, motorcycles, jeeps (Are horses, motorcycles, and jeeps allowed on this road?)
2. Boy Scouts, (acid) freaks, couple, family (Did six Boy Scouts, two acid freaks, a retired couple, and a family of four ride the lift to the top of the mountain?)
3. Sue, Betty, I (Did Sue, Betty, and I go along?)
4. man, woman (Did a very large man and a tiny woman enter the restaurant?)

Exercise A-5

1. snow (Was there snow on the ground this morning?)
2. apples (Were there two apples in the refrigerator?)
3. horses, cows, sow (Were there three horses, two cows, and a fat sow with an uncountable number of squirming piglets in the barn?)

Exercise A-6

1. life	4. tongue	7. windows, door
2. record	5. chance	
3. reasons	6. effort	

Exercise A-7

1. <u>George Jim</u> <u>decided</u>
2. <u>perseverance</u> <u>patience</u> <u>will be</u>
3. <u>contestant</u> <u>was being flown</u>
4. <u>speaker</u> <u>was</u>   <u>it was</u>   <u>who won</u>
5. <u>graduates</u> <u>are having</u>   <u>competition is</u>
6. <u>Marvin</u> <u>was</u>   <u>he started</u>
7. <u>college</u> <u>should have won</u>   <u>it</u> <u>would have put</u>
8. <u>are reasons</u>   <u>one lives</u>
9. <u>decision</u> <u>has focused</u>
10. <u>president</u> <u>rigged</u>

Exercise A-8

1. buy   4. run
2. tells   5. dashes
3. go   6. cooperate

Exercise A-9

1. are   6. is
2. has   7. go
3. thinks 8. come
4. is   9. sounds
5. runs   10. was

Check Yourself Section A

1. it is
   we took
   trouble exists
   country has produced
   that are
   coal wood were
   came gas oil
   country has been industrialized
   we have used
   We import
   companies assure
   are areas
   that may yield
   they have been discovered
   are we going
   we run can import

2. look   doesn't   was
   feel   aren't   are
   appears   are   are
   are   look
   has   make

KEY TO MINIGRAMMAR B

Diagnostic Section B

I didn't want to start band, but they ~~convince~~ convinced me to play. At the first lesson I ~~takes~~ took

out my horn, <u>showed</u> it to my teacher and <u>was</u> curtly ~~inform~~ it ~~ain't~~ worth five dollars.
(above: informed   wasn't)

But somehow, with lessons, practice sessions, and tears, I <u>managed</u> <u>to get</u> through the first lesson book and into the band. I ~~learn~~ fast that <u>sitting</u> at the end of the trumpet section in the junior high band <u>wasn't</u> enjoyable. Finally, thoroughly <u>frustrated</u>, I ~~begun~~
(above "learn": learned) (above "begun": began)

to show up at study hall instead of band class. My band instructor, very angry when he ~~finds~~ out, ~~yank~~ me out of study hall. I <u>went</u> back to band and ~~hate~~ it, but I ~~kepted~~ at it. From last chair in junior high I ~~progress~~ to first in senior high. That's how I ~~learn~~ the truth of the old <u>saying</u>, "Anything <u>is</u> possible."
(above "finds": found) (above "yank": yanked) (above "hate": hated) (above "kepted": kept) (above "progress": progressed) (above "learn": learned)

Exercise B-1

1. past		**6.** present
2. present		**7.** present
3. past		**8.** present
4. present		**9.** past
5. past		**10.** present

Exercise B-2

It is a discouraging start. In eighth grade, I persuade my parents to let me have a better horn. Just when I get the hang of playing, we begin to march outside. I can't keep in line, let alone play and stay in step. I still need a better horn, so I start delivering papers to save up for the trumpet I have my eye on. I have been looking forward to high school, but right away I find out that band is tougher than I expect. People who sit at the top of each section usually have three years under their belts. Heading down to a music camp the next summer is great. Only a lone senior sits ahead of me my sophomore year; his sound is silky smooth. My trumpet screams out high notes and finishes with a flurry that leaves the air shimmering; the crowd loves it!

Exercise B-3

It was a discouraging start. In eighth grade, I persuaded my parents to let me have a better horn. Just when I got the hang of playing, we began to march outside. I couldn't keep in line, let alone play and stay in step. I still needed a better horn, so I started delivering papers to save up for the trumpet I had my eye on. I had been looking forward to high school, but right away I found out that band was tougher than I expected. People who sat at the top of each section usually had three years under their belts. Heading down to a music camp the next summer was great. Only a lone senior sat ahead of me my sophomore year; his sound was silky smooth. My trumpet screamed out high notes and finished with a flurry that left the air shimmering; the crowd loved it!

Exercise B-4

Consult the list in the minigrammar.

Exercise B-5

Infinitive (present)	Past tense	Past participle
try	tried	tried
hunt	hunted	hunted
judge	judged	judged
urge	urged	urged
cast	cast	cast
satisfy	satisfied	satisfied
troll	trolled	trolled
hide	hid	hidden
sprout	sprouted	sprouted
wash	washed	washed
mount	mounted	mounted
run	ran	run
plead	pleaded	pleaded
flop	flopped	flopped
conceive	conceived	conceived
pay	paid	paid
set	set	set
sit	sat	sat
plow	plowed	plowed
choose	chose	chosen
catch	caught	caught
bring	brought	brought

Exercise B-6

Traveling with the carnival, we came to a small town with a population of about a thousand. This was the last county fair we were supposed to play in this year's circuit of the north. When we arrived, it was cold and damp. Soon it began to rain. What a drag, another hick town! But that was where the money was.

The fellows started setting up the rides and concession stands. There came the clang, clang sound of iron against iron. Someone yelled, "You s.o.b., watch it!" Up came the steel skeletons of the rides above the building, outlined against the sky and trees. Everyone was hurrying, for the opening was only a few hours away.

Exercise B-7

At last, opening! The night is bright with colorful lights from the rides and they seem to say, "Come take a ride on me, and I'll give you the thrill of your life!" From the carousel comes the sound of the calliope playing a catching tune, and before I know it, I am humming: de-de-dum, de-de-dum, da-da-dum.

Across the way, a girl yells, "Snow cones, snow cones, get your snow cones!" Ah, what is that smell? It's (It is) onions frying. I envision the hamburgers and French fries. The aroma floats through the air and makes me hungry. Growl, there goes my stomach!

(Make a value judgment here: do you like this carnival story better in present tense or past tense? The writer did it originally in present tense.)

Exercise B-8

Nouns	Predicates
Observing	can be
To perform	is
to talk	is
to smile	can do
to tell	is intended
Watching	is
being hypnotized	would be
	is
	is
	feel
	am becoming

Exercise B-9

Adjectives	Predicates
performing	reminds
controlled	were looked
malfunctioning	did work
dancing	were considered
singing	think
forbidding	look
	know
	is
	can hide

Check Yourself Section B

I conned the fellows into spending their money. "Come on in. Take a chance. Win

     couldn't help

a giant teddy bear!" I ~~can't help~~ but watch the confidence on their faces and then the

     thought

disappointment. I ~~thinks,~~ Sucker!"

    came

  Here ~~come~~ my relief. I could take a break and see how the others were doing.

 started

I ~~starts~~ walking amidst the spectators and came upon the rides. The sound of tapes

      was   flirted

blasting out hard rock songs ~~is~~ enough to make me deaf. The ride boys ~~flirt~~ and

tried   used

~~try~~ to make the locals. I ~~use~~ to fall for them myself, but not any more. I reached my

                 were

my destination, the cook shack, and some of the fellows ~~are~~ already there for their

   asked   it was

break. Sam ~~asks~~ "How about some carney steak?" Would you believe ~~it's~~ fried

bologna? It sure tasted good with lettuce and mayonnaise.

KEY TO MINIGRAMMAR C

Diagnostic Section C

1.

1. S	**6.** SF	**11.** SF	**16.** SF
2. S	**7.** SF	**12.** SF	**17.** SF
3. S	**8.** S	**13.** S	**18.** S
4. S	**9.** S	**14.** SF	**19.** SF
5. S	**10.** S	**15.** S	**20.** S

2.

1. S	**5.** SF
2. ROS	**6.** S
3. S	**7.** ROS
4. S	**8.** ROS

Exercise C-1

Shutting V	Forgetting V	feeling N
Shutting V	crooning A	breathing V
locked A	relaxed A	soaring V
Relaxing V		

Exercise C-2

1. S	**4.** S	**7.** S
2. SF	**5.** SF	**8.** S
3. S	**6.** S	**9.** SF

Exercise C-3

We were having a good day, doing just what we wanted to do. The wind was blowing up a storm. But we were having too much fun to pay any attention. Soon, however, noticing the quickening gale, the stirring of the leaves in the trees, the rain beginning to patter down on the sand, we ran for shelter. But we had waited too long and were soaked before we reached the old barn on the hill. We had learned our lesson, and the next time the weather began to threaten, we gathered up our things quickly and escaped the downpour, proving you can teach young dogs new tricks.

Exercise C-4

1. S	**6.** SF	**11.** SF
2. SF	**7.** S	**12.** S
3. S	**8.** SF	**13.** SF
4. S	**9.** SF	**14.** S
5. SF	**10.** S	**15.** SF

Exercise C-5

All of us think and act the way we do for various reasons, which to a large extent depend on the way we grew up. We have been greatly influenced by our families and friends. I would like to tell you about one of the greatest influences on me, one which most people never have, one which I have rarely talked about and have never written about. She was one of those unfortunate people born mentally retarded, those with no real muscle control, who can never walk, talk, or even sit up. Yet she was a constant source of joy for us and was easily entertained, which we would spend hours doing, entertaining ourselves at the same time. She loved to be held or petted or talked to, and I learned much about patience and love by caring for her, things that I might otherwise never have understood. There is one thing I know: that my little sister, who died suddenly on a cold night last winter, made me more appreciative of life and how lucky I am.

Exercise C-6

1. S	**5.** SF	**8.** SF
2. S	**6.** S	**9.** S
3. SF	**7.** S	**10.** SF
4. S		

Exercise C-7

Should certain classes be required of every person who graduates from college? I don't think so, because in some of the specific courses which are required we students "don't learn a thing." Sometimes we put forth very little effort, especially when we didn't elect the course in the first place. Some required courses are rinky-dink, general in perspective, and too simple for many students from good high schools. Instead of particular courses, we should be required to choose a certain number of hours in each subject group from a published list of courses, where the courses would be described in enough detail so we would know what to expect. With this information we could choose classes which would expand our minds and prove a challenge, although I suppose some students would still be looking for the easiest way out of any requirements.

Exercise C-8

1. ROS	**5.** ROS
2. S	**6.** S
3. ROS	**7.** S
4. S	**8.** ROS

Exercise C-9

Several possible revisions are given for each sentence. If you have a different one, check it with your instructor.
1. I was furious with my uncle; when I started thinking, I was sure I could have dug in that stupid hole all night and never reached China.
   I was furious with my uncle, because when I started thinking, I was sure . . .
   When I started thinking about it, I was furious with my uncle, as I was sure I could have dug . . .
   I was furious with my uncle. When I started thinking, I was . . .
2. I came to the conclusion grown-ups weren't really so smart; they had a lot of dumb ideas and didn't know much about anything.
   I came to the conclusion grown-ups weren't really so smart, since they had a lot dumb ideas and . . .
   I came to the conclusion grown-ups weren't really so smart. They had a lot of dumb ideas and . . .
3. Ever since, I've only half believed ideas that sounded a little fishy, and I usually check out advice before I follow it.
   Ever since, I've only half believed ideas that sounded a little fishy; I usually check out . . .
   Ever since, because I've only half believed ideas that sounded a little fishy, I usually check out . . .

Exercise C-10

1. Everyone would like to become famous; however, only a few actually do.
   Although everyone would like to become famous, only a few actually do.
   Everyone would like to become famous. However, only a few actually do.

2. It was a dark, cloudy day; therefore we stayed in and played cards.
It was a dark cloudy day. Therefore we stayed in and played cards.
Since it was a dark, cloudy day, we stayed in and played cards.

3. Mary did everything she could to block Tom's appointment. Nevertheless, he was given the position.
Mary did everything she could to block Tom's appointment; nevertheless, he was given the position.
Though Mary did everything she could to block Tom's appointment, he was given the position.

4. The children dashed across the bridge and then they saw the danger they were in.
The children dashed across the bridge. Then they saw the danger they were in.
The children dashed across the bridge; then they saw the danger they were in.

5. I couldn't see his point, however; I still had the same opinion as when I began talking to him.
I couldn't see his point, however. I still had the same opinion as when I began talking to him.

Check Yourself Section C

1.

1. S	**6.** S	**11.** S
2. SF	**7.** SF	**12.** SF
3. SF	**8.** S	**13.** SF
4. S	**9.** SF	**14.** S
5. S	**10.** S	**15.** SF

The world is a strange and often difficult place in which to live, a world in which we see many diversities, such as men landing on the moon one second and men starving in our own country the next. We are supposed to live in the richest country in the world. But we still have hungry kids who don't have enough energy to go to school. The unfortunate fact is that rich, affluent people don't open their eyes to what is going on around them, although we are not exactly opening our eyes to the facts either. Until we do, the world will remain its old, poor, starving self, where children die at a rate that would astound us if we knew. And we sit here doing nothing about it. While you have been reading this, nine children have died in the United States, and somewhere in the world, thirty children, of starvation alone. Isn't it time to be doing something, like writing your congressman or helping through CARE or UNESCO?

Note: Minor differences in composing this paragraph are, of course, acceptable, providing you have eliminated all sentence fragments. If you are not sure, check your paragraph with your instructor.

2.

1. S	**5.** ROS
2. ROS	**6.** S
3. ROS	**7.** ROS
4. S	

I will never know how someone can flatly state "Boy! I just hate to write," or "Teacher, teacher! I just L-O-V-E to write." Writing is such a broad and diverse activity that it's impossible to give a 100-percent truthful opinion in a few words. For a month and a half this summer I kept a journal while I was out west traveling; it was no chore for me to pick up a pen and write three pages of events, experiences, and emotions in that journal. I don't think I enjoyed anything as much on that trip as lying by the campfire, writing about all the wonderful and miserable things that had happened that day. The best part is now that I'm home I have a set of memories inside that beat-up, blue notebook worth more than a thousand color slides. But my feelings can jump to the other spectrum too: if you have ever filled out an application that wanted you to state in three hundred words what your future occupational plans were, you know what I mean. Or maybe you have had an experience such as I did with the epitome of all miserable writing assignments. An old, senile teacher wanted a five-page combination report and reaction to present-day draft dodgers. After four nights in the library and a lot of B.S., I had a paper that got me an A. More important, I had developed a lasting dislike for composition classes.

Note: This is one way to revise and "correct" this passage; there are others. The main thing is to eliminate all run-on sentences, of course. If you are not sure you have done that, check with your instructor. A little rewording and some added punctuation have also been included here in an effort to make the passage read more clearly and communicate better with the reader.

KEY TO MINIGRAMMAR D

Note: Increasingly, there are alternate ways of "solving" the exercises, and the one given here will be only one of several possible ways. Increasingly, however, you should also be growing more sophisticated, more sure of yourself, and you should be able to see the basic purposes behind the "solutions" and be able to judge whether yours meets the criteria just as well. If you have any doubt, talk to your instructor. Discussing the things that arise as real problems to *you* is a valuable activity, and you may learn far more from asking about things you don't understand than from pages of exercises that you can handle with relative ease.

Diagnostic Section D

1. *my:* the referent is "I"; *they:* the referent is "teacher"; *them:* the referent is "words." *They* is faulty, as the referent "teacher" is singular.
2. *my:* the referent is "I"; *that:* None. *That* is an example of a vague pronoun reference; it does not refer clearly to any one thing. It could be the whole foregoing paragraph, or only the last sentence, or anything in between.
3. No pronouns.
4. *It:* the referent is "good writing"; *yourself:* None. Both these pronouns are used poorly. *It* could refer to either "good writing" or "free writing" and is therefore an example of a vague pronoun reference. *Yourself* has no antecedent at all, because the rest of the essay has been done in the first person (*I, my, myself,* etc.) and there is here a sudden shift to second person (*you, your, yourself,* etc.). Avoid such a shift in most instances.

5. *my:* the referent is "I."
6. No pronouns.
7. No pronouns.
8. *it:* None. Faulty pronoun use. There is nothing *it* could refer to.
9. No pronouns.
10. *it:* None. Faulty pronoun use. No referent to show what *it* means.

Exercise D-1

1. (*they* has a vague referent.) The eight—sometimes nine—hours of slumber ebb away and the cramped areas of my body begin to come alive as I wake up in the morning and stretch.
2. No vague pronoun.
3. (*its* has a vague referent.) The brisk, blue February sky spawns spent white pillows of God in the dawn of a new day which seems to rejoice in its unveiling as golden strands of sunlight shower warmth and beauty upon the earth.
4. (the first *it* has a vague referent.) As I draw the curtains to shut out the beauty of the morning . . .
5. No vague pronoun.
6. No vague pronoun.
7. No vague pronoun.
8. (*it* has a vague referent.) Then I find myself at my desk writing to ease the angry thoughts swelling in my head.
9. No vague pronoun.
10. (*It* has a vague referent.) My writing isn't laid down according to strict rules and regulations, but spews forth thoughts as they come—careless, sincere thoughts of anger!

Exercise D-2

1. No faulty agreement.
2. No faulty agreement.
3. I'll bet way back in elementary and junior high school, everyone was like me and thought writing was a pain, probably not understanding its significance.
4. Sometimes people can have fun and learn to appreciate writing more if they play around with words a little.
5. (There is a question here: the switch to *you* is rather abrupt, though it doesn't interfere as much as in some contexts. Possibly it would work better to revise this sentence to something like: Everyone may have written a silly poem at least once, but if you haven't, try one.)
6. No faulty agreement.
7. No faulty agreement.
8. Of course, each person may have his or her own way of getting past that first reluctance to start using language as an effective tool.
9. No faulty agreement.
10. Writers run into trouble if neither they nor their readers can understand what is being talked about.

11. If ideas come out scattered as in the poem above, how then can anyone know what a writer is trying to say?

12. (This is a borderline case, in that *which* rather clearly refers to *principle for writing* and not to *writing* alone. But be on the lookout for this kind of difficulty.)

13. No faulty agreement.

14 (*one* is awkward here; this is a place where this kind of shifting for variety doesn't work well. And things get worse as the sentence goes on; the second person, which has been carried throughout this paragraph, is dropped and the whole thing shifts from singular to plural.) If you have to, prop your feet up on a chair, but don't let other ideas and thoughts hinder what you wish to express on paper.

15. No faulty agreement.

Check Yourself Section D

Teachers Unite

It's no wonder students are mixed up about writing by the time they get to college. Here's how their earlier schooling probably has gone. In kindergarten they are taught writing consists of printing the alphabet in large capital letters, an idea that seems pretty reasonable at the time. But then in first grade they find out about lowercase letters, and when and where to use them. By the end of the first year, all students know how to hold their pencils correctly and how to print perfectly, accomplishments they are proud of.

Alas, to their surprise upon entering second grade, these same children are *punished* for printing, while in third grade all they hear is "Don't write backhand," "Sit up straight," "Don't hold your fingers too close to the lead."

In the next three grades, they learn mostly about putting writing skills into practice. Among other things, they learn to write reports about something or somebody that really means nothing to them. It doesn't matter how good the report is, only if it is long enough.

In junior high, students find out it is against the law to copy what someone else has written without giving credit to the author. Also, English isn't English any more; it's Grammar. About this time, students begin to think writing is pretty heavy and wonder if they want to write anymore. In high school, more things are thrown at the student: principally big papers with an introduction, five to ten footnotes, a bibliography with at least five sources used, an outline, and a summary.

Finally in college there is an emphasis on the student's using his or her own mind. Each teacher expects something different. Some day all the teachers in all the schools and colleges should get together and decide what they expect of students!

Note: If you are pretty sure your revisions solve the pronoun problems of the foregoing exercises, fine. If not, check with your instructor.

KEY TO MINIGRAMMAR E

Diagnostic Section E

The following "solution" is not the only one possible. If you are not sure about your version, check with your instructor.

1. When I was in the eighth grade, Saturday afternoon excitement consisted of going to a local shopping mall for a day.   2. Watching people and hanging around the stores was fun, but shoplifting was what particularly excited us.   3. Seeing who could steal most in one day was what made it fun.   4. We stole all sorts of things, ranging from candy to perfume.   5. But we didn't bother with big things like clothes and typewriters, because they were too dangerous to try to steal.   6. We concentrated on candy, cosmetics, and jewelry.

7. One Saturday morning, as we were browsing around Montgomery Ward's makeup counter, a new type of mascara caught our eyes.   8. It was hanging on a rack right in front of us.   9. There it was, staring us in the face, and, with no sales lady behind the counter, each of us knew what the others were thinking.   10. Linda, Peggy, Martha, and I drew straws; I was elected.

Exercise E-1

As before, you may have a different version. Make your own choice about which of the two ideas should be in the independent clause in order to gain the best emphasis; there is no "right" answer.

1. Linda grabbed two more tubes and dropped them in her purse, after which we nonchalantly looked around a few minutes and then walked away.   2. We stayed in the store for a while, feeling successful about our rip-off, after which we left.
3. When we were outside the store, we heard a man talking to us.   4. He said in an accusing voice, as he pointed to a corner, "Girls, come with me."   5. We walked the way he directed, while he followed us.   6. When we were in the corner, he asked, "What do you have in those bags that doesn't belong to you?"

Exercise E-2

1. Feeling stupid and scared, we continued to cower there in the corner.
2. People were staring curiously at us as they walked by.   3. I forced my eyes, which kept wandering toward Linda's purse, to look in a different direction.   4. Finally, the man motioned for us to go inside and walk through the store.   5. Feeling like a criminal as he stayed close behind us, I thought we would never reach the elevator.   6. All the way up, I tried to keep myself from crying. (No misplaced modifier.)

Exercise E-3

1. After what seemed ages, the elevator stopped at the third floor, where the offices were.   2. As we walked miserably down the hall, the man kept right behind us.   3. We entered the office and saw a heavyset man sitting at a cluttered desk; he

looked as if he expected us.   **4.** The mean look on his face frightened us all the more.   **5.** Motioning us to sit down in chairs, he leaned forward and studied our faces intently.

Exercise E-4

1. As we sat there imagining what our parents' reaction would be, I wondered if I would be grounded and whether my dad would hit me.   **2.** Hearing his voice come over the phone in reply to the manager did not make me feel any better. (Or: When I heard his voice coming over the phone in reply to the manager, I didn't feel any better.)   **3.** His voice sounded both shaky and angry.   **4.** I couldn't hear what he said but I did hear the manager's reply. "No. No mistake. It's your daughter. We caught her shoplifting."   **5.** As I strained to hear, the manager paused again and then said, "Please come down to pick her up. It's routine."

Exercise E-5

1. There is no worse feeling than wanting the ground to open up and swallow you.   **2.** I wanted to disappear into thin air when my father arrived.   **3.** The importance of having my parents' respect hit me hard.   **4.** To say I was overcome with guilt all the way home is to put it mildly.   **5.** Since that Saturday, I have never stolen another thing.

Check Yourself Section E

Death is one of the hardest things to understand. Accepting it is one thing, but understanding it is another. I have been hit with death in many different ways, and each time it hurt me and left me with an empty feeling. As time went on, the pain lessened; however, there were always certain things that reminded me of it. I was reminded especially by accounts of murders and accidents in the newspapers. Death, I always had thought, happened only to the old and the sick. I wanted to believe it never hit young and healthy people and only took place in James Bond movies or some far-off place, never in our small, quiet safe town. Then one Sunday, a seventeen-year-old friend of mine, while riding his motorcycle, was hit by a car and died instantly. He never had a chance; he was thrown completely off his bike about twenty feet. All I could think of was "Why should it have taken place? Why did God take him when he had only begun his life?"

(If you are not sure of your version, check with your instructor.)

KEY TO MINIGRAMMAR F

Suggested "solutions" follow. If you have a different one about which you are not sure, check it with your instructor.

Exercise F-1

I love camping and go at least once every summer. Usually we camp in the mountains, though sometimes we go to the ocean. My favorite place is by a swift mountain stream bordered by tall evergreens through which I can see a snow-capped mountain. It is a beautiful scene. At night, I can hear the rushing water, and through the open tent flap I see stars twinkling in the dark sky and the outline of the mountain barely visible in the moonlight.

Exercise F-2

1. The moon shone brightly on the lake and lighted up the whole scene almost as if it were day.
2. Dark clouds began to rise off on the horizon; soon they began to creep upward.
3. As it rode serenely in the night sky, the moon continued to shed its brilliance over the lake.
4. Rising ever higher, the clouds soon covered the moon completely.
5. The wind began to blow, and waves appeared on the lake.
6. The houses on the shore and the little boats bobbing at the dock disappeared from view in the driving rain.
7. The wind coming out of the west grew stronger.
8. Soon we realized we were in a real storm; our little boat was in terrible danger of being swamped.
9. After what seemed like an age, at last we heard the sound of a powerful motor coming out of the rain.
10. We headed homeward in the motor boat, towing our little rowboat behind.

Exercise F-3

No suggested solution. Check your version according to the instructions.

Exercise F-4

Rows of pale brown lockers stood along simple concrete walls of a dull, off-white color. Pieces of tape, someone's phone number, and other messages festooned the lockers, beside which ran a couple of thin, narrow wooden benches. On the blackboard in front, different offensive and defensive plays looked like a four-year-old's chalk scribbles.

Sinks and mirrors lined the wall in front of the showers where the soap in the soap dishes softened, like mounds of semimelted snow. Papers, used strips of tape, and pieces of dried mud from yesterday's practice littered the floor; the benches looked like canoes floating in a polluted stream.

The players drifted in exchanging comments, usually foul and sarcastic. The sound of clicking, cleated footsteps on the cement floor and the slamming shudder of the outside door meant, "Hurry. It's time for practice."

Check Yourself Section F

You're on your own. Do your best.

KEY TO REVISING ACTIVITY 3-2 (p. 46)

Note: Not all the commas included in this key are absolutely necessary, but the ones shown here, in general, help a reader follow more easily.

1. The student should be required to type every paper he hands in, particularly for the English class.
2. This would not only conserve the eyesight and sweeten the disposition of the professor, but it would help the student learn.
3. He will no longer be able to hide his spelling errors behind blots and erasures and unrecognizable squiggles, and he will learn to spell better.
4. If he can't fatten his essays simply by enlarging his handwriting, he may be forced to come up with some real ideas.
5. And he will be less likely to dash off just any kind of nonsense in order to fill up space; silly statements have a way of looking very silly indeed, even to their author, when they are neatly lined up in precise and impersonal black type.
6. Thus he will be able to see his own errors in a new and painful clarity, deprived of his usual subterfuges: unrecognizable handwriting, great scrawls, and lots of empty words to make up the required five hundred.

KEY TO ACTIVITY 4-3 (p. 59)

The first rays danced in circles around the room. They leaped from my bed onto the floor and waltzed in time with my vanity stool. Tiring of this slow-paced dance, they threw themselves at the wall, climbing up and down, then racing all around the corners. The beauty and radiance of the rays gave a mystical glow to the room.

Suddenly there was a loud tremble outside the room, and a dark, mystical shadow appeared before the window. His angry face looked in and scorned the gaity taking place. He blew a sharp, bitter wind through the open window, which frightened my new friends. Upon seeing the cold, unfriendly face, they scattered in all directions. Their lights whizzed by and out the window. Once again I was left in the darkened stillness.

KEY TO ACTIVITY 4-4 (p. 60)

Paddles dipping quickly into the rushing waters, trees and bushes flashing by, the deep, clean smell of the outdoors assailing one's senses, and the bobwhite's call are all part of that oncoming sport—canoeing. Today everyone is canoeing, causing a growth to twenty percent more canoers on American rivers each year. Senior citizens, families, and young people are discovering the need to get back to the earth, and they are doing just that through canoeing. There are many reasons for the increasing popularity of this sport. The retiree and his wife, after a hectic week of golf and teas, arrive at the river with their Starcraft canoe, ready to get away and leave it all behind them. There are also the families, hoping to increase their togetherness through the outdoors, screaming and yelling at each other all the way down the river, not to mention the many young people looking for the challenge involved in avoiding river obstacles. "But," you say, "I thought canoeing was for the rugged, and I'm not that type at all." You don't have to be. With two people to a canoe, one guiding and the other steering, the trip can be smooth and enjoyable.

Making
Groups Work

S ometime during the term you may be assigned to a group, either for one day to work on a particular paper or for a longer time, during which you and the others will meet consistently for a while.

Group work can be a waste of time or it can be valuable. It can serve several worthwhile purposes. For one thing, you probably have a tendency, if you think about a reader at all, to think "What does my instructor want?" When what you write is to be read by a group, your audience is broadened and you have to take other readers into consideration. It isn't enough to write merely for an instructor. An instructor is only one person, with an inescapably biased outlook. A group can act as a more typical sounding board.

Second, a group gives you an initial hearing before the paper is handed in and can often pinpoint problems you didn't notice yourself. It is easier to see problems in other people's writing than in your own. Then you can revise your work and improve it before handing it in.

Third, by sharpening your own awareness through trying to help other people find their problems, you become increasingly able to look objectively and critically at your own work. You become a better writer; there is a distinct relation between criticizing well and writing well.

Several things must be kept in mind. First you need to understand what is meant by "criticizing" a work. It does not mean to rip it apart and find all the bad things in it. The best criticism is constructive criticism, criticism that helps someone else improve. Since people learn by developing their strengths as well as by correcting their weaknesses, you have a responsibility to point out both. Just as writers have trouble seeing their own problems, they often are not sure when their writing works well. *Make it a habit to say something nice first,* but don't shirk your responsibility to say how you think the writing could be improved.

Many students hesitate to criticize someone else's work because they don't feel they know enough. You aren't expected to be an expert. But if you have paid attention, you know what to look for in the particular piece of writing you are working on. At the very least, you know when your interest suddenly picks up; tell the writer, "This is particularly interesting," even if you can't tell why. You know too when you are bored, when the piece of writing just "lies there" on the page. You can at least say, "This needs something, but I'm not sure what." Maybe someone else in the group can suggest what the problem is. Then the writer has something to go on. When you find a paper dull or you know it hasn't been worked on much, it is dishonest to say, "Pretty good paper, I liked it." (If people say that to *you*, don't let them get away with it. You can be fairly sure your paper is not interesting. Make them tell you why.)

You probably will run into conflicting points of view in your group. Often someone couldn't care less and offers nothing worthwhile. Or someone thinks he or she knows *every* rule in the book and doesn't let you forget it. These people have problems; try to be understanding. As members of a group, you should all realize you are there to help one another. You should take the group work seriously but with enough sense of humor not to give it a touch of death. A group works if all of you respect and enjoy one another.

Use your common sense. If you feel ill at ease in your group, probably others do too. Make it your responsibility to help loosen things up. Some attitudes make a group function poorly; try to help overcome them if you recognize them. An aggressive person who tries to dominate, a negative person who tries to belittle, an excessively shy person, a person who is merely passive, sitting there like a lump on a log: any one of these can spoil a group. Most of these attitudes stem from a feeling of inferiority. Instead of rejecting the person who exhibits them, try to help him or her feel more secure.

Positive attitudes can be cultivated. You can be open and friendly, as well as businesslike, so that the work gets done. Be a good listener; if you serve as a receptive audience for others, they will reciprocate. If something is wrong with the group, start a frank talk to try to solve the problem. Encourage others to enter into the discussions. Above all, be honest and helpful.

All of us are sensitive about having our writing read and criticized. Try to be as objective as possible. If you feel someone is not being honest with you, you have every right to ignore what that person says. If, on the other hand, you know the criticism is serious and well-meaning, swallow that little prick of hurt pride and give serious consideration to what has been said. But feel free to reject the criticism tactfully if you don't feel it is justified. After all, the writing is yours, and you know what you want in it; you must make your own decision. If two or more people have the same comment, however, you had better rethink what you are doing.

By the same token, don't be put off if someone rejects *your* suggestions; others also have the right to make up their own minds. Sometimes they will react defensively at first and later decide you were right after all. Or perhaps you just weren't right. Everyone makes mistakes, so why not you?

Like everything else, a group works when each person assumes a responsibility to make it work. One person can ruin it. Don't let that person be you.

Taking Examinations

The ability to take examinations well is crucial to succeeding in college. Writing isn't much involved in taking objective examinations. To prepare for them, about all you can do is anticipate questions as much as possible and memorize the material. When taking the exam, the most important thing is to *read the instructions carefully and follow them exactly*. Second: *Don't panic*. The mass of material isn't as formidable as it looks at first glance. Often there is more there than anyone is expected to do. Start in and do what you can. Take time to read carefully and think the question through. If a question gives you trouble, skip it and go to the next one. When you've done everything about which you are reasonably certain, come back and start over on the harder questions. You may feel more secure by now, less paralyzed, and be thinking more clearly. If you're not sure, as a last resort, guess. On multiple choice, you have at least a chance to be right. Third: *Don't despair*. Lots of students leave an exam thinking they've failed miserably, only to find most of the others did *worse*. On the curve, you may show up all right after all.

Don't undersell yourself: figure that if someone else can succeed, you can too.

Most of the above holds true in greater or lesser degree when preparing for and taking essay examinations, where your skill in writing *is* involved to a great degree. Your memory is one of your most valuable assets; cultivate it and use it. The professor usually gives you a pretty good idea of what to expect; isolate the things that can be memorized and memorize as much as you can.

Usually you don't know exactly what questions will be asked, though sometimes you will be given a list from which they will be chosen. The professor wants you to review the material and retain more of it in your head than you otherwise would; this is one good reason for giving exams. The other reason is that in a big class the professor may have no other way to grade you. The fact is that when you have to review, you may see new patterns and you will remember more things than you otherwise would have, even though it seems as if you forget everything the moment you walk out the door of the examination room.

Once you have decided what types of questions will be asked, try to frame the *exact* questions as if you were the professor. Then organize material to answer the question you've framed, exactly as if you were going to write a paper on the subject. What facts and figures will you need? What specific instructions can you include? Are there quotations you can memorize to help you support your answer? If you are likely to be asked to compare one thing with another, what specific points can you compare?

Write a sample answer. Chances are the instructor will not ask exactly that question, but writing out answers gives you practice, increases your self-confidence at the time of the exam, and usually helps you retain information you can use to answer similar questions.

Practicing in the relative security of your own room can go far toward increasing your ability to perform well under the tensions of the exam room.

Work out ways of retaining information. Here's how one person does it. First he formulates the questions, then writes the answer. Then he lists the main points in his answer and *memorizes how many main points there are.* Next he memorizes the main points themselves. When he sees the question or one similar to it on the examination, he thinks, "How many points did I have for that? Five." Then he quickly jots down the five points. If he can't remember one, it doesn't matter too much. He has at least four to work with as he answers. Don't expect to remember *everything;* no one does. This procedure may not work for you, but it may give you an idea for your own system.

When taking the examination, remember the following points.

1. As with objective examinations, *read the instructions carefully.* Many an exam is blown simply because the student plows ahead without fully understanding what he or she is supposed to do. *The time taken to be absolutely accurate is not wasted!*

2. Also take time to *look over the entire examination and plan your best approach.* You have a limited time in which to work. Choose which questions you can answer best and start with those. Then go on to the ones you feel less certain about. If the professor tells you how long to take with each question, try to follow that timetable, answering the questions given longer time allotments as fully as you can and preparing briefer answers for the others. If there are no time allotments, write longest on the questions you know most about. But don't ramble on leaving insufficient time for the rest of the exam. Learn to time your answers to fit the overall time limits of the exam.

3. Once you have your general operation planned, begin to prepare the actual answer. If you are starting with the third question and will have to go back to the first two, leave room in your blue book or on your paper for the first two answers. *Be sure to number your answer so that it corresponds ex-*

actly to the question on the exam. Otherwise, your professor may not be able to tell which question you are responding to. Take time to jot down some main points so that you can organize the material better and also for later reference. If you don't jot down the main points, you may forget some in the heat of writing. Keep your answer concise and to the point but be sure to include supporting evidence for general statements. It is often helpful to start the answer by reframing the question; i.e., if the question is "Trace the major steps that led to World War II," start your answer with "The first of the major steps that led to World War II was . . . " Don't pad; say what you know and get on to something else. A long, rambling answer to try to disguise the small extent of your knowledge doesn't fool many professors. When you finish one answer, go quickly to the next. Don't lose your momentum or agonize over the answer you've just written.

4. *Leave at least five minutes at the end to check over your work.* Correct your grammar and mechanics where necessary. Be sure your sentences are sentences. Add extra information as neatly as possible.

5. Go home and forget about the exam. You'll learn soon enough how you did. You prepared as well as you could and wrote the answers as well as you could. If you do your best at any given moment, that's all you can do.

One last word: The most careful preparation won't save you from an occasional moment when you simply can't write on a question you are confronted with. If there is more than one question, leave a blank space and go on to another question; maybe something will come to you in the meantime. If it doesn't or if this is the only question on the exam, first try doodling a bit. Jot down anything that comes to your mind that is vaguely related; ideas may begin to form. If *that* doesn't work and you *do* know something about the subject, try honesty. Write, "Dr. _____, I'm sorry, but I can't write on that question. I'll tell you what I do know about the subject." You may not get full credit, but it's better than leaving the paper blank.

Index

808   Hoover, Regina M.
Hoo   Making your writing   810320
                count...

DATE DUE

DATE DUE

DEC. 1 8 1987

JAN. 2 1 1988

MAR. 1 0 1988
APR. 1 3 1990
APR. 2 5 1988

SEP 2 8 1988

PRINTED IN U. S. A.
NO. 23-247

Please Do Not Remove This Card From Pocket

CLARKSTOWN SOUTH
HIGH SCHOOL
MEDIA CENTER